Rediscovering the Constitution

A Reader for Jefferson Meeting Debates

Rediscovering the Constitution

A Reader for Jefferson Meeting Debates

The Jefferson Foundation

Alice O'Connor
Mary L. Henze
W. Richard Merriman, Jr.

Congressional Quarterly Inc.
1414 22nd Street N.W.
Washington, D.C. 20037

Congressional Quarterly Inc., an editorial research service and publishing company, serves clients in the fields of news, education, business and government. It combines Congressional Quarterly's specific coverage of Congress, government and politics with the more general subject range of an affiliated service, Editorial Research Reports.

Congressional Quarterly publishes the *Congressional Quarterly Weekly Report* and a variety of books, including college political science textbooks under the CQ Press imprint and public affairs paperbacks designed as timely reports to keep journalists, scholars and the public abreast of developing issues and events. CQ also publishes information directories and reference books on the federal government, national elections and politics, including the *Guide to Congress,* the *Guide to the U.S. Supreme Court,* the *Guide to U.S. Elections* and *Politics in America.* The *CQ Almanac,* a compendium of legislation for one session of Congress, is published each year. *Congress and the Nation,* a record of government for a presidential term, is published every four years.

CQ publishes *The Congressional Monitor,* a daily report on current and future activities of congressional committees, and several newsletters including *Congressional Insight,* a weekly analysis of congressional action, and *Campaign Practices Reports,* a semimonthly update on campaign laws.

An electronic online information system, the Washington Alert Service, provides immediate access to CQ's databases of legislative action, votes, schedules, profiles and analyses.

Copyright © 1987 Congressional Quarterly Inc.

Printed in the United States of America

Acknowledgments appear on page 221, which constitutes an extension of the copyright page.

Library of Congress Cataloging in Publication Data

Rediscovering the Constitution.

    1. United States—Constitutional law. I. Jefferson Foundation (Washington, D.C.)
KF4550.A2R43   1987   342.73'029   86-32852
ISBN 0-87187-407-5   347.30229

Contents

Preface

While working recently on a videotape about the Jefferson Meeting on the Constitution, I asked a number of citizens on the streets of Washington, D.C., "Who does the Constitution belong to?" Among the answers: "the government," "the Congress," "the president," and "I just read that in my book, do you want me to look it up for you?" The most frequent answer, though, and the one given with the greatest conviction, was that the Constitution belongs to "the people of the United States."

While Americans assert that the Constitution belongs to them, it is clear that many do not know very much about how it was made, what is in it, and how it has changed over the course of two hundred years. Americans, moreover, have a tendency to think of the Constitution not as a living document that shapes every aspect of our national political life, but as a gift from great men, long dead, that is now being safely preserved under glass at the National Archives.

The Jefferson Foundation

In 1983 a group came together to find a way to give a fresh and real meaning to the assertion that the Constitution belongs to the people of the United States. We wanted to enhance citizens' understanding of the Constitution and its history. And we wanted to enlarge Americans' sense of ownership of the Constitution by involving them in discussions that take the Constitution out from under glass for an examination of how it shapes the contemporary performance of our government.

We thought these goals of education and involvement made it appropriate to adopt the name the Jefferson Foundation. Thomas Jefferson wrote this of the connection between government and education:

> I know of no safe depository of the ultimate powers of the society but the people themselves; and if we think them not enlightened enough to exercise their control with a wholesome discretion, the remedy is not to take it from them, but to inform their discretion by education.

Jefferson also emphasized that it was important for each generation of Americans to review the Constitution and its plan for government to ensure that it provides them a proper government. Jefferson was not afraid of the results of such a review. He wrote,

> Some men look at constitutions with sanctimonious reverence, and deem them like the ark of the covenant, too sacred to be touched. They ascribe to the men of the preceding age a wisdom more than human, and suppose what they did to be beyond amendment.... I am certainly not an advocate for frequent and untried changes in laws and constitutions.... But ... laws and institutions must go hand in hand with the progress of the human mind.

The Jefferson Meeting on the Constitution

With these ideals in mind, Alice O'Connor, the first director of the Jefferson Foundation, designed the Jefferson Meeting on the Constitution. The Jefferson Meeting brings students and adults together to study and discuss the Constitution. Among the questions raised and debated are the following:

- Would abolishing the electoral college be a desirable change in the presidential selection process?
- Would a single six-year presidential term make the chief executive more or less effective?
- Would the performance of Congress be improved by setting constitutional limits on length of service?
- Would Congress perform better if members of the House of Representatives had longer terms?
- Is the separation of powers, so carefully crafted by the Constitution's framers, an asset or hindrance to the effective performance of government today?
- Would the judicial system be improved by establishing terms of office or a retirement age for Supreme Court justices and federal judges?
- Should the processes by which citizens make laws by direct popular votes in many states be adopted at the national level?
- Would it be advisable to call a constitutional convention, as provided by Article V, for the purpose of proposing amendments to the Constitution?
- Can the expenses of political campaigns be curbed without endangering rights of free speech and association?

The Jefferson Foundation does not advocate any changes in the Constitution, but experience at Jefferson Meetings has vindicated our expectations that debating the pros and cons of concrete proposals for constitutional change would inspire participants to learn about the

Constitution and to rationally evaluate the performance of the national government.

The Jefferson Meeting on the Constitution opens with discussion in "issue committees," each of which examines a particular proposal for changing the Constitution. After some discussion members of each issue committee divide naturally into "pro" and "con" groups, with the pro group favoring a proposed change and the con group opposing it. These groups work to prepare a series of brief speeches that will set out the key arguments supporting their point of view.

During the plenary session all the participants from the various issue committees come together for debate and discussion. Each issue is called to the floor in turn. Members of the pro and con groups from the relevant issue committee kick off the debate by giving a series of alternating pro and con speeches setting out their points of view. The floor is then opened to comments and questions. No motions or parliamentary maneuvers are used. No vote is taken at the end of the debate. The object of discussion is not to win, but to learn.

The Jefferson Meeting is for everyone because the Constitution belongs to everyone. It reflects our belief that the average citizen has both the ability and the interest to participate in a meaningful discussion of the Constitution. One of the great treats of attending a Jefferson Meeting is to see homemakers, farmers, and small-business owners more than hold their own in discussions.

The results of the Jefferson Meetings held so far have been spectacular. Not only do participants report that their involvement was a stimulating experience, but they also leave the Jefferson Meeting determined to share that experience with their fellow citizens. Such enthusiasm, combined with the 1987 bicentennial of the Constitution, has spread the Jefferson Meeting across the country.

About This Book

The Jefferson Foundation has prepared discussion guides on the constitutional issues that are debated during the Jefferson Meeting. These guides, furnished before the meeting begins, provide participants with a shared pool of knowledge that they can use in discussing the Constitution.

The Jefferson Foundation is pleased that Congressional Quarterly has published the texts of these guides, which are presented here as separate chapters. At the end of the book is a brief guide to organizing a Jefferson Meeting. Also included is the text of the U.S. Constitution as amended. You have in your hand, then, all the basic ingredients you will need to begin planning for a Jefferson Meeting. Jefferson Foundation staff members would be happy to talk with you about your plans and offer any additional information or assistance we can. Our address is: The Jefferson Foundation, 1529 18th Street, N.W., Washington, D.C., 20036; phone (202) 234-3689. Even if you do not plan to organize or become involved in a Jefferson Meeting, we think the substantive chapters of this book will stimulate and challenge you.

Charles L. Bartlett
President of the Jefferson Foundation

1. Article V and Amendment by Convention

Introduction

Constitutional conventions played a singular role in the creation of American government. Americans held the first national assembly to determine the fundamental law of the land. Nowhere since then has the right been so steadfastly upheld or, as the number of state constitutional assemblies shows, so frequently practiced.

The principle of popular consent to government dates back to colonial days. With their declaration of independence from Great Britain, the colonists claimed the additional right to make their own laws, and exercised it in the revolutionary state constitutional conventions. The Philadelphia Convention and the ratifying bodies of 1787-89 officially recognized the convention as a basic tenet of American republicanism. The founding generation thereby established a tradition that has been as much a source of fear and controversy as it has been a symbol of liberty.

The convention has historically been the expression of the people's right to create their own governing authority and to consent actively to that authority. It is also one way to make fundamental changes in the government. In addition to giving Congress the power to propose amendments, Article V of the Constitution says the Congress shall call a convention for the purpose of amending the Constitution whenever two-thirds of the states request it. The right has never been exercised even though Congress has received over three hundred petitions calling for a national convention.

The prospect of a national amending convention is frightening to some, remote to others, and unknown to many people. But reform groups throughout history have looked to Article V for the key to constructive change. Today supporters of the balanced budget amendment have succeeded in making a second constitutional convention too

by Alice O'Connor and Mary L. Henze

imminent to ignore. Already, thirty-two of the required thirty-four states have petitioned Congress to call a convention to consider an amendment requiring a balanced federal budget.

Amending the Constitution by convention is a much larger issue over and above the issue of a balanced budget. As a fundamental right it is always relevant. But realizing it in practical terms has been elusive because it is not entirely clear what the founders intended when they included the convention method in the amendment clause. The unanswered questions arouse debate over the very principles of the Union. Does Article V give the people the power to rewrite the fundamental law of the land? Or does the supremacy of the Constitution prevent an amending convention from changing it completely? What is actually the source of the right to change the Constitution? Does it come from the Constitution itself or does it come from a source outside the Constitution? The answers to these questions will determine the meaning of the convention to Americans today—is it revolutionary or can it be controlled?

Historical Roots of the Convention

We can understand the controversy over the power of the amending convention by tracing its development in the American revolutionary and constitutional traditions.

The Convention and Revolution

In the American revolutionary tradition, set forth in the Declaration of Independence and the writings of eighteenth century republican agitators, the popular constitutional assembly was the most basic expression of the people's supremacy over the governing body. Thomas Paine wrote that

> government has no right to make itself a party in any debate respecting the principles or modes of forming, or of changing, Constitutions. It is not for the benefit of those who exercise the powers of government that Constitutions, and the governments issueing from them, are established. In all these matters the right of judging and acting are in those who pay, not those who receive. (Paine, *The Rights of Man*)

Paine's distinction between the day-to-day governing body and the principles underlying government was a very important one to the framers of the American Constitution. It challenged the traditional relationship between the ruler and the ruled to rest ultimate authority with the people. The revolutionary potential of making the people the supreme authority is nowhere more eloquently expressed than in the Declaration of Independence. To read beyond the famous first lines is to see how the right to join together to realize self-government could become the right to overthrow the existing government:

> We hold these truths to be self-evident: that all men are created equal; that they are endowed by their creator with inalienable rights; that among these are life, liberty and the pursuit of happiness; that to secure these rights, governments are instituted among men, deriving their just powers from the consent of the governed; that whenever any form of government becomes destructive of these ends, *it is the right of the people to alter or abolish it, and to institute a new government,* laying its foundation on such principles and organizing its powers in such form, as to them shall seem most likely to effect their safety and happiness. Prudence, indeed, will dictate that governments long established should not be changed for light and transient causes; and accordingly all experience hath shown that mankind are more disposed to suffer while evils are sufferable, than to right themselves by abolishing the forms to which they are accustomed. *But when a long train of abuses and usurpation, pursuing invariably the same object evinces a design to reduce them under absolute despotism, it is their right, it is their duty to throw off such government, and to provide new guards for their future security.* (Declaration of Independence, emphasis added)

Americans exercised the right to "institute new government" by mutual consent when they met to frame the state constitutions that overthrew the colonial charters. These first constitutional bodies were indeed revolutionary.

Article V made this revolutionary right part of the Constitution itself. It stands as a constant reminder to government officials that they are bound by the people through the Constitution:

> The important distinction so well understood in America, between a constitution established by the people, and unaltered by the government; and a law established by the government and altered by the government, seems to have been little understood and less observed in any other country. Wherever the supreme power of the legislature has resided, has been supposed to reside also, a full power to change the form of the government. (*Federalist* No. 53)

The United States Constitution is supreme law because it stands above government. By leaving the people with the right to change the Constitution, the framers provided a defense against "usurpation" and reconfirmed the ultimate authority of the governed.

The Convention and Stability

The founders' inclusion of an amendment provision was also a reaction to the inflexibility of the Articles of Confederation, where it is stated that

> the Articles of Confederation shall be inviolably observed by every state, and the Union shall be perpetual; nor shall any alteration at any

> time hereafter be made in any of them, unless such alteration is agreed
> to in a Congress of the United States, and be afterward confirmed by
> the legislature of every state. (Articles of Confederation, Article 13)

While they may not have called themselves "radicals," most of the
delegates to the Philadelphia Convention believed that radical changes
were necessary to make the Union work. The proposals they made
undermined the fundamental law they had pledged to uphold, without
requiring the approval of every state to do it.

Their frustration with the Articles could only convince the framers
that good government required flexibility and room for growth. An
institutional avenue for change acted as a safety valve; desire for reform
could be satisfied systematically instead of through revolution. Thomas
Paine praised the amending clauses of the state constitutions because of
their stabilizing effect:

> One of the greatest improvements that has been made for the perpetual
> security and progress of constitutional liberty, is the provision which
> the new constitutions make for occasionally revising, altering, and
> amending them.
> . . . The Rights of Man are the rights of all generations of men, and
> cannot be monopolized by any. That which is worth following will be
> followed for the sake of its worth, and it is in this that security lies, and
> not in any conditions with which it may be encumbered. When a man
> leaves property to his heirs, he does not connect it with an obligation
> that they shall accept it. Why then, should we do otherwise with
> respect to the Constitution? (Paine, *The Rights of Man*)

By institutionalizing the people's right to change parts of the fundamental law, the founders were protecting the Constitution and avoiding
future upheavals. In effect, they took what was the most revolutionary
aspect of the new republic—the power to call a convention— and tamed
it.

The Genesis of Article V

The Virginia Plan, submitted by Edmund Randolph to the Philadelphia Convention, contained the first recommendation for an amendable
constitution:

> Resolved, that provision ought to be made for the amendment of the
> articles of the union, whensoever it shall seem necessary; and that the
> assent of the National Legislature ought not be required thereto. (Pole
> 1970, 172)

The purpose of the amending provision was clear: to provide against
future upheaval and to keep the legislature in check. But the actual
procedure was more difficult to determine. The major question faced by
the delegates was whether the power to initiate change should rest with

the national government or with the state governments. They were aware that the power to amend could be as much a weapon against as a protection of liberty.

Until September 10, one week before the Convention approved the Constitution, the framers' position on amendment procedure was not fully formulated. The provision that emerged from final debate was a compromise between those who thought revision should be strictly in the hands of federal government and those who wanted to leave it to the states. While Congress could propose specific amendments, the states could petition for a convention of unspecified powers to consider amendments. The national legislature would not have exclusive control over the Constitution. In addition, the state government could not make specific proposals that might increase their power. In either case, Article V of the Constitution makes it clear that the people would have the final word.

> The Congress, whenever two thirds of both Houses shall deem it necessary, shall propose Amendments to this Constitution, or, on the Application of the Legislatures of two thirds of the several States, shall call a Convention for proposing Amendments, which, in either Case, shall be valid to all Intents and Purposes, as Part of this Constitution, when ratified by the Legislatures of three fourths of the several States, or by Conventions in three fourths thereof, as the one or the other Mode of Ratification may be proposed by the Congress. (U. S. Const. Art. V)

The framers made no judgment as to which amending procedure was the better one. But tradition and the language of the Virginia Plan suggest that they considered the need to establish a peaceful way for the people to bypass the national legislature as their primary concern. It is also interesting to note that Article VI, which binds all officials of the government—judges, senators, representatives, and both judicial and executive officers—to uphold the Constitution, leaves the people and their conventions free of such restraint:

> 2. This Constitution, and the Laws of the United States which shall be made in Pursuance thereof; and all Treaties made, or which shall be made, under the Authority of the United States, shall be the supreme Law of the Land; and the Judges in every State shall be bound thereby, any Thing in the Constitution or Laws of any State to the Contrary notwithstanding.
>
> 3. The Senators and Representatives before mentioned, and the Members of the several State Legislatures, and all the executive and judicial Officers, both of the United States and of the several States, shall be bound by Oath or Affirmation to support this Constitution; but no religious Test shall ever be required as a Qualification to any Office of public Trust under the United States. (U. S. Const. Art. VI)

The "Runaway Convention"?

The Anti-Federalists objected to many of the particulars of the proposed Constitution, but one of the most powerful arguments against it was a challenge to the legitimacy of the Philadelphia Convention itself. The very phrase "We the People," which opened the Preamble, offended those who believed that the convention had overstepped its bounds and ignored its instruction to the point where it violated the trust of the people and therefore had no right to pretend to speak for them.

The original resolutions calling for a constitutional convention supported the Anti-Federalist argument over legitimacy. Alexander Hamilton made the original suggestion at the Annapolis Convention of 1786, which had been called by Virginia to discuss commercial matters between the states. The Convention recommended

> ... the appointment of Commissioners ... to take into consideration, the situation of the United States, to devise such further provisions as shall appear to be necessary to render the Constitution of the Federal Government adequate to the exigencies of the Union; and to report such an Act for that purpose to the United States in Congress assembled, as when agreed to, by them, and afterwards confirmed by the Legislature of every State, will effectually provide for the same. (Pole 1970, 163)

This recommendation led to the congressional resolution that formally mandated and instructed the Philadelphia Convention:

> Resolved that in the opinion of Congress, it is expedient, that on the second Monday in May next a Convention of delegates, who shall have been appointed by the several states be held at Philadelphia for the sole and express purpose of revising the Articles of Confederation and reporting to Congress and the several legislatures, such alterations and provisions therein as shall, when agreed to in Congress, and confirmed by the states, render the federal constitution adequate to the exigencies of Government and the preservation of the Union. (Pole 1970, 166)

Congress called for a revision of the existing Articles of Confederation. The Convention delivered an entirely new government. Taken on these terms, the Philadelphia Convention might be called a "runaway convention." William Grayson, arguing at the Virginia ratifying debates, accused the framers of just that:

> How were the sentiments of the people before the meeting of the Convention at Philadelphia? They had only one object in view. Their ideas reached no farther than to give the general government the five per centum impost, and the regulation of trade. When it was agitated in Congress, in a committee of the whole, this was all that was asked, or was deemed necessary. (Kenyon 1966, 280)

Not only had the founders violated the Articles' sacred trust, Grayson went on, they were creating "phantoms" to justify their violation:

> Since that period, their views have extended much farther. Horrors have been greatly magnified since the rising of the Convention. We are now told by the honorable gentleman [Governor Randolph] that we shall have wars and rumors of wars, that every calamity is to attend us, and that we shall be ruined and disunited forever, unless we adopt this Constitution. Pennsylvania and Maryland are to fall upon us from the north, like the Goths and Vandals of old; the Algerines, whose flat-sided vessels never came farther than Madeira, are to fill the Chesapeake with mighty fleets, and to attack us on our front; the Indians are to invade us with numerous armies on our rear, in order to convert our cleared lands into hunting grounds; and the Carolinians from the South (mounted on alligators, I presume) are to come and destroy our cornfields, and eat up our little children! These, sir, are the mighty dangers which await us if we reject—dangers which are merely imaginary, and ludicrous in the extreme! Are we to be destroyed by Maryland and Pennsylvania? What will democratic states make war for, and how long since they have imbibed a hostile spirit? But the generality are to attack us. Will they attack us after violating their faith in the first Union? Will they not violate their faith if they do not take us into their confederacy? Have they not agreed, by the old Confederation, that the Union shall be perpetual, and that no alteration should take place without the consent of Congress, and the confirmation of the legislatures of every State? I cannot think that there is such depravity in mankind as that, after violating public faith so flagrantly, they should make war upon us, also, for not following their example. (Kenyon 1966, 280-81)

Alexander Hamilton, writing as "Publius" in *The Federalist Papers*, replied to these objections with an appeal to the larger duty of the delegates to overcome the restrictions of the Articles in order to secure the happiness of the people. He expressed the revolutionary tradition of the convention: overthrow laws to attain the higher good.

> ... if [the framers] exceeded their powers, they were not only warranted but required, as the confidential servants of their country, by the circumstances in which they were placed, to exercise the liberty which they assumed, and that finally, if they had violated both their powers, and their obligations in proposing a Constitution, this ought nevertheless to be embraced, if it be calculated to accomplish the views and happiness of the people of America. (*Federalist* No. 40)

The Unanswered Questions

The framers left a myriad of troublesome questions buried within Article V. James Madison pointed this out at the Philadelphia Convention when it considered the article in September 1787. How, he asked, was a convention to be formed? And what would be the force of its acts?

CONSTITUTIONAL CONVENTION: THE STATE EXAMPLES

The convention has been called the "American style" of constitution-making, even though there is only one example of a federal constitutional convention in our history. It gets its reputation from the states where conventions have been used to write and subsequently rewrite many state charters. Thousands of amendments have been proposed and adopted; some state constitutions even require periodic review by convention. The history of these state conventions reveals both the significance and the potential of the people's right to make and remake their fundamental governing document.

• During the formative years of the Union, 1776-98, eleven of the thirteen states wrote and revised a total of twenty-one constitutions. (Rhode Island and Connecticut kept their colonial charters until 1818 and 1842, respectively.) These early state constitutions contained the seeds of the federal republic, for time and again the founders turned to them for guidance.

• The trend in pre-Civil War America was toward creating more democratic state constitutions. Conventions extended popular sovereignty and in some states provided for universal male suffrage. State judges, executive branch officials, and even the prison inspector of New York became subject to election. Conventions were clearly being used to control the power of state governments and to assert the power of the people, as a statement from the Illinois Constitutional Convention of 1847 demonstrates:

> We are here, the sovereignty of the state. We are what the people of the state would be if they were congregated here in one mass meeting. We are what Louis XIV said he was—"We are the state."

But the delegation never addressed the vagueness of the provision to "call a convention for the purpose," leaving it to future generations to clarify. Debate has raged over what, exactly, the framers intended—how much change they wanted to open the Constitution to, and whether they would have approved of the prospect of another convention. The controversy stems from what is unspoken in Article V. It is clear that Congress has the duty to call the convention when the specified number of states petition for a convention. But can Congress exercise any control

We can trample the constitution under our feet as waste paper, and, no one can call us to an account save the people. (*Politics Today* 1979, 31)

●The major conflicts of the Civil War and Reconstruction period were, to some extent, played out in the state conventions held during 1860-80. The secession from the Union and the subsequent confederation of the southern states were accomplished by conventions, as was their initial restoration to the Union. The Reconstruction Congress imposed strict requirements on the southern states to revise their constitutions to reflect federal policy. In reaction against this, state conventions of the 1870s revised their constitutions to return power to the state governments. State constitutions in the north also reflected changing attitudes toward the central government. Initially supportive of the activist role that government took in engineering social change, by the 1870s northern states were calling conventions in reaction against activist policy.

●By the late nineteenth and early twentieth centuries, an increasingly diverse population made it more difficult for a convention to reflect a popular mandate, and fewer states looked to the convention method of proposing amendments. In an interesting contrast to the democratizing trends of the early nineteenth century, conventions of this period instituted restrictions on suffrage, such as the poll tax, and some even refused to submit their proposals to the electorate for approval.

●In recent years, state constitutional revision has taken alternate routes. While there have been several conventions, the interpretation of the courts, legislative alternatives, governor's commissions, and mechanisms such as the initiative and referendum have proven more successful in securing change.

over the convention after it is called into existence? Important questions come up every time a movement to call a convention gains momentum.

●Can Congress limit the convention to an agenda of proposals specified in the state petitions?

●How will delegates to a convention be chosen and who will set the procedures for choosing them?

●How long does a state's petition for a convention remain valid and can a state rescind its petition?

• Once a convention is called, does it have the power to set its own rules and, if so, is it accountable to anyone?

The answers to these questions are far from clear, but it is clear that they would have a great effect on whether the convention is indeed a "principle of melioration, contentment and peace" or one of revolution. Can a constitutional right subvert the Constitution itself?

A Convention: Historical Precedents

Those who are anxious over the prospect of a convention ask: What would the people do if given free reign over our basic charter? Would they get rid of the Bill of Rights? Limit the Supreme Court? Install "tyranny of the majority"? Examples from the past do more to fuel the arguments of convention opponents than to quell their fears, for the convention has historically been associated with times of upheaval, sectionalism, and, eventually, disunion.

• The Philadelphia Convention went far beyond the instructions of the Continental Congress to rewrite entirely the basic charter of government.

• Anti-Federalist agitation during the ratification debates almost prevented ratification. Some Anti-Federalists called for a second convention to rewrite the proposed Constitution even before it was adopted. Anti-Federalists from Virginia proposed "that a convention be immediately called ... with full power to take into their consideration the defects of this constitution that have been suggested by the state conventions ... and secure to ourselves and our latest posterity the great and inalienable rights of mankind." Advocates of a second convention to secure the addition of the Bill of Rights applied steady pressure to the first Congress until it passed, and the states ratified the first ten constitutional amendments in 1792.

• Still rankled over the "expansionist" policies of the Republican administration of Thomas Jefferson, and the Louisiana Purchase in particular, Federalist Josiah Quincy called for a convention to initiate secession in Massachusetts in 1811. Federalist agitation reached its peak in 1815 when representatives from the New England states gathered at the Hartford Convention to discuss mutual grievances over the conduct of the War of 1812 and Republican embargo policies. Although the only action of the Hartford rebels was to propose constitutional amendments designed to protect the states' economic and political interests, secession was definitely an issue.

• Federal economic policy again provoked near secession in the 1830s when a South Carolina convention issued a nullification proclamation to signal its protest over tariffs of 1828 and 1832. In an extreme interpretation of the states' rights doctrine, the radical convention claimed the right to declare null and void federal laws that "assumed undelegated powers" and were contrary to the interests of its citizens.

● A South Carolina convention again took the radical lead in 1860 when it assembled to rescind the act of the original ratifying convention:

> We the people of South Carolina in convention assembled do declare and ordain and it is hereby declared and ordained that the ordinance adopted by us in convention on the twenty-third of May in the year of our Lord one thousand seven hundred and eighty-eight whereby the Constitution of the United States of America was ratified and also all acts and parts of acts of the General Assembly of this state ratifying amendments to the said Constitution are hereby repealed; and that the union now subsisting between South Carolina and the other states under the name of the "United States of America" is hereby dissolved. (Commager 1950, 6-7)

The South Carolina Convention claimed the right to empower as well:

> . . . the State of South Carolina has resumed her position among the nations of the world as a separate and independent state with full power to levy war, conclude peace, contract alliances, establish commerce, and to do all other acts and things which independent states may of right do. (Commager 1950, 6-7)

● On February 4, 1861, delegates from the seceded states assembled in a constitutional convention in Montgomery, Alabama. They unanimously adopted the constitution of the Confederacy on March 11, 1861, which was very similar to the United States Constitution but was easier to amend: three states could petition for a convention on a specific agenda of amendments and two-thirds of the states were required for ratification.

From Constitutional Right to Constitutional Threat

More than three hundred state petitions calling for an amending convention have been submitted since 1789, most of them during the twentieth century. The earliest petitions called for a general convention, but the majority have called for specific amendments, ranging in subject from anti-polygamy measures after Utah was admitted as a state, to the repeal of Prohibition, to structural reforms such as the direct election of senators and the two-term limitation on presidents. Each new wave of petitions has produced a counter wave of resistance to the convention method of amendment. As resistance has built up, particularly over the past decade, one thing has become clear: the convention is as much a threat as it is a right.

As we move closer to realizing this right to convene we seem to lose the confidence Lincoln exhibited in his first inaugural address when he stated that

> ... the convention mode seems preferable in that it allows amendments to originate with the people themselves, instead of only permitting them to take or reject propositions originated by others. ... (Manning and Potter 1949, 282)

Today the prevailing attitude toward a convention is fear—fear that it would undermine the very principles of the constitutional system.

> ... the realistic fact remains that 200 years later there is no certainty that our nation would survive a modern-day convention with its basic structures intact and its citizens' traditional rights retained. The convening of a federal constitutional convention would be an act of the greatest magnitude for our nation. I believe it would be an act fraught with danger and recklessness. (Melvin Laird, *Washington Post*, 13 February 1984)

Opponents of calling a convention are apprehensive of what that convention might recommend. They hesitate to open up the carefully crafted system of checks and balances, the Bill of Rights, and minority protections to the whims of a popular forum. And they are generally pessimistic about the power of Congress to control the convention in any way. Senator Heyburn expressed this view before the Senate in 1911 when the movement to call a convention to consider direct election of senators was gaining ground:

> When the people of the United States meet in a Constitutional Convention there is no power to limit their action. They are greater than the Constitution; and they can repeal the provision that limits the right of amendment. They can repeal every section of it, because they are the peers of the people who made it.

Not everyone believes the Constitution is so vulnerable. Those who fear that a convention makes it thus may be underestimating the American people and their commitment to the basic principles, rights, and freedoms of the republic. Milton S. Eisenhower takes this view:

> Objections to a constitutional convention called to draft a balanced budget amendment have been more emotional than logical. I know of no reason to expect that delegates to a convention would be any less responsible or committed to upholding our basic liberties than are members of Congress. (Eisenhower 1982)

Some think there may be more to fear from elected officials than there is to fear from the people. Sen. William V. Roth echoed the Virginia Plan's resolution for an amending device that did not "require the consent of the national legislature" when he called for a general convention in 1979:

> [The Constitution] is the living, breathing consensus of American democracy. It not only guarantees the rights of the governed and the process by which their right to be governed is obtained, it also provides the means by which the governed can regain their rights if their representatives govern without their consent. (Roth 1979)

However, to some opponents, the prospect of a convention threatens more than internal stability. Just as the founders believed they were setting a republican example for the entire world, those who wish to protect it from a general convention might agree with Melvin Laird, who adds to his objections:

> If a convention were called, our allies and foes alike would soon realize the new pressures imposed upon our Republic. The mere act of convening a constitutional convention would send tremors through all those economies that depend on the dollar; would undermine our neighbors' confidence in our constitutional integrity; and would weaken not only our economic stability but the stability of the free world. (Melvin Laird, *Washington Post*, 13 February 1984)

The Convention as a Tactic

The widespread fear of convention has endowed petition movements with considerable political leverage. In 1912, Congress preferred to pass the Seventeenth Amendment rather than face the consequences of the convention petitioned for by supporters of direct election of the Senate. Other strong petition campaigns were launched to pass the Twenty-first Amendment repealing Prohibition and, after Franklin Roosevelt's fourth election, in support of the Twenty-second Amendment. In both cases, Congress acted before a convention was necessary. The most controversial petition campaigns have been over the Supreme Court's reapportionment decision in the 1960s and the balanced budget amendment, which in 1986 had thirty-two petitions before Congress.

The fear of a "runaway convention" and uncertainty about rules and procedures have persisted as important preventive factors. A report issued by Common Cause, a Washington-based citizens' interest group, stated:

> A constitutional convention is uncharted political territory. There are no precedents for it except the constitutional convention of 1787, when the Articles of Confederation were thrown out and replaced by the United States Constitution, despite the convention delegates' much more limited mandate. That precedent of wholesale revision of the nation's governing charter raises serious questions about the limits that

could bind a second constitutional convention. But state legislators (who have called for a balanced budget convention) appear to have given those implications little thought. (Common Cause 1977)

Balanced budget convention advocates see no basis for these apprehensions. They point to the "seven checks on a constitutional convention" listed by the National Taxpayers Union in calling a "runaway convention" a "hoax":

1. Congress could avoid the convention by acting itself.
2. Congress establishes the convention procedures.
3. The voters themselves would demand that a convention be limited.
4. Even if delegates did favor opening the convention to another issue, it is unlikely they would all favor opening it to the same issue.
5. The Congress would have the power to refuse to send a non-conforming amendment to ratification.
6. Proposals which stray beyond the convention call would be subject to court challenge.
7. Thirty-eight states must ratify.
(National Taxpayers Union 1985)

With the exception of the first and the seventh, these "checks" are all open to question. There are currently no laws to regulate a convention, and some question whether it is valid for Congress to pass regulations at all.

Constitutional Convention Implementation Bills

If we fail to deal now with the uncertainties of the convention method, we could be courting a constitutional crisis of grave proportions. We could be running the enormous risk that procedures for a national constitutional convention would have to be forged in a time of divisive controversy and confusion when there would be a high premium on obstructive and result-oriented tactics. (American Bar Association 1974)

As the reapportionment and balanced budget petitions climbed closer to the necessary two-thirds level, members of Congress introduced several bills to set rules, regulations, and procedures for a national convention. Hearings were held in 1979. Two major Senate bills have been proposed, one by Sam Ervin in 1971 and the other by Orrin Hatch in the Ninety-eighth Congress. Senator Hatch's bill attempts to set the procedures for calling a limited constitutional convention. It features the following:

● A requirement that state legislatures give their reasons for wanting a convention in specific enough terms to determine whether there is a "consensus" on the need for change but without requiring that all petitions be identical in language.

• A seven-year effectiveness clause for petitions and recognition of the state legislatures' right to rescind petitions.

• Delegate selection would be up to the states, with each state allotted the same number of delegates as it has presidential electors. No member of Congress could be a delegate and delegates would be required to take an oath to comply with the Constitution and the limitations of the convention as called by Congress.

• Congress could refuse to submit proposed amendments to the states if they were contrary to or outside the mandate of the convention.

• Proposed amendments would be subject to judicial review.

While recognizing the powers of the states to call a convention for broad unspecified constitutional revision, Hatch's bill is based on the assumption that Congress does have the power to call and regulate a limited convention if the states specifically request it in their petitions:

> The constitutional convention, while clearly remaining a unique and separate element of the Government—a new branch of Government, so to speak—is subject to the same limitations and checks and balances as the other, permanent branches of the Government. A constitutional convention, as its name clearly implies, is a constitutional entity; it is appointed under the terms of the Constitution and is subject to all of the express and implied limitations imposed by that document. (Sen. Orrin Hatch, statement before the Senate, 5 September 1979)

This assumption is disputed by many legislators and legal scholars. Debates and hearings on implementation bills rarely get beyond the basic point of contention expressed by Walter E. Dellinger of Duke University Law School:

> . . . I am persuaded that any Article V convention was intended to be free of the control of both Congress and the state legislatures. One theme that emerges from the Philadelphia debates in 1787 is that Congress should not be given the exclusive authority to propose amendments. Another is the fear expressed by Hamilton and others that state legislatures would propose amendments that would seek to enhance their own power at the expense of the national government. The framers of Article V therefore rejected a plan which would have permitted state legislatures to propose particular amendments for ratification. They created instead an alternative amendment free of congressional or state control: a constitutional convention free to determine the nature of the problem, free to define the subject matter and free to compromise the competing interests at stake in the process of drafting a corrective amendment. State legislatures may call for such a convention, but neither they nor Congress may control it. (Dellinger 1979)

It is difficult to say how, if ever, this debate will be resolved, since it rests so heavily on varying interpretations of what the founders intended. Some doubt that Congress will face the issue on convention regulation because that might clear the way to calling one. In the meantime, as legislators confront the very real possibility of having to call a convention, they continually return for some reassurance to the moderate words of Publius:

> That useful alterations [in the Constitution] will be suggested by experience, could not but be foreseen. It was requisite therefore that a mode for introducing them should be provided. The mode preferred by the Convention seems to be stamped with every mark of propriety. It guards equally against that extreme facility which would render the Constitution too mutable; and that extreme difficulty which might perpetuate its discovered faults. It moreover equally enables the general and state governments to originate the amendment of errors as they may be pointed out by the experience on one side or on the other. (*Federalist* No. 43)

References

American Bar Association. *Amendment of the Constitution by the Convention Method Under Article V.* Chicago, Ill.: American Bar Association Press, 1974.

Commager, Henry Steele, ed. *The Blue and the Gray.* Indianapolis: Bobbs-Merrill, 1950.

Common Cause. "Is the U.S. Ready for a Constitutional Convention?" *In Common* 10 (Winter 1979).

Dellinger, Walter E. *Prepared Statement Concerning S. 1710 and Related Bills.* Testimony given before the Subcommittee on the Constitution, Committee on the Judiciary, United States Senate, 29 November 1979.

Eisenhower, Milton. Preface to *The Runaway Convention or Proving a Preposterous Negative.* Taxpayers Foundation, 1982.

Hamilton, Alexander, John Jay, and James Madison. *The Federalist Papers.* Available in various editions.

Kenyon, Cecelia M., ed. *The Antifederalists.* Indianapolis: Bobbs-Merrill, 1966.

Manning, Thomas G., and David M. Potter, eds. *Nationalism and Sectionalism in America, 1775-1877.* New York: Holt, Rinehart & Winston, 1949.

National Taxpayers Union. *Hoax of a Runaway Convention.* 1985.

Paine, Thomas. *The Rights of Man.* Available in various editions.

Pole, J. R., ed. *The Revolution in America, 1754-1788.* Stanford, Ca.: Stanford University Press, 1970.

Politics Today. "The Con[stitutional] Con[vention] Papers: Memos to Jimmy Carter and Jerry Brown." May-June 1979.

Roth, William V., Jr. "Revitalizing Democracy." Speech given at The University of Virginia Legal Forum. 1979.

Suggested Readings

American Historical Association and The American Political Science Association. *The Constitutional Convention as an Amending Device.* Project '87 publication, 1981.

Walter E. Dellinger. "The Recurring Question of the 'Limited' Constitutional Convention." *Yale Law Journal* 88 (1979): 1623-40.

Jonathan Elliott, ed. *The Debates in the Several State Conventions on the Adoption of the Federal Constitution,* vol. III, the Virginia Debates. J. B. Lippincott, 1859.

J. Franklin Jameson, ed. *Essays in the Constitutional History of the United States in the Formative Period.* Houghton, 1889.

Thomas Jefferson. "Draft Constitution for Virginia, Declaration of Independence" (1776), "The Kentucky Resolutions" (1798), collected in Merrill D. Peterson, ed. *The Portable Thomas Jefferson.* New York: Penguin Books, 1975.

Merrill D. Peterson, ed. *Democracy, Liberty and Property: The State Constitutional Conventions of the 1820's.* Indianapolis: Bobbs-Merrill, 1966.

Edward P. Smith. "The Movement Towards a Second Constitutional Convention in 1788." In *Essays in the Constitutional History of the United States in the Formative Period.* J. Franklin Jameson, ed. Houghton, 1889.

Gordon Wood. *The Creation of the American Republic 1776-1787.* Durham, N.C.: University of North Carolina Press, 1967.

U.S. Congress, Senate Committee on the Judiciary, Subcommittee on the Constitution. *The Constitutional Convention Implementation Act of 1979.* Hearings on S. 1710, 29 November 1979.

2. Presidential Election and the Republican Principle

How many voters realize that when they pull the lever for a presidential candidate they are actually choosing a slate of electors who will in turn cast votes directly for the president? The reality of the electoral college system is easily lost in the campaign fray that precedes presidential elections. Most voters are reminded of its existence only if they tune into television coverage of election returns. Recent nationwide surveys, however, indicate that a majority of voters who are aware of the electoral college system would prefer a system where each and every vote counted directly and carried the same weight.

It might seem like simple common sense to tally each vote directly as it is cast, but supporters of the electoral college have a point, too. A system of indirect voting, they say, corrects the natural imbalances that exist in a large nation of diverse people and interest, all of which must be represented.

The argument over how we should elect our president has been one of the most heated and persistent in our political system. No other feature of American government has been the target of so many reforms. Direct election and the electoral college are only two of the dozens of methods which have been proposed over the last two hundred years. And yet the electoral college system has remained intact. Why?

Electing the president is far more than an administrative necessity. The methods by which the choice is made is a mirror of the most fundamental principles of government. The statesmen who gathered in Philadelphia in the summer of 1787 to draft a new Constitution debated long and hard over how to appoint the "Chief Magistrate," and those who reopen the discussion today find themselves confronted with the same difficult questions. Reviewing the original debate is the best way to comprehend the challenge posed by the need to find an equitable, democratic, representative way of electing a president. It is also the best

by Alice O'Connor and Mary L. Henze

way to prepare for considering reform of the electoral college in light of changes that have occurred in the United States political system. How have changes in who votes for president and who runs for president affected the founders' electoral device? Does the electoral college still produce the fairest and best choice or is it time to overhaul our presidential election process?

The Electoral College—How it Works

Only the basic structure of the electoral college is set forth in the Constitution—many of the functional details of the system are left to the individual state legislatures to design and implement. Although opponents of the electoral college fear the vagueness of the Constitution and the free rein it gives the states, the electoral college has evolved into a relatively stable and uniform institution. Not all states fill their electoral college obligations in the same way, but a series of amendments, federal and state laws, and political party rules have provided the framework for this complex system.

In accordance with the constitutional provision, each state must appoint a number of electors equal to the number of representatives and senators it has in Congress. The District of Columbia did not have electoral college representation until 1961 when the Twenty-third Amendment gave it three electors. The electoral college, therefore, has 538 members and works, with some variations, in the following manner:

● In every state, prior to the election, each political party with a presidential candidate selects a full slate of electors who are pledged to vote for the party's candidate. The selection process is accomplished through a party convention, a designated selection committee, or by primary. Candidates who are not the nominee of a party can name a slate of electors by filing a petition with the required number of signatures.

● When an individual voter casts a ballot for a presidential candidate, he or she is actually voting for the party's slate of electors and not directly for the president. Most states list only the names of the presidential and vice-presidential candidates on the ballot. Less than half require the names of the electors to be listed on the ballot, thus many Americans believe they vote directly for a candidate.

● The slate of electors that wins the popular vote wins membership to the electoral college and the opportunity to cast its state electoral votes for the presidential candidate of its choice. The slate of electors wins as a unit so all of the state's electoral votes are awarded to only one candidate. Candidates who do not win the popular vote will not receive any electoral votes. Every state except Maine uses this "winner take all" method of awarding electoral votes. Maine uses a proportional plan whereby electoral votes are awarded according to the percentage of the popular vote cast for each candidate.

● On the Monday following the second Wednesday in December (a date set by federal statute), the winning slate of electors meets in each state to cast two ballots, one for president and one for vice-president. Electors are not bound by the Constitution to vote for the candidates they are pledged to although the large majority of them do. The fear that "faithless electors" (those who cast votes against their pledge) could change the outcome of a close race has caused one-third of the states to enact laws binding electors to their pledges.

● The ballots cast by the state electors are tallied and the results sent to Congress, where they are counted in the presence of the new Senate and House of Representatives on January 6. The candidate for president who gets at least 270 votes, the majority of the total 538 votes, is declared the president elect. The same procedure is followed for counting the ballots for vice-president.

If no candidate receives a majority of the electoral college votes, the election is thrown into the House and Senate for resolution. The Twelfth Amendment states the procedure for this so-called "contingent election." The House selects the president according to the following rules:

● Only the top three vote-getters in the electoral college are to be considered.

● Regardless of its population and number of representatives, each state delegation in the House has one vote, for a total of fifty votes. The District of Columbia, which sends a nonvoting delegate to the House, has no vote.

● The state's choice is determined by a vote within its delegation. If that vote is a tie, the state loses its vote.

● A winning candidate must receive the votes of a majority—twenty-six—of the states.

● There is no limit to the number of ballots in the House.

The following rules apply to the Senate's selection of a vice-president:

● The choice is between the top two vice-presidential vote-getters in the electoral college.

● Each senator has one vote, for a total of one hundred votes (no vote for the District of Columbia).

● A vice-president must be elected by a majority—fifty-one—of the whole Senate.

If the House fails to elect a president by January 20, the vice-president elect serves as president until the House makes its choice. If the Senate has not elected a vice-president either, then the Speaker of the House will act as president.

The Constitution sets these procedures for "contingent elections" but places no restrictions on how the members of Congress must vote. They are free to vote for the candidate of their choice regardless of the preferences voiced by their constituents at the polls. It is even conceivable, under this system, that the House will elect a president from one party and the Senate a vice-president from another.

Why the Electoral College? — 1787

"The Convention, sir, were perplexed with no part of this plan so much as with the mode of choosing the president of the United States," said James Wilson to his fellow Pennsylvanians, who were gathered to approve or disapprove the work of the Constitutional Convention. As a delegate to the Philadelphia Convention, Wilson had been one of the strongest voices in favor of popular election of the president. And yet he defended the proposed electoral college system during the ratification process. Wilson, like many of his fellow delegates, put ideology aside to accept an experimental but "practicable" solution to the task of electing a chief magistrate. A solution which was the product of long hours of heated debate, the electoral college (as it came to be known early in the nineteenth century) was a compromise among practical men.

Much of the difficulty the founders had in finding an electoral process they could agree on can be traced to a wariness of centralized power in general. Their models of centralized executive power did not exactly inspire confidence—the British crown being the most immediate example.

To many of the delegates the obvious way to counteract some of the danger of central executive power was to have the legislature elect the president. The founders all shared a deep republican conviction that the real power in government should be vested in the legislature, the branch of government that most closely represented the people. This conviction had already been put to practice in most of the revolutionary state constitutions which provided for legislative election and legislative-judicial review of the governor. Appointment of the president by the national legislature would act as a check on centralized power and keep the government in the hands of the people through their representatives. It would ensure that the interests of the states would play a part in choosing the president. Delegates from smaller states were particularly supportive of the legislative method because they felt it would give them a voice in the selection process that others would not.

The same body of republican theory that suggested election by the legislature also provided ammunition for arguments against it. In a republican system the legislature acted as a buffer between the people and the executive power, but, as James Wilson pointed out in Philadelphia, it was also important to have some check on legislature:

> A particular objection against an absolute election by the legislature was that the Executive in that case would be too dependent to stand as the mediator between the intrigues and sinister views of the Representatives and the general liberties of the people. (Farrand 1937, 2:29)

Wilson, James Madison, and Gouverneur Morris, among other delegates, felt that to be strong an executive had to be independent. Their experience with the Articles of Confederation convinced them that the nation needed a strong leader to survive. The need for a new Constitution was largely due to the lack of central authority under the Articles—the national government had no power to levy taxes, raise an army, or even to represent the United States as a whole. If the president were dependent upon the legislature for election and reelection, he would not be strong enough to rise above its "cabals," conflicts, and petty intrigues and set the nation on a stable course.

Gouverneur Morris and others who supported popular election believed that there was such a thing as "the national interest," distinct from state interests and embodied in the people and the president. It made sense, therefore, for the people to elect their own representative. Morris was confident that the method would avert the danger of a dependent president and ensure the country an able leader:

> If the people should elect, they will never fail to prefer some man of distinguished character, or services; some man ... of continental reputation. If the legislature elects, it will be the work of intrigue, of cabal, of faction: it will be like the election of a pope by a conclave of cardinals; real merit will rarely be the title to the appointment. (Farrand 1937, 2:29)

Opponents of popular election were reluctant to accept the idea of a distinct national interest for fear that the states would be overshadowed by the central government. They kept returning to the idea of election by Congress, believing that conspiracy between the executive and the legislature would be better controlled by making the executive ineligible for a second term than by instituting popular election.

At the root of much of this argument was a difference of opinion about how the size of the country would affect the success of a republican system. George Mason and other opponents of popular election have been accused of anti-democratic elitism and lack of faith in the people. Mason believed "it would be unnatural to refer the choice of a proper magistrate to the people, as it would to refer a trial of colors to a blind man." His belief that the people were an inappropriate electorate can more accurately be attributed to a very practical consideration:

> The extent of the country renders it impossible that the people can have the requisite capacity to judge ... the candidates. (Farrand 1937, 2:29)

As well as being too disbursed to be informed about the candidates, the people were too far away to control the president once he was elected. The country would be without guard against despotism.

In the developing argument, supporters of popular election turned this fear on its head and credited the size of the country with ensuring a safe popular election. Corruption and intrigue could never affect a large enough section of the country to influence the outcome of the election. The expanse of the country was its own best safeguard against tyranny.

Proponents of legislative election and popular election seemed to be at loggerheads. Many of the delegates were uneasy about popular election but did not feel the legislative branch was the appropriate body to elect the president either. As a result, ideas for an alternative intermediary electoral body began to take shape. Elbridge Gerry offered one version of the proposal. Prefacing his remarks with an attack on popular election because "the people are uninformed and would be misled by a few designing men," Gerry then

> ...urged the expediency of an appointment of the Executive by Electors to be chosen by the State Executives. The people of the States will then choose the first branch: the legislatures of the States the second branch of the National Legislature, and the Executives of the States the National Executive. This ... would form a strong attachment in the states to the National System. (Farrand 1937, 2:57)

James Madison put the idea of an intermediate body of presidential electors in the context of the debate which had already taken place. His comments reflect the attitude of much of the Convention—here was a compromise of a very practical nature:

> It is essential ... that the appointment of the Executive should either be drawn from some source, or held by some tenure, that will give him a free agency with regard to the legislature. This could not be if he was to be appointed from time to time by the legislature. It was not clear that an appointment in the first instance, even with an ineligibility afterwards, would not establish an improper connection between the two departments. Certain it was that the appointment would be attended with intrigues and contentions that ought not be unnecessarily admitted. He was disposed for these reasons to refer the appointment to some other source. The people at large was in itself the fittest. It would be as likely as any that could be devised to produce an Executive Magistrate of distinguished character. There was one difficulty, however, of a serious nature. The right of suffrage was much more diffusive

in the Northern than the Southern states. The substitution of electors obviated this difficulty and seemed on the whole to be liable to the fewest objections. (Farrand 1937, 2:56-57)

Without a history of success or a body of republican theory to recommend it, the electoral college was established as a practical solution to a difficult problem that had threatened to create an irreconcilable gap. Late in the Convention, the Committee of Eleven, which had been appointed to forge a compromise, proposed a device with which the Convention could live:

> 2. Each State shall appoint, in such Manner as the Legislature thereof may direct, a Number of Electors, equal to the whole Number of Senators and Representatives to which the State may be entitled in the Congress: but no Senator or Representative, or Person holding an Office of Trust or Profit under the United States, shall be appointed an Elector.
>
> 3. The Electors shall meet in their respective States, and vote by Ballot for two Persons, of whom one at least shall not be an Inhabitant of the same State with themselves. And they shall make a List of all the Persons voted for, and of the Number of Votes for each; which List they shall sign and certify, and transmit sealed to the Seat of the Government of the United States, directed to the President of the Senate. The President of the Senate shall, in the Presence of the Senate and House of Representatives, open all the Certificates, and the Votes shall then be counted. The Person having the greatest Number of Votes shall be the President, if such Number be a Majority of the whole Number of Electors appointed; and if there be more than one who have such Majority, and have an equal Number of Votes, then the House of Representatives shall immediately chuse by Ballot one of them for President; and if no Person has a Majority, then from the five highest on the list the said House shall in like Manner chuse the President. But in choosing the President, the Votes shall be taken by States, the Representation from each State having one Vote; a quorum for this Purpose shall consist of a Member or Members from two thirds of the States, and a Majority of all the States shall be necessary to a Choice. In every Case, after the Choice of the President, the Person having the greatest Number of Votes of the Electors shall be the Vice President. But if there should remain two or more who have equal votes, the Senate shall chuse from them by Ballot the Vice President. (U. S. Const. Art. II, sec. 1)

The electoral college system was, therefore, the result of a truly creative compromise and it offered something to every faction involved in the debate. For those who favored states' rights, there was the provision that state legislatures could decide how electors would be chosen; small states were guaranteed at least three electoral votes—one per senator and one per representative—and equality in case of an election in the House of Representatives; large states had the advantage of population-based apportionment of electoral votes; southern states could apportion electoral votes according to the white population plus three-fifths of the slave population. There was even an element of popular vote in the election, albeit indirect.

The Ratification Debates

> The mode of appointment of the chief magistrate of the United States is almost the only part of the system, of any consequence, which has escaped without severe censure, or which has received the slightest mark of approbation from its opponents. (*Federalist* No. 68)

So wrote Alexander Hamilton to the people of New York in the series of pro-ratification newspaper articles known today as *The Federalist Papers*. There is a certain irony in his statement, in light of the difficulty the Convention had in forming the system in the first place, and the subsequent frequency with which the electoral college has come under attack. Hamilton's statement is also not unreservedly true. Anti-Federalists did object to the electoral college, and on some very fundamental grounds. No longer tied to the practical demands of the Philadelphia Convention, the debate over presidential election during the ratification process focused more directly on principles. The philosophical differences between the Federalists and the Anti-Federalists were evident in the objections raised against the indirect presidential election process.

"Refined Democracy" or the "Simple Business of Election"?

Many Anti-Federalists accused the Constitution, as a whole, of violating republican theory because it attempted to instate a representative system which, they felt, was unworkable in a nation so large and diverse. Self-government was impossible unless the government was closer to the people. The electoral college was another example of how the Constitution was sowing the seeds of tyranny—it reinforced a central government by taking the selection of the president, and therefore any control over him, out of the hands of the people.

James Madison responded to these kinds of objections in *Federalist* No. 10 by developing an argument that was crucial to the justification of the entire representative system and the electoral college in particular. The system was not meant to rob the people of their democratic role in government; its purpose was

> to refine and enlarge the public views, by passing them through the medium of a chosen body of citizens, whose wisdom may best discern the true interest of their country, and whose patriotism and love of justice, will be least likely to sacrifice it to temporary or partial considerations. Under such a regulation, it may well happen that the public voice pronounced by the representatives of the people, will be more consonant to the public good, than if pronounced by the people themselves convened for that purpose. (*Federalist* No. 10)

But Madison's "refined" democracy looked like no democracy at all to "Republicus," a Kentucky Anti-Federalist. In a sharp and lengthy criticism of the electoral college system, Republicus sneered at the "refinement" it represented and displayed a tone that would be echoed in future criticisms as well:

> An extraordinary refinement, this, on the plain simple business of election and of which the grand convention have certainly the honor of being the first inventors; and that for an officer, too, of so much importance as a President . . . who is to continue four years, and is only removable on conviction of treason or bribery, and triable only by the Senate, who are to be his own council, whose interests in every instance runs parallel with his own, and who are neither the officers of the people nor accountable to them. (*Kentucky Gazette*, 1 March 1788)

Thus what appeared to Madison to be an enhancement of the popular will to make it somehow a better representation of the true popular interests of the people was to Republicus an unnecessary and dangerous feature of the system that could only distort the voice of the people. It was a question of how direct self-government could be.

Smokescreen

The theoretical groundwork laid down by Madison gave the Federalists a basis for justifying the electoral college both as a democratic institution (because it refined the choice of the people) and as a republican institution (because it represented the various interests of the states). When it came time to extol the virtues of the electoral college during the ratification debates, the Federalists seemed to overlook the practicalities it had so apparently offered to the Philadelphia Convention and instead focused on the high moral standards they believed the system ensured. Gone was the sense of compromise and imperfection expressed by Madison at the Convention. Instead, Hamilton attested that

> this process of election affords a moral certainty, that the office of President will seldom fall to the lot of any man, who is not in an eminent degree endowed with the requisite qualifications. (*Federalist* No. 68)

Hamilton went on to explain how a system of electors was conducive to the selection of an able and virtuous executive:

> [While it is] desirable, that the sense of the people should operate in the choice of the person to whom so important a trust was to be confided, [it is] equally desirable, that the immediate election should be made by men most capable of analyzing the qualities adapted to the station. A small number of persons selected by their fellow citizens from the general mass, will be most likely to possess the information and discernment requisite to so complicated an investigation. (*Federalist* No. 68)

While Hamilton praised the electoral system as an enhancement of the people's will, "Philadelphiansis" voiced the Anti-Federalist suspicion that the whole invention was merely a smokescreen for the schemes of the elite. The system retained just enough of the trappings of popular election to appease the demands of the people, while in fact, Anti-Federalists claimed, the selection of an executive would be made in the House of Representatives, thereby laying the foundation of tyranny:

> There is not a tincture of democracy in the proposed Constitution, except the nominal elections of the President general and the illustrious Congress be supposed to have some colour of that nature; but this is a mere deception, invented to gull the people into its adoption. Its framers were well aware that some appearance of election ought to be observed, especially in regard to the first Congress; for without such an appearance there was not the smallest probability of their having it organized and set in operation. But let the wheels of this government be once cleverly set in motion, and I'll answer for it, that the people shall not be much troubled with future elections, especially in choosing the *king*, the *standing army* will do that business for them. (*Independent Gazetteer*, 7 February 1788)

If the Federalists were able to invest the electoral system with a hitherto-absent moral and theoretical virtue during the ratification debates, some people, at least, weren't convinced.

Threat from Above or Below?

Distrust was at the root of the arguments of both the Anti-Federalists and the Federalists. Philadelphiansis and his cohorts did not trust a centralized government with a structure that put it out of the reach of the people. The electoral college was just such a structure, they felt, designed with dictatorship as its ultimate goal. The Federalists, on the other hand, distrusted the masses. Not only did they concur with the opinion expressed at the Philadelphia Convention that the people were not adequately informed to choose a president, but they generally feared the "tumult and disorder" that could result from too much democracy. The electoral college, in their view, was the perfect buffer against the "excesses" of the people:

> The choice of *several* to form an intermediate body of electors will be much less apt to convulse the community, with any extraordinary or violent movements, than the choice of *one* who was himself to be the final object of the public wishes. And as the electors, chosen in each state, are to assemble and vote in the state, in which they are chosen, this detached and divided situation will expose them much less to heats and ferments, which might be communicated from them to the people, than if they were all to be convened at one time, in one place. (*Federalist* No. 68)

The Anti-Federalists rejected the whole notion that the community needed to be protected from itself. As far as Republicus was concerned, the electoral college system reflected a blatant disregard for the basic rights and freedoms of citizens, and a disintegration of those rights was much more to be feared than "heats and ferments":

> Is it then become necessary, that a free people should first resign their right to suffrage into other hands besides their own, and then, secondly, that they to whom they resign it should be compelled to choose men, whose persons, characters, manners, or principles they know nothing of? And, after all . . . to intrust Congress with the final decision at last? Is it necessary, is it rational, that the sacred rights of mankind should thus dwindle down to the elector of electors, and those again electors of other electors? This seems to be degrading them even below the prophetical curse denounced by the good old patriarch, on the offspring of his degenerate son: 'servant' of servants. . . ."
> To conclude, I can think of but one source of right to government or any branch of it—and that is THE PEOPLE. They and only they, have a right to determine whether they will make laws or execute them, or do both in a collective body, or by a delegated authority. Delegation is a positive actual investiture. Therefore if any people are subjected to an authority which they leave not thus actually chosen—even though they may have tamely submitted to it—yet it is not their legitimate government. They are wholly passive, and as far as they are so, are in a state of slavery. (*Kentucky Gazette*, 1 March 1788)

A Question of Numbers

William Grayson argued against the electoral college at the Virginia ratifying convention by taking an approach that was echoed in other southern states in 1787-88 and continues to be heard to this day:

> I presume . . . that seven Eastern states will always elect him. As he is vested with the power of making treaties, and as there is a material distinction between the carrying and productive states, the latter will be disposed to have him to themselves. He will accommodate himself to their interests in forming treaties, and they will continue him perpetually in office . . . I have made an estimate which shows with what facility they will be able to reelect him. (Elliott 1888, 3:492)

Grayson then presented what may have been the first in a long history of calculations which "proved" that the electoral college would allow a small number of states with powerful interest to elect the president of their choice. Grayson complained that the election process did not adequately counteract the power of state coalitions and therefore could not ensure that the president would reflect a truly national choice, as its defenders claimed it would. This danger was particularly acute if no candidate received a majority of electoral votes and the election of the president was sent to the House of Representatives. That possibility

CONTROVERSIAL ELECTIONS

> I can return to private life with the consciousness that I shall receive from posterity the credit of having been elected to the highest position in the gift of the people, without any of the cares and responsibilities of the office. (Hyman 1954, 29-30)

So said Samuel J. Tilden after losing the election of 1876 to Rutherford B. Hayes. He is not alone in the annals of history; his distinction—winning the popular vote but losing the electoral vote—was shared by Andrew Jackson in 1824 and Grover Cleveland in 1888. These elections all caused surges of reform proposals but no change in the electoral college system. The first problem election of 1800 did.

● **1800**—The contingent election provision of the Constitution was first tested after a vituperative campaign between the Federalists with President John Adams at their head and the Republicans led by then Vice-president Thomas Jefferson. On February 11, 1801, Jefferson presided over the joint session of Congress in which the state electoral votes were opened and counted, revealing an unsatisfactory result to say the least: Jefferson and Aaron Burr each had 73 votes; Adams, 65; Charles Cotesworth Pinkney, 63; and John Jay, 1. Under the rules, it was up to the House to choose the president from among those five. Each of the sixteen states had one vote, with nine needed to win. The first ballot on February 11 was a portent of things to come. Jefferson received 8 votes and Burr received 6 votes. (The congressional delegations from Maryland and Vermont were divided, so they lost their votes.) After a tremendous amount of jockeying and despite the scathing commentary of arch rival Alexander Hamilton, Thomas Jefferson was elected on the thirtieth ballot and the seventh day of continuous session. Under the provisions of the Constitution, Burr as the runner-up became vice-president. The Twelfth Amendment changed the rules for contingency elections in 1804.

● **1824**—The second test of the contingent election came in 1824. Since by then eighteen of the twenty-four states chose electors by popular vote, the people's choice for president could be estimated. Both the popular and the electoral returns gave Andrew Jackson a plurality with John Quincy Adams running second,

William H. Crawford running third, and Henry Clay running fourth in the electoral vote (even though Clay received more popular votes than Crawford). Since no one received a majority in the electoral college, however, the election went to the House. Just before the contingent election, a story in the *Columbian Observer* alleged that Adams had promised Clay an appointment as the Secretary of State in return for his support. Despite their denials, Adams did win with Clay states, and Clay did become Secretary of State. In 1828, Jackson's popular win was vindicated by a sweeping victory over Adams.

● **1876**—The election of 1876 held a series of surprises in a nation barely beginning to recover from the Civil War. The first surprise came in early returns when Democrat Samuel J. Tilden received the electoral votes of Republican states in the north. It looked like he would win with the backing of the solidly Democratic south, but his opponent, Rutherford B. Hayes, had a chance in the states where Reconstruction was still in effect and Republicans controlled the state machinery. What happened is unprecedented in United States history: four states, South Carolina, Louisiana (Reconstruction states), Florida, and Oregon, each sent in two conflicting sets of electoral votes in a year when neither candidate could afford to lose a single electoral vote.

To complicate matters, it was up to the Democratic House and the Republican Senate to resolve the dispute. The electoral commission subsequently appointed by Congress to judge the conflicting state returns was composed of five senators, five representatives, and five members of the judiciary, eight of whom were Republican and seven of whom were Democratic. In every instance, the disputes were decided in the Republican's favor by an 8-7 vote. Hayes won the election, 185-184 electoral votes. Tilden had won the popular vote by half a million.

● **1888**—It was an era of extremely close presidential elections. After a relatively lackluster campaign, Republican Benjamin Harrison received 233 electoral votes and won over Democratic incumbent Grover Cleveland. Cleveland received only 168 electoral votes despite his popular victory by a margin of 95,096 votes. Like the campaign, however, this result caused relatively little excitement at the time.

seems remote to us now but it was generally believed, by the founders themselves, that no one other than George Washington could win an outright majority and that most subsequent elections would, indeed, be decided in the House.

An Imperfect Solution

Despite the high praise given the electoral system by its defenders in the ratifying debates, the records show that it was regarded as an imperfect solution to the very real dilemma of choosing an "Executive Magistrate" in an equitable, representative, and peaceful way. The question then, as now, is whether any other solution would be "more perfect."

Major Electoral Alternatives

Many different alternatives to the electoral college have been proposed, beginning soon after the Constitution was finally ratified in 1789. The major approaches to reform over the years, which can be summed up in a few categories, were formulated in the early nineteenth century and for the most part remain the basis of the discussion today.

The District Method

First proposed in Congress in 1800, the district method of choosing electors has been touted by supporters as the one most favored by the founders themselves, because of Madison's statement in 1823 that "the district mode was mostly, if not exclusively, in view when the Constitution was framed and adopted" (letter to George Hay, 1823). Under this system, each of the nation's congressional districts would have one elector and each state would have two at-large electors, with the District of Columbia allotted the same number as the least populous state. Electors would be chosen by popular vote in each district, and the at-large electors would be chosen according to the overall state vote. A number of states used the district method in the first decades of the nineteenth century and it was a prominent reform supported by Thomas Hart Benton in the 1820s and 30s, during the 1870s by Sen. Oliver P. Morton, and was revived during the 1950s in the Mundt-Coudert amendment.

The Proportional Plan

This plan would abolish the office of elector and automatically assign a state's electoral votes to a candidate in direct proportion to the popular vote in the state. While approaching the popular vote principle, the proportional plan seeks to preserve the federal principle of distributing electoral power among the states. It was first introduced in Congress in 1848 and considered again in the aftermath of the uncertain presidential election of 1876. It is primarily known to twentieth-century reformers as the Lodge-Gossett amendment, reported favorably in 1948 and 1949 by House and Senate Judiciary committees. In 1950 it passed the Senate by a 62-27 vote, thereby achieving the two-thirds majority necessary for constitutional amendment, but was defeated in the House, 210-134.

Direct Popular Election

The most frequently proposed alternative would do away with the indirect vote and the electoral college altogether, and establish a national election of the president by a popular majority. Recently added to the plan have been provisions that the winning candidate must receive only forty percent of the popular vote and that if no candidate wins forty percent the president will be chosen by the people in a second runoff election between the top two candidates, rather than by a vote in Congress.

First proposed in 1816, direct election met with resistance from the states' rights advocates, smaller states, and the slave-holding states, which would lose electoral votes apportioned to three-fifths of the slave population. Andrew Jackson, defeated by John Quincy Adams in the controversial election of 1824, advocated a popular vote in his first annual address to Congress after he was elected in 1828. After a lull in interest, the idea was revived in the post Civil War Congress by Sen. Charles Sumner on the basis of civil rights and during the 1870s by representatives from western states who favored more direct forms of democracy. The proposal slipped into the background again until the 1960s when renewed interest resulted in many resolutions and hearings in the House and Senate. Direct election has been the most prominent reform proposal ever since.

Other Changes

Several changes short of fundamental reform have been proposed to correct what are widely perceived as flaws in the electoral college system. The automatic plan would correct the "faithless elector" problem by abolishing the office of elector and automatically assigning all the state electoral votes to the popular vote winner. Its opponents say the automatic plan is worse than no change at all, because it would institute the winner take all system everywhere. Other reforms, such as the National Bonus Plan, seek to eliminate the possibility that the popular vote winner can lose the election.

The Modern Debate

Early Changes in the Electoral College

Despite the reform efforts of almost two hundred years, the constitutional provisions regulating the electoral college have changed very little. In 1804, the Twelfth Amendment changed the procedures governing the selection of the president by the House of Representatives when no candidate wins a majority of electoral votes. Passed in the aftermath of the troubled election of 1800, the Twelfth Amendment created the contingent election procedure we have today and made a separate ballot for the vice-president rather than assigning that office to the runner-up of the presidential ballot. Since George Grayson had complained from the start that the contingent election was "rather founded on accident than any principle of government I ever heard of," the amendment was timely. It was clearly inspired by practicality rather than principle: the thirty ballots required to elect Thomas Jefferson were evidence enough of the need for change.

Other electoral college changes have been made in the states, which under the Constitution have broad discretion in the method of choosing presidential electors. By the 1830s, most states had changed from legislative appointment to popular election of slates of electors. All the states, except South Carolina, adopted the "general ticket," "unit vote," or "winner take all" system, as it is variously known, by 1836. This method is used everywhere except Maine today. The dominant political parties in the states were early proponents of this system, since they stood to gain even more strength by not having to concede any votes to the opposition party. Once a few states instituted the winner take all rule, it made sense for others to maximize their relative electoral clout by adopting it, too.

The influence of politics on early electoral college change is ironic in light of James Wilson's argument in its favor in 1787. With the electoral college, he said,

> ... we avoid corruption; and we are little exposed to the lesser evils of party intrigue; and when the government shall be organized, proper care will undoubtedly be taken to counteract influence even of that nature. (Elliott 1888, 2:511)

In its original form, the electoral college did not anticipate the political extravaganzas presidential elections would become. However, the electoral college *has* adapted with changing times into a more political, party-dominated, and nonelitist institution. Is it a suitable way for Americans to elect a president in the late twentieth century and beyond? Its supporters, arguing practicality, say yes, it can be adapted. Its opponents, invoking the principles of an evolving democratic system, say no.

Electoral college reform has a long and varied history of its own. By no means part of a single or unified movement, attempts to change the way we elect the president have been inspired by larger developments in American history—in particular, the changing nature of the right to vote and the rise of what has been called the "People's Presidency." The recent history of electoral college reform, from the debates over the Lodge-Gossett proportional plan in the 1940s and 50s to the rise of a new interest in direct popular election in the 1960s and 70s, provides a good example of how attempts to change the electoral college have been, and continue to be, influenced by the principles and politics of suffrage, relative state power, and representative government.

Votes Given and Votes Taken Away

The gradual democratization of the franchise is a trend that spans two hundred years of United States history. What began as a strictly limited franchise expanded in the early eighteenth century as the states extended the right to vote to all white men whether they owned property or not. The use of the Constitution to extend voting rights began after the Civil War, when the Thirteenth Amendment (1865) outlawed slavery, the Fourteenth Amendment (1868) established citizenship and equal protection under the law for blacks, and the Fifteenth Amendment (1870) guaranteed that "the right of citizens of the United States to vote shall not be denied or abridged by the United States or by any state on account of race, color, or previous condition of servitude."

Extension of voting rights continued into the twentieth century. The Seventeenth Amendment (1913) gave citizens the right to elect their senators directly. The Nineteenth Amendment (1920) recognized the right of women to vote. The District of Columbia was allotted presidential electors by the Twenty-third Amendment (1961), and the franchise was extended to eighteen-year-olds in the Twenty-sixth Amendment (1971).

Through the amendment process the Constitution has played the central role in extending the franchise beyond society's privileged and beyond the majority. One longstanding criticism of the electoral college, however, charges that the Constitution, with its loose provision allowing states to decide how electors are chosen, in effect denies the vote to a different kind of minority: those who oppose the winner. Sen. Thomas Hart Benton of Missouri, for whom electoral reform was a lifelong commitment, made this charge as early as the 1820s:

> To lose their votes, is the fate of all minorities, and it is their duty to
> submit; but this is not a case of votes lost, but of votes taken away,
> added to those of the majority, and given to a person to whom the
> minority is opposed. (*Annals of Congress, 1823-24*, 41)

Benton aimed his criticism directly at the winner take all system of
awarding electoral votes in the states, which effectively gives the
popular vote winner the electoral votes of citizens who oppose him.
Benton suggested a variation on the district plan as an alternative, but
his larger point went beyond state regulations to the heart of the
electoral system itself: the very idea of an intermediary between the
president and the people makes inequality inevitable.

The Lodge-Gossett Proportional Plan

Benton's reasoning and his direct plan were an important part of
the spurt of interest in electoral college reform more than 125 years later
when considerable congressional attention was paid to a host of
proposals to get rid of the winner take all system in the states and, in
some cases, to get rid of the office of elector itself. Perhaps the most
widely known was the Lodge-Gossett amendment, a joint resolution
sponsored by Sen. Henry Cabot Lodge and Rep. Ed Gossett, which
passed the Senate by a more than two-thirds majority but failed in the
House in 1950.

The Lodge-Gossett amendment was a proportional plan and its
main target was the winner take all system. Unlike Benton, its
supporters now had a history of constitutional amendments to add
weight to their case for change. Had not amendments successfully
expanded the electorate and made the Senate subject to popular
election? The American people were accustomed to electing their
leaders directly. Why should the dangers of the electoral college
continue to exist?

The "dangers" that the Lodge-Gossett bill tried to avert were those
brought on by the fact that the electoral college and winner take all
systems ran contrary to the democratizing direction of the evolving
Constitution. It violated the sanctity of the individual's vote by crediting
the winner with the votes cast against him and it placed an intermediary
between the people and the president, an intermediary which many did
not even realize existed. The bill's sponsors were not willing to advocate
direct popular election, however. They wanted to preserve the element
of state participation and the essentially federalist nature of the presidential election process. Ironically, the federalism question of relative
state power in presidential elections created the controversy that has-
tened the demise of the Lodge-Gossett proportional plan.

The Civil Rights Objection

The road to an extended franchise has been far from straight and smooth. The Thirteenth, Fourteenth, and Fifteenth amendments recognized blacks as citizens with the right to vote, but measures to enforce them met with resistance and countermeasures in many southern states. Devices such as poll taxes, literacy tests, strict residency requirements, "grandfather clauses," and restrictive primary regulations denied the rights guaranteed by the Constitution. These devices worked because of the dominance of the Democratic party in the post-Reconstruction South. If blacks, for example, were kept from participating in the Democratic party primaries, and therefore had no voice in the selection of a candidate, they in effect had no vote because the Democratic candidate was sure to win the general election with or without black support.

During the debate over the Lodge-Gossett amendment and related plans in the 1950s, the tradition of state resistance ran head-on into that of extending voting rights. The immediate issue at hand was a familiar one within electoral college discussions: Which states stood to benefit most from the proportional plan? In the course of the sometimes heated exchange, this issue spawned a clash over civil rights and pitted conservative southern Democrats against northern liberals from both parties. Representative Gossett brought the conflict to center stage when he asked, on the floor of the House, and "at the risk of stepping on a few toes":

> Is it fair, is it honest, is it democratic, is it in the best interest of anyone, in fact, to place such a premium on a few thousand labor votes, or Italian votes, or Irish votes, or Negro votes, or Jewish votes, or Polish votes, or Communist votes, or big-city machine votes, simply because they happen to be located in two or three large industrial pivotal states? (*Congressional Record* 1950, 10416)

Gossett's appeal to the majority only verified the suspicions of liberal Democrats and Republicans that the southern Democrats were trying to inflate their power in presidential elections at the expense of the liberal wing of the party and as a threat to the political voice of minorities. Representative Clifford Case, a Republican from New Jersey, warned that the proposal would "reduce the Republican Party to impotence" (Peirce 1968, 170). Case added that any weakening of two-party competition would have important consequences for the emerging politics of civil rights. NAACP representative John A. Davis and NAACP executive director Clarence Mitchell charged more overtly in their 1955 testimony against the Daniel-Humphrey proportional plan bill: it would give free rein to southern states to continue and reinforce

"BLOODSHED ... OR REVOLUTION"
THE CASE OF THE PROBLEM ELECTOR

Representative Walter: Suppose a sufficient number of electors were for some reason prevailed upon to vote contrary to the wishes of the voters in their states? I could see possibilities of bloodshed.

Senator Kefauver: ... or revolution.

By the early nineteenth century, the original notion of electors as detached and thoughtful leaders designated by the people to exercise independent judgment was a thing of the past. They had become agents of the people's or, more accurately, of their party's will, and were chosen not for their learning but for their pledges.

The fact remains, however, that an elector is a free agent empowered by the Constitution to vote for any candidate. Despite some state and party regulations attempting to bind an elector to his pledge, that free agent can, and has, become a problem elector in a number of ways.

● The *faithless elector* has appeared in a few isolated cases in the past, making enough noise to send out warning signals to those who fear the consequences of a widespread "bolting" of pledged electors. A pledge was broken as early as 1796 when Federalist Samuel Miles voted for Republican Thomas Jefferson. The most recent bolt was in 1960 when Republican Henry D. Irwin of Oklahoma voted for Harry Byrd instead of Richard Nixon and defended his action on national television as a stand against the "socialist-labor leadership."

● The *unpledged elector* was used as a device in the elections of 1948 by the Dixiecrats and in 1960 by southern conservatives who sought bargaining power by threatening to prevent either major party candidate from winning a majority of electoral votes, a

their efforts to deny the black vote. One-party southern states with few minorities would have an inordinate effect on the presidential election because all their electoral votes would go to the conservative Democrat while the electoral votes of the more diverse north would be divided among many candidates. As Davis said, the plan

... will kill directly the political influence of the Negro and the minority group votes in pivotal states. Second, it will reduce the importance of the Northern states as a whole and the great industrial states specifically. Third, it will destroy the liberal Democratic Party, for it will once again establish the power of the solid South over the

strategy that, if successful, would have thrown the election into the House of Representatives and given its architects virtual power to determine the election results.

● The *uncertain elector* cropped up in the elections of 1860 and 1912. In 1860 the Democratic Convention nominated Steven Douglas, but only after thirteen southern states had broken away to nominate John Breckinridge. Since neither candidate had the two-thirds support required by party rules, some states actually had electoral tickets split between Douglas and Breckinridge. In 1912, the Republicans nominated Taft without the renegade delegates who withdrew to become part of the Progressive Party backing Theodore Roosevelt. An *Outlook* magazine editorial described their dilemma this way:

> For whom should the presidential electors in these [progressive] states vote, provided they are elected in November? Should they vote for the conservative candidate of the 18th of June convention or for the Progressive candidate of the 5th of August Convention? On the one hand, it is claimed that by a tradition existing for over a century, presidential electors are chosen to perform a purely ministerial act, and therefore the electors already nominated by the Republican Party are under a moral obligation to vote for Mr. Taft. On the other hand, it is claimed that the presidential electors in the several states do not represent the National Convention, or the National Party, but the state which elects them, and therefore they should vote for the candidate who is favored by that state. (*Outlook* 12 [1912], 656)

None of these problem electors has had a measurable effect on the presidency. But the potential danger is clear and they are part of the case against the electoral college.

> Democratic Party. Fourth, many independent groups, liberal groups, and even labor groups will begin to take less interest in the problems of the Negro and other minorities. Fifthly, the Daniel-Humphrey proposal will kill the influence of the great urban pivotal states. (Testimony, Senate Judiciary Committee, 1 April 1955)

The director of the NAACP, Clarence Mitchell, accused the sponsors of proportional and district plans of making a "blatantly racial appeal" to achieve reform for the sake of political power rather than principle. Commenting on Gossett's 1950 floor statement, Mitchell said:

I would get the impression from Mr. Gossett's statement that about the only people in the United States who are not minorities and not, therefore, a menace to the national welfare are the people of Texas. (Testimony, Senate Judiciary Committee, 1 April 1955)

Valuing principle over politics, Mitchell claimed, would lead reformers to oppose the proportional plan, which not only essentially disenfranchised minorities but retained the possibility of electing a president who did not have a majority of popular votes. Only the direct election alternative, he believed, combined with a positive commitment to getting rid of poll taxes, literacy tests, residency requirements, and other restrictive state measures, would represent a true extension of the constitutionally recognized right of every citizen to vote.

Toward Direct Election

Proportional and district plan amendments had been proposed long before the 1950s and continue to attract support today. The 1950s' debate is particularly significant, however, because it brought together the issues of extended suffrage, civil rights, and the balance of state power within the electoral college system. In many ways, these clashes set the stage for a new direction in the electoral college debate during the 1960s: toward renewed support for the direct election alternative.

One Person, One Vote

"All of these proposed reforms have one fault in common," commented Tom Wicker in discussing the proportional, district, and similar plans. "In some form each of them retains the electoral college, and that is the root of the trouble." Wicker, writing in 1968 in the foreword to journalist Neil Peirce's book *The People's Presidency*, agreed with the author's carefully argued support of direct election for the president:

The single reform that removes the inequities and perils of the present system without substituting others, that conforms to the long-range trend of American politics and society, is to eliminate the electoral college altogether and give the election of their President directly to the American people. (Peirce 1968, 11-12)

Wicker's opinion reflects a basic shift in attitude toward electoral college alternatives, a shift which indicated a profound change in the conception of a citizen's right to vote in the United States. Beginning in 1962, with the *Baker v. Carr* case, a series of Supreme Court decisions on legislative apportionment and voting rights had an enormous effect on the law of the land and gave added impetus to civil rights legislation in the battle to enforce the guarantees of the Thirteenth, Fourteenth, and Fifteenth amendments. These decisions also stimulated efforts to gain electoral college reform, this time with a renewed interest in a century-old proposal: direct popular election of the president.

In the *Baker v. Carr* decision the Court claimed the jurisdiction to review questions of apportionment of state legislatures in light of the equal protection clause of the Fourteenth Amendment:

> All persons from or naturalized in the United States and subject to jurisdiction thereof, are citizens of the United States and of the State wherein they reside. No State shall make or enforce any law which shall abridge the privileges or immunities of citizens of the United States; nor shall any State deprive any person of life, liberty, or property without due process of law; nor deny to any person within its jurisdiction the equal protection of the laws. (U. S. Const. Amend. XIV, sec. 1)

In extending the equal protection clause to include the political rights of individuals, the court was declaring, in the words of Justice William O. Douglas, that "the concept of 'we the people' under the Constitution visualized no preferred class of voters but equality among those who meet the basic qualifications. . . ." Douglas continues:

> The concept of political equality from the Declaration of Independence to Lincoln's Gettysburg Address, to the 15th, 17th and 19th amendments can mean only one thing—*one person, one vote.* (Peirce 1968, 246; emphasis added)

Justice Douglas made this statement in the majority opinion of the Court ruling that the state of Georgia, which had a winner take all system of choosing candidates in statewide and congressional primaries, was denying its city residents equal protection under the law. Georgia modelled its system on the presidential electoral college: each county had a certain number of electoral votes, and the candidate who won the majority within the county won all its electoral votes. The system not only enabled a candidate to win the electoral count without having won the popular vote, but it was heavily in favor of rural counties, which had more electoral votes than cities.

The "concept of political equality" and its doctrine of "one person, one vote" invoked by the Court in its Georgia decision set a standard for state legislatures which had direct significance for the individual voter. Justice Earl Warren spelled it out in the majority opinion of a related case in 1964:

> A citizen, a qualified voter, is no more nor no less so because he lives in the city or on the farm. This is the clear and strong command of our Constitution's Equal Protection clause. This is an essential part of the

concept of a government of laws and not men. This is at the heart of Lincoln's vision of 'government of the people, by the people [and] for the people.' The Equal Protection clause demands no less than substantially equal state legislative representation for all citizens, of all places as well as of all races. (Cushman 1975, 659)

If It's Not Good Enough for the States...

The Court's actions and opinions in state apportionment decisions set a precedent that the state of Delaware tried to extend to the electoral college method of choosing presidents. Delaware, later joined by twelve other states, petitioned the Supreme Court in 1966 to hear its case against the electoral college. Based on the principle of "one person, one vote" and the Court's application of equal protection under the law to the political rights of citizens, it contended that the electoral college system was biased against the citizens of small states and denied them equal protection under the law. The plaintiffs in *Delaware v. New York* sought justice against the winner take all system, which, they claimed, gave their votes as citizens less weight than the votes of citizens in New York and other states with large electoral vote blocs. The immediate aim of the case was to have the winner take all system declared unconstitutional, but the brief filed by Delaware revealed a preference for the direct election alternative. The Court declined to hear the case, but the point had been made on behalf of small states.

Despite its refusal to consider extending its standards for state elections to national elections, the Court's opinions in the apportionment decisions laid the groundwork for the application of the one person, one vote principle to civil rights legislation, and for the passage of the Twenty-fourth Amendment (1964) which proclaims that

> The right of a citizen of the United States to vote in any primary or other election for President or Vice President, for electors for President or Vice President, or for Senator or Representative in Congress, shall not be denied or abridged by the United States or any State by reason of failure to pay any poll tax or other tax. (U. S. Const. Amend. XXIV, sec. 1)

The attention to political equality stimulated by the Court and the Congress made the alleged inequalities of the electoral college more glaring and fueled a new round of challenges to the electoral college system. The failure of persistent efforts to reform it seemed more paradoxical than ever before, as Neil Peirce, writing near the end of the decade of change, pointed out:

> Today the United States is approaching universal suffrage, so that every adult American, regardless of wealth, race or residence, will be able to

vote, and to have his vote counted equally and fairly. Suddenly, with the civil rights acts of the last decade, the death of the poll tax and the voting decisions of the Courts, it is upon. *It is the basic political fact of our times. And it is reflected in every American political institution—except the way we elect our President.* (Peirce 1968, 205; emphasis added)

Congress Takes Another Look

On the legislative front, what Peirce referred to as the "basic political fact of our time" caused a distinct shift in emphasis away from reform attempting to reapportion and equalize a still-indirect vote. Instead of juggling with the mechanics of the electoral system, reform proposals of the 1960s and 70s went for all or nothing: abolish the electoral college and replace it with direct popular election, or don't change it at all.

In the late 1960s direct election suddenly became a feasible and timely alternative. For decades, "closet" supporters of direct election shied away from it under the assumption that it would never be ratified by three-fourths of the states because they stood to lose the most from the abolition of the electoral vote. For example, Henry Cabot Lodge, of Lodge-Gossett fame, was in favor of direct election, but threw his weight behind the proportional plan in 1960 because he thought it had a better chance for success. A decade and a half later, it began to look as if direct election commanded enough support to make it all the way. Endorsement by a growing number of groups, including the Chamber of Commerce in 1966 and the American Bar Association in 1967, gave the reform added exposure and credibility. Polls conducted of the general public and the members of the state legislatures indicated a substantial majority were in favor of direct election. Of particular significance was Chairman of the Senate Judiciary Committee Amendments sub-committee Sen. Birch Bayh's announcement on May 18, 1966, that he would sponsor a direct election plan. (This was the same day a Gallup poll showed that sixty-three percent of the American public favored an amendment to abolish the electoral college and establish direct popular election.)

In making this announcement, Bayh reversed his earlier stand against direct election, an opposition which was based on his fear that it would encourage and strengthen splinter parties. Bayh said he had been "wrong" and offered a way to discourage the proliferation of splinter parties. He endorsed a plan calling for direct popular election where only forty percent of the popular vote, instead of a majority, would be enough to win. This would make it much harder for splinter parties to prevent either majority party candidate from winning. One year later, Bayh went a step further and endorsed the American Bar Association plan, which, in addition to the forty percent rule, replaced the contingent election provision with one requiring a runoff between the two highest polling candidates. The popular vote winner would become president.

The Electoral College and the New Math

The feasibility of direct election was also enhanced in the 1960s by the breakdown of the old argument that the states had everything to gain from the electoral college and everything to lose from its abolition. New scholarship sought to prove that smaller states in fact lost out in the electoral college system (and therefore in the campaign) because their numbers didn't mean as much. One piece of scholarly evidence used in the *Delaware v. New York* case (1966) made creative use of a line of argument which had been part of the presidential election debate since the Constitution's ratification: the mathematical inequality. Using a computer analysis which calculated the relative weight of individual votes, political scientist John Banzhaf concluded that a New York vote had 3.312 times the voting power of a voter in Delaware. This formed the basis of Delaware's claim that the winner take all system denied its citizens equal protection. The results of this numerical analysis were later published in an article entitled "One Man, 3.312 Votes: A Mathematical Analysis of the Electoral College."

Louis Koenig made a similar point, without the aid of a computer:

> A national popular election of the President could best harmonize with the ideal proclaimed by the United States Supreme Court in its reapportionment decisions, of one man, one vote, or of equal voting influence for all Americans regardless of geographical location. Under the workings of the electoral college system, this ideal is grossly violated; a popular voter in Nevada can command a far greater percentage of an electoral vote than a voter in the far more heavily populated state of California . . . with the Senate now strongly representative of the urban factor, and with the growing reflection, in the House and the state legislatures, of the Supreme Court's ideals of one man, one vote, the undeniable logic of political progress requires that the Presidency too be brought into accord with that ideal. (Stedman 1968, 20-21)

Growing Support

The flurry of congressional activity on direct election proposals in the late 1960s did not get an amendment through Congress, but did convince many people of the legitimacy of direct election as a viable alternative to the electoral college. It was during this period that the framework of today's reform debate was established. While many proposals short of direct election still exist and have support, the major contemporary arguments revolve around the direct election option.

In September 1969, the House passed a direct election amendment by a vote of 338-70. Ten years later, in July 1979, a similar amendment received a 51-49 favorable vote in the Senate, but failed to receive the necessary two-thirds vote required for constitutional amendments. In between those votes, hearings, endorsements, and opinion polls indicated broadening support for the idea. Presidents Nixon, Carter, and Ford endorsed direct election because disparities between the electoral and the popular vote margins in their elections stirred renewed efforts to reform the existing system. Public opinion polls showed as much as seventy-seven percent of the general public in favor of direct election at the end of 1979. The League of Women Voters has made a continuous effort to achieve direct election, and various interest groups have joined the ranks of the reform's supporters. In 1972, for example, the United Auto Workers convention passed a resolution advocating direct election:

> The UAW's interest in electoral college reform is a logical one that springs directly from the basic principle on which UAW was founded and on which it has always operated. That is the principle of equality of individuals, equality of economic opportunity, equality of educational opportunity, equality of social opportunity, and equality of political participation.
>
> The proposed [direct election] amendment involves the basic principle of equality—of the right of every citizen of age to vote and have his vote count exactly the same as that of every other voter. This is, of course, the theoretical basis of the one man, one vote decisions that the Courts have handed down. The logic and morality of those decisions is inescapable. (Schlossberg, Testimony, Senate Judiciary Committee, 27 September 1973)

As the opinion polls indicate, direct election seems, quite simply, to make sense to many people who, as citizens of the United States, believe they have a right to choose those who govern. Echoing the words of "Republicus," Nancy Newman of the League of Women Voters argues that depriving the people of this right is not only unnecessary, but dangerous:

> The 1976 election showed once again the real chances that our electoral system would elect a candidate who was not the popular vote winner. A switch of only 9,245 votes in Ohio and Hawaii would have put an individual in the White House who was not the popular choice of the voters of our country. (League of Women Voters 1979, 1-2)

Even though support for direct election has broadened since the 1950s and 60s, arguments against it—some new and some old—persist and keep the amendment from getting anywhere. Objections to the direct election system and arguments that insist on the continued viability of the electoral college system are the other half of the dialogue, which, after two hundred years and more than five hundred proposals, has the longevity of the electoral college itself.

The Case for the Electoral College

Defending the electoral college system against its many opponents over the years has never been a simple task. Opponents believe they have the trend of history and the specter of the election of a president who is not the people's choice on their side. Defenders, on the other hand, have the status quo and a record of peaceful (if not perfect) presidential successions to support them. The case for the electoral college today, unlike that in the Philadelphia Convention of 1787, goes beyond practical considerations and links it to the preservation of the founding principles of American government: the balance between central power and local autonomy, the recognition of state identity, and the combination of direct democracy and the representation that protects the minority against the tyranny of the majority.

The Federal Principle and the Dangers of Democracy

The electoral college has been called obsolete and useless because it serves no function in our more democratic and centralized system. Challenging that assumption, its defenders claim it is largely responsible for the continued vitality of the federalist principle which keeps the American system from becoming centralized to the point of no return.

A witness to the 1949 congressional hearings on electoral reform blamed the uninformed public for the ridicule heaped on the electoral college and warned of the consequences of losing a great "national resource":

> The electoral college in late years has become a stranger to most people. The constant shrinkage of public knowledge concerning the functions of government in general, the disinterest and lack of understanding with respect to the fundamentals of the American system, has resulted very largely in this attitude. The electoral college makes its appearance every four years, clothed, it is true, in the ruffles and lace of a period almost forgotten by young and old alike. Its quadrennial appearance induces the mirth, even of some persons in high public office ... It is looked upon as grotesque.
>
> The present system is not grotesque, Mr. Chairman. Rather, it is we who have become grotesque in our present failure to do more than we have to preserve the two most fundamental principles underlying our dual system of government: the principle of state sovereignty and the concept of a Federal Union. The electoral college system of indirect

presidential elections is keyed to that principle by an indissoluable bond. We may laugh it out of existence, but in doing so we will only be destroying one of our greatest national resources. Like the ancient republics mentioned by Dickinson, our scorn for the rights and integrity of the states will only invite the same diseases that destroyed them. (Tawney, Hearings, 11 February 1949)

This vision of doom has been contested by those who agree with Neil Peirce that "if one wants to preserve 'states rights' and the American federal system, there are many better ways to do so than by preserving fictional advantages of the electoral college" (Peirce, 1968). Sen. Mike Mansfield elaborated on this point in 1961:

The Federal System is not strengthened through an antiquated device which has not worked as it was intended to work when it was included in the Constitution and which, if anything, has become a divisive force in the Federal System by pitting groups of states against groups of states. As I see the Federal System in contemporary practice, the House of Representatives is the key to the protection of district interests as district interests, just as the Senate is the key to the protection of state interests as state interests. These instrumentalities, and particularly the Senate, are the principal Constitutional safeguards of the Federal System; but the Presidency has evolved, out of necessity, into the principal political office, as the Courts have become the principal legal bulwark beyond districts, beyond states, for safeguarding the interests of all the people in all the States. And since such is the case, in my opinion, the Presidency should be subject to the direct and equal control of all people. (*Congressional Record* 1961, 147-50)

From an institutional point of view—and in light of the changing roles of governing institutions within the federal system—Mansfield argued that it was logical and right to change the mode of electing presidents. But another important defense of the electoral system, articulated by Raymond Moley in 1955, when the Lodge-Gossett plan was again under discussion in Congress, cautioned would-be reformers to look beyond the institutional point of view to the principle involved in changing the system. Arguing with the logic of consistency, Moley warned that the proportional principle in the electoral college would lead to proportional representation in Congress. Similarly, direct election "would assume that this is a single, unitary national government." Moley wrote:

If we grant that this should be a democracy and to that end prefer a direct popular election of the President, let us be consistent. Let us then abolish the Senate, deny to the Courts the right to pass upon the Constitutionality of legislation, establish a nationwide initiative and referendum on legislation by Congress, and elect a national assembly by proportional representation. This, in effect, would abolish Constitutional government. (Moley 1955)

A Question of Identity

In defense of the as yet unratified Constitution in 1787, Alexander Hamilton tried to reassure states' rights advocates that the people would, no doubt, gain a sense of identity and attach their allegiances to the state and local, rather than the national, government. The role of states and state identity is another aspect of the federalism issue that has appeared in debates over the electoral college. For some, the old idea of filtering the will of the people through electors to find "the best man" runs contrary to the historical development of a national identity embodied in the one national official who is not only a leader, but also a protector of the aspirations and ideals of all Americans:

> Can it any longer be pretended that this great people needs the electors to choose wisely for it? Of course not. Yet that was the original theory. The President is the only American official who represents the American people entire—the whole constituency, every one of us, from Maine to California, Dixiecrat and New Left, white and black, man and woman—and what real reason is there that we should not vote directly for him and have our votes counted directly for him? We may be 50 states in Congress but we are one people in the White House—or should be—and the President ought to be ours to choose. (Wicker, Foreword in Peirce 1968, 15)

Resisting a vision of undifferentiated national unity, Theodore White, in an article entitled "Direct Elections: An Invitation to National Chaos," hearkens back to Hamilton in insisting that the states do have a role in the creation of an American identity. Among the faults of the direct election system, which was characterized as "a proposal to abolish the federal system" that would promote a degree of "centralization" that "breaches all American tradition," White predicted a loss, not just of federalism, but of the identity that only the states could provide:

> What is right about the old system is the sense of identity it gives Americans. As they march to the polls, Bay Staters should feel Massachusetts is speaking, Hoosiers should feel Indiana is speaking; blacks and other minorities should feel their votes count; so, too, should Southerners from Tidewater to the Gulf. The Federal System has worked superbly for almost two centuries. It can and should be speedily improved. But to reduce Americans to faceless digits on an enormous tote board, in a plebiscite swept by demagoguery, manipulated by TV, at the mercy of crooked counters—this is an absurdity for which goodwill and able theory are not justification. (White 1970)

In a very real sense, then, the electoral college and federalism debate is over what is the more essentially American tradition—the growth of nationhood or the retention of state identity—and whether the indirect vote for president would elevate "this great people" or degrade them into "faceless digits." Would it create the kind of democracy the founders wanted to avoid—one that would promote tyranny of the majority at the expense of the diversity our system of mixed government was created to preserve? Or would it in fact preserve the vitality of that tradition by recognizing the new reality of the "People's Presidency"?

To Protect the Minority

Supporters of the electoral college have recently added a new twist to their argument against direct election—they claim it would hurt minority groups more than it would hurt anyone else. This represents a change from the days when the civil rights groups, which so strongly opposed the proportional plans of the 1950s, favored direct election in the name of making every individual vote count equally. Now, however, a growing number of scholars believe that direct election would hurt minorities more than it would help them. A reform instituted in the name of "more democracy" would actually eliminate any political leverage minority groups now have in presidential elections. Theodore White asserted in his 1970 criticism of direct election proposals that:

> if the states are abolished as voting units, the chief political leverage of Negroes is abolished. Whenever a race issue has been settled by plebiscite . . . the plebiscite vote has put the blacks down. (White 1970)

Denied the ability to swing a pool of electoral votes to one candidate or another, minorities would be at the mercy of the majority and they would, invariably, suffer as a result.

In a 1979 article entitled "The Plebiscitary Presidency: Direct Election as Class Legislation," political scientist Aaron Wildavsky explains the gradual disenfranchisement which he fears direct election would create. The electoral college system as it stands now forces the political parties to build broad coalitions of supporters who span a range of geographic areas, professions, and interest. The parties need the votes of the disadvantaged and less educated as well as the educated elite. Thus they pay attention to the needs of the disadvantaged and, more importantly, serve as "intermediaries" between the people and the candidates. With a direct election method, Wildavsky argues, parties would not need the broad coalitions as long as they could appeal to a sufficient number of like-minded voters. Nobody would care about the people who need parties to educate them. Elections would become a contest of stark numbers rather than a process of building coalitions based on real issues and interests.

Critics of Wildavsky's approach to the issue say that it is mere speculation. No one really knows whether parties would decline and certain groups would suffer with direct election. Furthermore, it is questionable whether the electoral college really does force parties to pay attention to minorities, or whether it leads them merely to focus on a few "key" states with large numbers of electoral votes. Sen. Birch Bayh takes note of these concerns, but returns attention to

> ... the most fundamental flaw: the fact that the present electoral vote system cannot guarantee that the candidate with the most popular votes will be elected.... How can we possibly justify the continued use of such a patchwork of inequity and chance? (Baum and Longley 1972, viii)

The development of the minority argument against direct election and related research into its effects on the federal principle seem to indicate a renewed concern for a system that is balanced rather than one that reflects the "one person, one vote" principle that so pervaded the 1960s' debate. Another indication of this concern appeared in 1978 in the form of a new plan to reform the electoral college, one which was forged and proposed as a genuine compromise between the seemingly irreconcilable positions of direct election or the status quo.

A New Compromise: The National Bonus Plan

In 1978, the Twentieth Century Fund issued the report of a task force composed of people from various scholarly, political, and professional backgrounds gathered to consider electoral college reform. The members of the task force began their deliberations divided into two camps: those who favored keeping the electoral college system with minor changes and those who favored abolishing it and instituting direct election. The experience of this modern-day committee bore a striking resemblance to that of the Committee of Eleven which created the original electoral system at the Philadelphia Convention. Like that committee, the task force started with two seemingly irreconcilable positions and ended up with a compromise.

The compromise is known as the National Bonus Plan, which represents an attempt to retain the current system of state electoral votes but eliminate what the task force saw as its major flaw by creating an extra "bonus" of votes which would be added automatically to the tally of the national popular vote winner. Specifically, the proposal would:

● Create an extra pool of national electoral votes in the ratio of two per state plus two for the District of Columbia for a total of 102. The winner of the national popular vote would be awarded this "bonus" on a winner take all basis. This would be sufficient to ensure that the electoral college winner was also the popular vote winner.

● Eliminate the office of elector and the college itself and institute an automatic winner take all electoral vote awarding system in every state. There would be no possibility of "faithless elector" and state electoral vote procedures would be uniform.

● In case no candidate wins an electoral majority, the plan calls for a second runoff election between the two highest contenders within thirty days, and the winner of the electoral vote wins.

The task force explained its compromise in the statement accompanying its report:

> [The] debate over its merits, and a careful comparison of its features to both the existing system and direct election, resulted in broad agreement, by a task force that was both diverse and bipartisan, that the national bonus plan was fairer than, and superior to, any other. It introduces novel features to the existing system, but it's a Constitutional innovation that is no more novel or ingenious than the original plan for the electoral college. There can be only one winner in a presidential election and the proposed provision of a bonus for the candidate with the majority votes is, in our view, in the Anglo-American tradition of winner take all. In every sense, it is a reform, not a radical restructuring of the system.
>
> We believe that our recommendations either minimize or eliminate the problems that plague the existing system. We also believe that the national bonus plan avoids potential problems and risks that might be encouraged with direct election. Because it both preserves traditional values and simplifies the presidential election process, it appealed to the task force as a whole. It is our hope that it will have a similar appeal to the nation. (Twentieth Century Fund 1978)

The balance the National Bonus Plan attempted to achieve was not unlike the balance achieved in 1787: it combined the elements of popular voting, preserved the states as electoral units, and deferred to the "Anglo-American tradition" in its nonrevolutionary proposal. In its concern for traditional values, it gave more attention to eliminating some of the obvious and agreed upon flaws of the system than to extending the principle of absolute equality of voting to the presidential election—the basic goal of direct election proponents. So far, this compromise has not appealed to the nation as much as direct election, which remains the major reform proposed as an alternative to the electoral college system.

Why No Change?

The issue of electoral college reform is raised at least once every four years, when the presidential election stimulates the press to explain, if not comment upon, the way the electoral college system works. Debate, proposed amendments, and hearings persist in Congress, but no amendment has reached either house of Congress for a vote since 1979.

After so many years and so many varied attempts to change the way we elect the president, it is only logical to wonder why there has been no change in the electoral college. Almost everyone agrees that the mechanics of the electoral college, as an institution composed of electors, could be improved. Historian Carl Becker looked at it in the context of the rest of the Constitution and concluded that

> of all the provisions of the federal Constitution, the electoral system was the most unrealistic—the one provision not based solidly on political experience and precedent. It was in the nature of an academic invention which ignored experience in the vain expectation that, in this one instance for this high purpose, politicians would divest themselves of party prejudice and class and sectional bias, and be all for the time being noble Brutuses inspired solely by pure love of liberty and the public good. (Becker 1945, 389)

But the mechanics of the college and the electoral principle are two different things. Despite the scathing review, Professor Becker concludes his argument in favor of retaining the electoral college, with minor changes. This dichotomy is no doubt largely responsible for lack of reform success: even when critics agree on the problem, they don't always agree on the solution.

It is also true that the odds are heavily weighted against any change in the American constitutional system. One of the reasons why the electoral college reform has remained a perennial queston can be summed up in a statement about change in general: it is risky, it is uncertain, and it is difficult.

The Practical Perspective

In the absence of any true consensus in favor of the current system, it is probably sheer practicality that has prevented reform. One "practical" argument is that the system has worked, at least in the sense that it has produced a succession of presidents in a peaceful process. Political scientist Martin Diamond weighed the relative success against the possible risk of change and concluded that

> like every political institution, the electoral college contains dangerous possibilities. But this much may be said about them: all the dangers critics claim to see in the electoral college are entirely matters of speculation. Some have never actually occurred and others have not occurred for nearly a century. Nothing whatever has actually gone wrong with the electoral college for a very long time. Experience has

demonstrated that the dangers incident to the present system are neither grave nor likely to occur. But what of the dangers incident to the proposed reform? It is as important to speculate about them as to frighten ourselves with imaginary possibilities under the electoral college. (Diamond 1977, 18-19)

One of the strongest of the practical arguments against change is that we would be exposing ourselves to the unknown. As Clinton Rossiter, one of the foremost authorities on the American presidency, wrote:

> There are several reasons, all of them convincing, why we should hesitate a long time before replacing a Humpty-Dumpty system that works with a neat one that may blow up in our faces. All the arguments for the system are practical; most of those against it are theoretical. Until we are sure that the Presidency itself will not suffer from a radical change in the method of election, we had best stand fast on tradition and prescription. (Rossiter 1960, 222)

Advocates of direct election disagree with Rossiter's characterization of their arguments as "theoretical" and point out that during the nineteenth century there were several instances in which the popular vote winner was defeated and many, more recent close calls. They also assert, as James MacGregor Burns did in 1948, that the electoral college is a dangerous anachronism in a democratic society:

> If [our electoral college system in action] were a perfectly harmless pastime, Americans might take as much delight in it as the English do in the opening of Parliament by the King. Unfortunately, the Electoral College is not harmless. A Senate Committee recently called it unfair, inaccurate, uncertain and undemocratic. (Burns 1948)

The "Most Difficult" Question

The one certain conclusion that can be drawn from electoral college reform attempts is that the question of its merit—what James Wilson called the "most difficult" question to face the Philadelphia Convention—has not yet been answered to everyone's satisfaction.

Arguments For the Electoral College

• The electoral method remains an essential part of the federal system and the only fair way to elect a president. It recognizes the important role of the states as political units and guarantees that a president will be supported by a geographically broad constituency.

• The electoral college method is also an accurate reflection of "mixed" government, which combines elements of popular democracy with representative democracy in recognition of the legitimate role of both the majority and the minority in American politics.

● The electoral vote margin has the effect of expanding the president's sense that he has a mandate to lead the country. For example, President Reagan won only fifty-one percent of the popular vote in 1980, and a whopping ninety-one percent of the electoral college vote.

● The electoral college enables minority groups to wield power in presidential elections because they can influence significant blocs of electoral votes in a state and therefore the candidates must pay attention to their legitimate interests. No other alternative retains this feature.

● The electoral college method discourages fraud. The direct election alternative would create a wide-open target for fraud in vote counting because there would be no way of facilitating a recount.

● The electoral college system has some defects, such as the "faithless elector," but they can be corrected without radical restructuring.

Arguments Against the Electoral College

● The system is archaic. It was created in a time when the people did not have access to the information they do now and based on the assumption that a few electors would be better equipped to choose a national leader wisely. It is completely counter to the historic trend toward one person, one vote in this country.

● The system is dangerous. The possibility of electing a president who is not the choice of the people is very real and could cause a constitutional crisis.

● There has been much debate over who benefits most from the current system: large states, industrial states, or urban minority groups? There is no doubt, however, that some groups and states benefit unduly and are the focus of attention in the presidential campaign to the exclusion of others. It is both more logical and more just that every vote carry equal weight.

● The electoral college system is complicated and inconsistent: different states choose their electors differently; there is no guarantee that electors will actually vote for the candidate they are pledged to.

● The indirect feature of the electoral college is discouraging to voter participation because every vote does not count. Because of the winner take all system in most states, a number of popular votes are actually nullified.

References

Banzhaf, John F., III. "One Man, 3.312 Votes: A Mathematical Analysis of the Electoral College." *Villanova Law Review* 13 (Winter 1968).

Baum, Alan G., and Lawrence D. Longley. *The Politics of Electoral College Reform.* New Haven, Conn.: Yale University Press, 1972.

Becker, Carl. "The Will of the People." *Yale Review* 34 (Spring 1945).

Burns, James MacGregor. "The Electoral College Meets—But Why?" *New York Times Magazine*, 12 December 1948.

Cushman, Robert. *Cases in Constitutional Law.* 4th ed. Englewood Cliffs, N.J.: Prentice-Hall, 1975.

Diamond, Martin. *The Electoral College and the American Idea of Democracy.* Washington, D. C.: American Enterprise Institute, 1977.

Elliott, Jonathan, ed. *The Debates in the Several State Conventions on the Adoption of the Federal Constitution.* 5 vols. New York: Burt Franklin, 1888.

Farrand, Max, ed. *The Records of the Federal Convention of 1787.* 4 vols. New Haven, Conn.: Yale University Press (revised edition), 1937.

Hamilton, Alexander, John Jay, and James Madison. *The Federalist Papers.* Especially numbers 10, 67-77. Available in various editions.

Hyman, Sidney. *The American President.* New York: Harper and Row, 1954.

League of Women Voters. "Testimony Before the Subcommittee on the Constitution of the Senate Judiciary Committee on the Direct Election of the President, by Nancy Newman, Vice-president League of Women Voters of the United States." Washington D. C.: League of Women Voters, 3 April 1979.

Moley, Raymond. "To Form a More Perfect Union." *Newsweek*, 4 April 1955.

Peirce, Neil. *The People's Presidency.* New York: Simon and Schuster, 1968.

Rossitor, Clinton. *The American Presidency.* New York: Harcourt Brace & World, 1960.

Stedman, Murray S., Jr., ed. *Modernizing American Government.* Englewood Cliffs, N.J.: Prentice-Hall, 1968.

Twentieth Century Fund. "Winner Take All." Task Force on Reform of the Presidential Election Process. New York: Twentieth Century Fund, 1978.

U.S. Congress, House Committee on the Judiciary. *Amend the Constitution with Respect to Elections of the President and Vice President.* Hearings, 82d Cong., 1st sess., 9-25 February 1949.

U.S. Congress, Senate Committee on the Judiciary. *Nomination and Election of President and Vice President.* Hearings, 84th Cong., 1st sess., 16 March-6 April 1955.

U.S. Congress, Senate Committee on the Judiciary. *Electoral Reform.* Hearings, 93d Cong., 1st sess., 26-27 September 1973.

White, Theodore. "Direct Elections: An Invitation to National Chaos." *Life,* 3 January 1970.

3. The Presidential Term and Executive Power

"Article— The term of office of the President and Vice-President of the United States shall be six years. No person shall be eligible for more than one term as President or Vice-President."

The founders created the president as the representative of the entire people, the one who would lead, protect, and uphold the American vision of its nationhood. The office has changed with the nation. In the last fifty years, the executive branch has increased in size and stature beyond all initial expectation.

Modern attempts to reform the presidency are responses to recent developments, but they are not a new phenomenon. Hundreds of constitutional amendments affecting the executive branch have been proposed since 1787. Of the few that have passed, the Twenty-second, which limits the president to two terms in office, has had the greatest impact and sparked the greatest controversy. The proposal to create a single term of six years is a closely related reform which has had supporters in every political generation since the one that produced the Constitution. With each renewal of interest in the single six-year term, the debate over principles formulated in the eighteenth century is revived in an evolving political environment.

The Formative Debate

Framing the Executive Branch

The framers of the Constitution looked to history for guidance as they confronted the task of creating an executive body. The ancient republics and the recent colonial experience supplied more negative examples than positive. The British monarch and the very idea of unappointed, hereditary power were completely contrary to the right of self-government symbolized in the revolutionary success. It was clear that extreme caution had to be exercised when investing any individual

by Alice O'Connor and Mary L. Henze

or body with executive powers, especially the power of the sword, control over foreign affairs, and the ability to pardon and appoint officers of the government.

On the eve of the Philadelphia Convention, the agitators for a change in the Articles of Confederation felt they were in danger of heading right for the "dictatorship" they had just escaped. The existing federal government was strapped by its lack of power and vulnerable to corruption, insolvency, and foreign attack. The situation demanded the attention of the framers and attracted the interest of the whole world. In their minds, the failure of the American experiment would signal the failure of self-government itself:

> It has been frequently remarked, that it seems to have been reserved to the people of this country, by their conduct and example, to decide the important question, whether societies of men are really capable or not, of establishing good government from reflection and choice or whether they are forever destined to depend, for their political constitutions, on accident and force. If there be any truth in the remark, the crisis, at which we are arrived, may with propriety be regarded as the era in which the decision is to be made; and a wrong election of the part we shall act, may, in this view, deserve to be considered as the general misfortune of mankind. (*Federalist* No. 1)

With the eyes of the world upon them and the fate of self-government in their hands, the founders were determined to avoid mistakes of the past and to leave no room for the rise of an arbitrary despot.

The founders knew clearly what they *did not* want in an executive: neither a despot nor a figurehead—a puppet of foreign governments and an officer too weak to protect them from bad laws and schemes of the legislature. They faced a paradoxical problem: stability required a strong leader yet liberty could not be sacrificed. Few agreed on how both these demands should be met. "Publius," however, argued that strength did not have to threaten liberty; on the contrary, it was a necessary ingredient of sound republican government:

> There is an idea, which is not without its advocates, that a vigorous executive is inconsistent with the genius of republican government. The enlightened well-wishers to this species of government must at least hope that the supposition is destitute of foundation; since they can never admit its truth, without at the same time admitting the condemnation of their own principles. Energy in the executive is a leading character in the definition of good government. It is essential to the protection of the community against foreign attacks. It is not less essential to the steady administration of the laws, to the protection of property against those irregular and high-handed combinations, which sometimes interrupt the ordinary course of justice, to the security of liberty against the enterprises and assaults of ambition, of faction, and of anarchy. (*Federalist* No. 70)

Could "good government" really be "free government" as well? "The true test of a good government is its aptitude and tendency to produce good administration," Publius said, and a good administration required an executive with the power to lead, the tools to manage, and sufficient time in office to become established. Benjamin Franklin emphasized a very different set of criteria for the executive of his free government: "In free governments the rulers are the servants and the people their superiors and sovereigns. For the former therefore to return among the latter is not to degrade but promote them."

The American executive, to satisfy the demands of stability and those of liberty, would have to be both energetic enough to lead and humble enough to follow.

The Presidential Term

The fear of creating too strong a central government was the major influence on the founders as they debated the presidential term. And yet the inability of their decentralized confederate system to protect their freedoms was painfully apparent. They were steering between two extremes. Publius feared that "disgraceful and ruinous mutability in the administration of government" would be the result of short presidential terms and frequent changes in government. At the other extreme was the lesson of history, as William Grayson of Virginia said in declaring the proposed four-year presidency dangerous:

> Whence comes this extreme confidence, that we disregard the example of ancient and modern nations? We find that aristocracies never invested in their officers with such immense powers. Rome had not only an aristocratical, but also a democratical branch; yet the consuls were in office only two years. This quadrennial power cannot be justified by ancient history. There is hardly an instance where a republic trusted its executive so long with much power; nor is it warranted by modern republics. The delegation of power is, in most of them only for one year. (Elliott 1888, 3:491)

A more positive example was set by the state governments, where short terms and limitations on eligibility were the rule. Most of the governors were appointed by the legislatures to one year terms. New York had a three-year term and, along with Massachusetts, provided for direct popular election of the governor. The proposals made at the Constitutional Convention mirrored the diversity found throughout the states.

● The Virginia Plan submitted by Edmund Randolph early in the convention proposed a president elected by the Congress with a single term of unspecified length. This plan was temporarily approved by the

Convention, which followed George Mason's advice and decided on seven years for the term length.

- Citing success with similar models in New York and Massachusetts, James Wilson of Pennsylvania argued for direct popular election of the president with a three-year renewable term.
- The New Jersey plan offered a plural executive elected by Congress for an unspecified term and ineligible for a second term.
- Alexander Hamilton and others proposed an executive chosen for life or "during good behavior." Hamilton's proposal, the first he made to the Convention, took over six hours to present. Its major point was to demonstrate that the life appointee would be a "safer depository of power" because he would have no "private emoluments" to tend and wouldn't have the anxiety of reelection as a temptation to usurp power.

Experience in the states also told the founders that the length of the president's term was inseparable from how and by whom the president was to be chosen. Terms and the electoral body were potential checks on the president, but they were also potential sources of power that had to be balanced against each other. The idea of providing a longer single presidential term was proposed when the president was to be chosen by the Congress. When the electoral college replaced the legislature as the electing body, the four-year renewable term was agreed upon. A four-year term was long enough to provide some strength and stability and short enough to make periodic renewal an effective check on power.

Basis for Reeligibility

The founders believed that a single term restriction was necessary when the president was to be chosen by the Congress so that he would be independent of the legislative branch. The legislative was the stronger of the two branches and would have too much power over the executive if he depended on it for reelection. The president was also supposed to protect the people from the "schemes and intrigues" that might arise in Congress; if looking to it for reelection, he might join in those schemes.

The electoral college lessened the threat of legislative domination and removed one major reason for limiting the presidency to a single term. The college was also a safeguard against another danger of unlimited reeligibility—despotism. It could never be a forum for "cabal, intrigue, and corruption," those "deadly adversaries of republican government," because it was a temporary body that would never meet in a single place. An institution structured to retain its virtue would ensure the regular election of virtuous executives, as Publius pointed out:

THE ELECTORAL COLLEGE

As created by the Constitution, the electoral college was envisioned as an independent body of enlightened men who, acting as trustees for the people, would choose the executive best qualified to lead the country. It was a compromise between election by the legislature and direct popular election.

Every four years the states were to "appoint, in such manner as the Legislatures thereof may direct, a number of electors, equal to the whole number of Senators and Representatives to which the state may be entitled in Congress: but no Senator or Representative, or person holding an office of trust or profit under the United States, shall be appointed an elector."

On a single day determined by Congress, electors were to meet in their respective states to "vote by ballot for two persons, of whom one at least shall not be an inhabitant of the same state with themselves. And they shall make a list of all the persons voted for, and of the number of votes for each; which list they shall sign and certify, and transmit sealed to the seat of government of the United States, directed to the President of the Senate."

In 1804 the Twelfth Amendment instructed electors to vote in separate ballots, one for president and one for vice-president. Beyond that, regulation of the college—how electors are chosen and by what criterion they cast votes—has been left up to the individual states.

The process of election affords a moral certainty, that the office of President, will seldom fall to the lot of any man, who is not in eminent degree endowed with the requisite qualifications. Talents for low intrigue and the little arts of popularity may alone suffice to elevate a man to the first honors in a single state; but it will require other talents and a different kind of merit to establish him in the esteem and confidence of the whole nation.... It will not be too strong to say, that there will be a constant probability of seeing the station filled by characters preeminent for ability and virtue. (*Federalist* No. 68)

With the electoral college there was no need for the auxiliary precaution of limitation: virtue would prevail.

The Anti-Federalist Response

The Anti-Federalist reaction to the proposed presidency was immediate and unfavorable. The sharpest criticism was aimed directly at unlimited reeligibility. By allowing for reelection, the framers had omitted the most obvious check on power available to them:

> You don't even put the same check on [the President] that you do on your own state governors; a man from and bred among you—a man over whom you have a continual and watchful eye—a man from the very nature of his situation, it is almost impossible can do you any injury; this man you say shall not be elected for more than four years and may be elected for years and years. (*South Carolina Daily Advertiser*, 1 February 1788)

Publius argued that indefinite reelection was a source of stability; the longer an official, especially the president, served, the more he would identify his interests with the good of the office. But Anti-Federalists saw something very different, as George Mason pointed out at the Virginia ratifying convention: "The great fundamental principle of responsibility in republicanism is here sapped. The president is elected without rotation ... he will be continued in office for life."

Throughout the ratifying debates, Anti-Federalists appealed to some of the most basic fears of their compatriots to point out the danger of the proposed charter. As George Mason continued his critique of the lack of a rotation provision, he played upon the ever-present anxiety of foreign invasion to paint a scenario of near destruction:

> Will not the great powers of Europe, as France, and Great Britain, be interested in having a friend in the President of the United State? ... the powers of Europe will interpose, and we shall have a civil war in the bowels of our country, and be subject to all the horrors and calamities of an elective monarchy.... (Elliott 1888, 3:484)

The electoral college was no protection against the foreign threat, as Federalists claimed it would be. Limitation was still necessary because the electors were just as liable to "intrigue" as the Congress and more vulnerable to foreign influence:

> The electors, who are to meet in each state and vote for him, may be easily influenced. To prevent the certain evils of attempting to elect a new President, it will be necessary to continue the old one. The only way to alter this would be to render him ineligible after a certain number of years, and then no foreign nation would interfere to keep in a man who was so utterly ineligible. (Elliott 1888, 3:484-85)

In a comparison that came up time and time again during the constitutional debate, Mason warned the new nation against becoming another Poland, a government installed and maintained by foreign intrigue.

President or Monarch?

Perhaps no Anti-Federalist specter was more effective, however, than that of the monarchy. Again, in direct opposition to Federalist logic that equated long tenure with "good government," Mason closed his argument against unrestricted eligibility with an appeal to the republican tenet of "free government"—a republican leader must be one of the people:

> Nothing is so essential to the preservation of a republic as a periodical rotation. Nothing so strongly impels a man to regard the interest of his constituents as the certainty of returning to the general mass of people, from whence he was taken, where he must participate in their burdens.... Some stated time ought to be fixed when the President ought to be reduced to private station ... as it now stands he may continue in office for life; or, in other words, it will be an elective monarchy. (Elliott 1888, 3:485)

The return of the king in the thin guise of a president was a powerful and recurring theme in Anti-Federalist arguments against ratification. It was a theme that was present at the Philadelphia Convention. But the framers were satisfied that the electoral college and the separation of powers were sufficient safeguards against an American monarchy. As far as critics were concerned, the lack of a term limitation provision made those checks useless. Publius' response to the Anti-Federalist prophecy reflects the near-hysteria their arguments created:

> Here the writers seem to have taken pains to signalize their talent of misrepresentation, calculating upon the aversion of the people to monarchy, they have endeavored to enlist their jealousies and apprehensions in opposition to the intended President of the United States; not merely as the embryo but as the full grown progeny of that detested parent. To establish the affinity they have not scrupled to draw resources even from the regions of fiction. The authorities of a magistrate, in a few instances greater and in some instances less, than a Governor of New York; have been magnified into more than royal prerogatives. He has been decorated with attributes superior in dignity and splendor to those of a King of Great Britain. He has been shown to us with the diadem sparkling on his brow, and the imperial purple flowing in his train. He has been seated on a throne surrounded with minions and mistresses; giving audience to the envoys of foreign potentates, in all the supercilious pomp of majesty. The images of Asiatic despotism and voluptuousness have scarcely been wanting to crown the exaggerated scene. We have been almost taught to tremble at the terrific visages of murdering janizaries; and to blush at the unveiled mysteries of a future seraglio. (*Federalist* No. 67)

ALEXANDER HAMILTON AND THE MONARCHY

While Alexander Hamilton wrote some of the strongest arguments for the four-year term as Publius in *The Federalist Papers*, he did not entirely relinquish his conviction that a long—if not life—tenure was wisest for the executive. The charge that Hamilton was at heart a monarchist could be supported without much difficulty by citing his many favorable references to life tenure in *The Federalist Papers*:

> However proper or safe it may be in governments where the executive magistrate is an hereditary monarch, to commit to him the entire power of making treaties, it would be utterly unsafe and improper to entrust that power to an elective magistrate of four years duration. . . . an hereditary monarch, though often the oppressor of his people, has personally too much at stake in the government to be in any material danger of being corrupted by foreign powers. But a man raised from the station of a private citizen to the rank of chief magistrate, possessed of but a moderate or slender fortune, and looking forward to a period of not very remote, when he may probably be obliged to return to the station from which he was taken, might sometimes be under temptations to sacrifice his duty to his interest, which it would require superlative virtue to withstand. (*Federalist* No. 75)

Hamilton's distrust of the ordinary citizen's ability to withstand temptation was not the only reason for his support of life tenure. If he had to accept periodic elections, he would never accept a restriction on perpetual reeligibility:

> Would it promote the peace of the community, or the stability of the government, to have half a dozen men who had had credit enough to be raised to the seat of the supreme magistracy, wandering among the people like discontented ghosts and sighing for a place which they were destined never more to possess? (*Federalist* No. 72)

Despite the fact that Hamilton was not the only one to favor a life term for presidents, the ghost of monarchism was to haunt him for the rest of his political career.

Accountability to the People

The relentless Anti-Federalist attack on the presidency served a constructive purpose: it added a new dimension to the conception of the presidency in the republic. While the members of the Philadelphia Convention had not ignored the idea of reelection as a way of keeping the president accountable to the people, they were more concerned about his independence from the legislature. Frequent elections and accountability were notions applied to the House of Representatives, the branch of the people. But in the public debate over the Constitution proposed by the framers, it became clear that the people would not trust a leader who was too independent. One worried citizen stated it thus:

> I would ask (considering how prone mankind are to engross power, and then to abuse it) is it not probable, at least possible, that the president who is to be invested with all this demi-omnipotence—who is not chosen by the community; and who, consequently, as to them, is irresponsible and independent—that he, I say, by a few artful and dependent emissaries in Congress, may not only perpetuate his own personal administration, but also make it hereditary? (*Kentucky Gazeteer*, 1 March 1788)

The idea of the president being directly accountable to his constituents through elections began to take stronger hold in the Anti-Federalist camp. Governor Randolph of Virginia originally supported term limitation because he believed reelection would tempt the executive scheme. By the time the issue came up in Virginia's ratifying convention he had changed his mind. Reelection was a positive influence, Randolph said, because it

> ... renders [the President] more independent in his place, and more solicitous of promoting the interest of his constituents; for, unless you put it in his power to be reelected, instead of being attentive to their interests, he will lean to the augmentation of his private emoluments. (Elliott 1888, 3: 485-86)

Accountability directly to the people has become a more integral part of the American system since the 1780s. The early debates over presidential term and reeligibility marked the beginning of the evolution of the presidency into an office of the people. Political parties, strengthened by the increase in eligible voters, became the bodies that discerned and refined the choice of the executive. The virtue of the electoral college, which had originally been based on its reputation as a detached body of wise men, became dependent on its ability to reflect the will of the people. The presidential election itself has become an important opportunity to answer the people's questions and gain the popular mandate. The executive has truly become a branch with its roots in the people.

But change should not obscure a good deal of continuity, especially in the republican concern that keeps Americans ever watchful of their political institutions and fearful of the dangers they might create. What is our fear of an "imperial presidency" if not an acknowledgment that the "monarchical"—or dictatorial—threat still lives as a check against giving the president too much power? The problem faced by the founders resurfaces with every discussion of the presidential term: how can "energy" and "safety" in the executive be combined? Publius answered as follows:

> The ingredients, which constitute energy in the executive, are first unity, second duration, thirdly an adequate provision for its support, fourthly, competent powers. The circumstances which constitute safety in the republican sense are first a due dependence on the people, secondly a due responsibility. (*Federalist* No. 70)

The Debate Continues

It was with a decisive air that Publius pronounced that

> there is an excess of refinement in the idea of disabling the people to continue in office men, who had entitled themselves, in their opinion, to approbation and confidence, the advantages of which are at best speculative and equivocal; and are overbalanced by disadvantages far more certain and decisive. (*Federalist* No. 72)

And yet his was far from the final word on the subject of presidential terms. Ratifying conventions in New York, where *The Federalist Papers* first appeared, and in North Carolina called for an amendment to limit the president to one term even as they gave their approval to the Constitution. These were the first in a steady stream of proposals to change presidential tenure. By far the most popular and frequently proposed has been a single six-year term that continues to have its proponents today.

"The Desire to Be Reelected"

As the American style of popular politics began to take shape in the nineteenth century, a new specter appeared in the comments of observers such as Alexis de Tocqueville: the specter of the demagogue, who intrigued for power not by scheming with Congress, as the founders suspected, but by courting popular favor. To this French visitor, writing in the 1840s,

> . . . it is impossible to consider any course of affairs in the United States without perceiving that the desire to be reelected dominates the thought of the president; that all the policies of his administration tend to this point; and that his least movements are subordinated to this object . . . . (Tocqueville 1945)

To Tocqueville, the danger of ineligibility was nothing compared to the danger reelection posed:

If reeligible (and this is especially true at the present day, when political morality is relaxed and when great men are rare), the president of the United States becomes an easy tool in the hands of the majority. He adopts its likings and its animosities, he anticipates its wishes, he forestalls its complaints, he yields to its idlest cravings, and instead of guiding it, as the legislature intended that he should do, he merely follows its bidding. Thus, in order not to deprive the state of the talents of an individual, those talents have been rendered almost useless; and to retain an expedient for extraordinary perils, the country has been exposed to continual dangers. (Tocqueville 1945, 142-43)

A similar awareness of this desire for reelection led president Andrew Jackson to "earnestly invite" consideration of a single-term limitation in every one of his eight annual addresses. Removal of the temptation to be reelected would save the country from the whims of mere popular favor and, Jackson seemed to be saying, save presidents from their own ambitions.

The People's Choice?

The proposal of a single six-year term continued to be part of nineteenth century attempts to promote "good government" by preserving the presidency from the schemes of politicians courting popular favor. There was a notable shift in the support for the reform during the late nineteenth and early twentieth centuries, when it became a Progressive cause and gained a decidedly populist ring. The schemers against the national interest were not the popular politicians but the monied interests and big corporations. The presidency was going to the highest bidder, and the highest bidder was inevitably the incumbent. Senator Works of California introduced a single six-year term bill in 1912. The bill gained considerable public attention and, after a year-long debate, passed the Senate in 1913. Prospects for passage in the House looked good until President Woodrow Wilson, who had won on the 1912 Democratic platform that called for the single six-year term, threw his weight against it to preserve his reelection options in 1916. While he cited numerous reasons for opposing the reform, one point in particular turned the "protection of the people" argument on its head. First, he argued, the president was the one who needed protection. Second, it would be anti-democratic to take away the people's right to vote for the person of their choice. Wilson stated:

If you wish to learn the result of Constitutional ineligibility to reelection, ask any former governor of New Jersey, for example, what the effect is in actual experience. He will tell you how cynically and with what complacence the politicians banded against him waited for the inevitable end of his term to take their chances with his successor. . . . We singularly bely our own principles by seeking to determine by fixed Constitutional provision what the people shall determine for themselves. We cast doubt upon the whole theory of popular government. (Cronon 1965, 83)

Whether swayed by Wilson's arguments or not, Progressive interest in the six-year term diminished after Works' bill and similar attempts failed.

Controlling the President

While a considerable part of the support for a six-year term is inspired by the desire to protect the presidency from too much politics, the proposal is also a part of attempts to control the presidency, one of which succeeded with the passage of the two-term limitation in the Twenty-second Amendment. During the 1947 hearings in Congress on the proposed Twenty-second Amendment, six-year term supporters argued that it would only be carrying the principle of limitation to its logical conclusion by removing the reelection option altogether. Their arguments, prompted largely by Franklin Delano Roosevelt's unprecedented election to four terms, focused on power and the need to control it. President Harry S. Truman later deemed limitation an outright effort to disable the president:

> You do not have to be very smart to know that an officeholder who is not eligible for reelection loses a lot of influence. So, what have you done? You have taken a man and put him in the hardest job in the world, and sent him out to fight with one hand tied behind his back; because everyone knows he cannot run for reelection. (FSPCT 1982, 2))

The fear of a "lame duck" presidency echoes the founders' concern for the independence of the president from the legislature. But in limiting the president's term, it was Congress that was gaining protection from the accumulated powers of the executive rather than the other way around. Protection was gained, perhaps, but not absolute control, as Sen. Mike Mansfield said in rejecting the idea that a single term could debilitate a president:

> Lameness is by no means inherent in a single term. It relates to the strength and quality of the man holding the office. If a president becomes a lame duck, it is not because of any inhibitions imposed by a single term. An unlimited number of terms would not sustain such a man. (FSPCT 1982, 2)

The Reform Today — Free the President

As its long history shows, the six-year term has become one of the "perennials" of the legislative process, and is to this day discussed frequently in Congress, state legislatures, and other public forums.

Support today is based on a combination of concerns of the past: the need to have a more efficient, less corruptible administration; to protect the people from the ambitions of a powerful incumbent; and to keep the office from being subordinated to the politics of reelection. But the overriding concern of current-day proponents is to free the president and his policies from what they see as a distraction from the real business of governing. The reelection campaign has grown to such length, cost, and proportions that the president starts running again as soon as he takes office, they argue. The new cadre of election "experts" insulates the president and has entirely too much say in determining policy. What is good for the country and what is good for reelection are growing farther and farther apart, and while public expectations of the president increase, the president's ability to be a good leader declines. What six-year term supporters are saying, then, is that reelection no longer serves the function it was intended to serve; rather than making the president independent of the legislature and accountable to his constituents, it threatens to turn the executive branch into a permanent campaign headquarters. Milton S. Eisenhower wrote:

> My reason for favoring a single term for the president is based on my conviction that we should expect the president to foster only those programs and policies which he is convinced are in the interest of the nation as a whole—that he should have no incentive to propose and fight for measures conceived solely to enhance his chances of reelection, or merely to confound the political opposition. I have seen too often the enormous power of the federal government employed by presidents in seeking approval of ill-conceived or wasteful programs that seemingly would add temporarily to their prestige but in the long run would be detrimental to the country. (Eisenhower 1974)

In response, opponents of the reform charge that "taking the president out of politics" may lead to unintended consequences:

> It is, of course, true that we would not have had the Watergate reelection scandal if we did not have reelections. Similarly, we could not have election scandals if we did not have elections. And that extreme solution flows from the anti-democratic logic of the argument for a single six-year term. (George Will, *Washington Post*, 1986)

The National Interest

Today's debate over the six-year term shows that fear of monarchy and unchecked power and suspicion of the private ambitions of public people are an ever-present part of the American political conscience. Likewise, every time the reform is discussed, the question of the national interest—what it is and who can discern it best—is raised once again:

THE TWO-TERM PRESIDENCY:
FROM TRADITION TO CONSTITUTIONAL AMENDMENT

The example of four Presidents voluntarily retiring at the end of their eight years, and the progress of public opinion that the principle is salutary, have given it in practice the form of precedent and usage; in so much that should a president consent to be a candidate for a third election, I trust he would be rejected on this demonstration of ambitious views. (Thomas Jefferson, *Autobiography*)

Jefferson's statement was more prescient than he might have realized, for what he suggested proved true in every instance of a president seeking more than two terms until Franklin D. Roosevelt broke with tradition. Beyond being rejected, in fact, almost every third-term candidate in our history has been the target of a legislative campaign to impose a two-term restriction by constitutional amendment. In the aftermath of Roosevelt's election to four terms, the Twenty-second Amendment to the Constitution was passed.

It has been said that the founders felt safe in giving the executive an unrestricted reeligibility because they had George Washington in mind to fill the post and they wanted him to serve indefinitely. Reelection would

... enable the people, when they see reason to approve of his conduct, to continue him in the station, in order to prolong the utility of his talents and virtues, and to secure to the government, the advantage of permanency in a wise system of administration. (*Federalist* No. 72)

Even though Washington's voluntary retirement may have

A one-term president makes for more courageous decisions uninfluenced by reelection concerns. It will avoid the spectacle of tactics acceptable in political campaigns yet demeaning to the office of the presidency. Thus, it will exalt the office in the eyes of the people. (Jaworski 1980)

The argument for insulating the presidency (with a single six-year term) is profoundly anti-democratic in its implication. It assumes that the president alone knows what is best for the country and that the voters are so wrong-headed and ignorant that a president should be enabled to disregard them. It assumes that the democratic process is the obstacle to wise decisions. ... it is hard to imagine a constitutional

been disappointing, the precedent seemed well secured in the early republic. Not until 1875 did the threat of a serious challenge to the "unwritten law" arise when Ulysses S. Grant looked with favor upon Republican talk of nominating him for a third term in office. Rumors spurred many petitions and statements against the idea, which encouraged the House to pass a resolution proposed by Illinois representative William M. Springer asserting that

> ... in the opinion of the House, the precedent established by Washington and other presidents of the United States, in retiring from the presidential office after their second term has become, by universal concurrence, a part of our republican system of government, and that any departure from this time-honored custom would be unwise, unpatriotic, and fraught with peril to our free institutions.

Sen. Robert LaFollette used these same words in 1928 after Theodore Roosevelt's campaign for a third (nonconsecutive) term in 1912 provoked an extended period of attention to term limitation proposals.

In 1947, during the session of the first new Congress since Franklin Roosevelt's death two years earlier, the debate on presidential tenure was renewed with proposals to institute either a two-term limitation or a single six-year term. By March the Twenty-second Amendment had passed both houses and was sent to the states for ratification, which was completed in 1951. Limited service, which many saw as a direct and heavily partisan backlash against Roosevelt, had become part of the Constitution.

Measures to repeal the two-term limitation were proposed as early as 1956.

change more efficiently designed than the six-year presidential term to release presidents from the discipline of consent and thereby to revive the imperial presidency. (Arthur Schlesinger, Jr., *Wall Street Journal*, 7 April 1981)

Related Reforms

The single six-year term has often been proposed as part of more comprehensive reform packages:

● In June, 1968, Sen. Mike Mansfield proposed the following package of amendments to correct "the inequities and inadequacies of our electoral system":

First. Abolish both the convention system and the electoral college.

Second. Extend the right to vote in primaries as well as general elections to 18-year-olds.

Third. Establish a nationwide primary to be held in all the states on the same day to be followed by the direct election of the president . . .

If the above proposals were adopted . . . it would mean that the people would be able to participate fully and directly in the electoral process, from nomination to election, rather than is now the case through intermediary state delegations. . . . It would strengthen the presidency by forbidding reelection and would allow the president to be his own man, so to speak, throughout his entire term of office.

● The idea of giving Congress or the people an opportunity to recall the president was discussed in relation to the six-year term in 1913. Recall would be a way of keeping the president accountable without the cost and distraction of a campaign.

● During the 1970s, in the aftermath of Watergate, measures similar to the recall were introduced in Congress to provide a way to remove the president, short of impeachment procedures, when he has lost the capacity to lead without actually having committed an impeachable offense.

● Others regard the six-year term as the first step toward a more parliamentary system that would be achieved by lengthening House terms to three years and placing candidates for federal elections on a single ballot so that when a president was elected his party would control Congress.

Arguments For the Single Six-Year Term

● First-term presidents are always looking to the next term and do not spend enough time truly leading the country. Six years could give the president enough time in office to carry out his policies in a single term, and remove the diversion and disruption caused by the campaign for reelection.

● The president would pay more attention to the national interest and less attention to political popularity in making and instituting policies. A single term would free him to make courageous decisions.

● Without the prospect of an approaching reelection campaign, the president would feel less obliged to satisfy the demands of special interest groups.

• At the advice of their political advisors, presidents now tend to put off hard or controversial decisions until after their reelection campaign. This causes waste and inaction where we most need leadership.

• The campaign is financially and personally costly to a president and takes away from the dignity of the office. This is not in the best interest of the people.

• A six-year term would promote more consistency in foreign and economic policy because the administration would not fluctuate according to the barometer of public opinion.

• The presidency has grown tremendously since 1787, and especially so since the New Deal. Reforming the presidential term would recognize the increased demands on the office and produce more efficient administrative leadership.

Arguments Against the Single Six-Year Term

• The single six-year term would make the president an automatic lame duck.

• The need to be reelected keeps the president accountable to the people—an important check on an office that wields so much power.

• The whole idea of term limitation is anti-democratic because it restricts the right of the people to decide for themselves whether a president should be continued in office. Its supporters assume that paying attention to public opinion and what the people want is a distraction when in fact it is what self-government is all about.

• Supporters of a six-year term are trying to take the president out of politics, when politics and reelection are integral parts of effective executive leadership. Giving up reelection for the sake of efficiency would further remove the president from his constituents.

• Six years is too long for a bad president to serve and too short for a good one. The single term limitation might arbitrarily remove a good leader from office in a time of crisis.

• Reelection is not the source of the troubled presidency, and the single six-year term is not the solution. We need better ways of attracting and nominating high-quality candidates for president.

• A single six-year term would be a step back in the direction of the "imperial presidency."

Questions to Guide Discussion

• Does the need for "energy" and efficiency in the executive branch conflict with the republican concern for "safety" and accountability?

THE PRESIDENTIAL TERM—A BRIEF LEGISLATIVE HISTORY

1826-89   First amendment calling for a single six-year term was proposed by Rep. John Hemphill of Texas.

President Andrew Jackson called for a single-term limit to "safeguard our liberties" in eight annual addresses during his two terms in office.

The proposal was featured in many nineteenth-century campaign platforms. Presidents Harrison, Buchanan, Johnson, Hayes, and Cleveland recommended the reform, which the Whig Party, and later the People's Party, included in their platforms.

Jefferson Davis was chosen for a single six-year term as president of the Southern Confederacy.

1890-1926   One hundred and seven proposals sought to limit the president to one or two terms.

President Taft and presidential candidate William Jennings Bryan endorsed a single six-year term, as did the Prohibition Party in 1912 and 1916.

1912-13 were the biggest years for the six-year term, when unprecedented legislative and public support nearly led to its passage. The Senate passed it, but it died in the House in 1913 after President Woodrow Wilson testified against it. The Democratic party included the six-year term on its 1912 platform.

1927-63   The reform was often proposed, but did not become the subject of congressional hearings again until 1940.

How did the founders balance these considerations and does their balance work today?

● Were the founders correct in assuming that in a republic the representative would be the more naturally powerful branch? Has their fear of "cabal, intrigue, and corruption" between the legislative

The states ratified the Twenty-second Amendment limiting presidents to two terms in office in 1951. The congressional party alignment on the issue set anti-limitation Democrats against pro-limitation Republicans. Everett Dirksen led a bipartisan coalition to press for a single six-year term amendment during the debate.

Hearings were held in Congress on repealing the Twenty-second Amendment in 1959.

1964-80   Three amendments called for a three-year presidential term.

Sen. Mike Mansfield and Sen. George Aiken led efforts to pass the six-year term starting in 1968. They succeeded in getting committee hearings in 1973.

More than sixty amendments called for a single six-year term; ten of them were proposed in 1979.

Presidents Johnson and Carter endorsed the change. Nixon specially referred the issue to his proposed nonpartisan Commission on Federal Election Reform in 1973.

1981-84   As congressional proposals continued, the issue again attracted public attention. A 1981 Gallup poll showed sixty-six percent of the general public opposed to the six-year term and forty-seven percent of the "informed" public in favor.

The Committee for a Single Six-Year Presidential Term, co-chaired by Griffin Bell, Milton Eisenhower, William Simon, and Cyrus Vance, was formed to press for a constitutional amendment.

and executive branches been justified?

● What is the function of reelection in the system today? Is it an instrument of accountability or merely an outlet for presidential ambitions?

● Does the two-term limitation on presidents protect the people

POINTS OF VIEW

I think, first of all, that the desire to liberate presidents from the temptations of ambition would, in fact, liberate presidents further from the disciplines of accountability.

The great motive to the public good, which Gouverneur Morris called it, or seeking reelection, helps keep the presidents responsive.

I think that the desire to free presidents from the pressure of interest will, in fact, leave them less concerned about building consensus, leave them less responsive to the views and values of voters, and produce a less representative government. (Jeane Kirkpatrick, *San Francisco Chronicle*, 2 September 1981)

If ineligible a second time, the president would not be independent of the people, for his responsibility would not cease; but the favor of the people would not be so necessary to him as to induce him to submit in every respect to its desires. (Tocqueville 1945, 143)

. . . a single term limit does not strip the voters of their rights. Rather, it offers the leader of their choice enough time and the proper environment to carry out the public's mandate. A new president barely begins to make his mark in office when virtually forced to start campaigning for a second term. By the time a president's budgetary proposals even begin to see daylight—well into the third fiscal year in office—the chief executive is inevitably transformed again into the candidate. There is certainly some gray area between these incompatible roles. But it is clear to me that, wherever the line between public and private interest is drawn, it is routinely crossed. The public interest cannot help but suffer. (Rep. Gerry E. Studds, Statement before the House of Representatives, 20 July 1980)

. . . the attempt to move toward the single six-year term really is an attempt to take the president out of politics. And I think it is neither possible nor desirable to take the president out of politics. To ask that the presidency be above or out of politics is very similar to asking the bishop to be out of or above religion; it is just not possible.

A president has to be a creative politician, has to be concerned with majorities, has to be concerned with the possibilities of being reaffirmed or turned out of office. I think that is, by and large, a healthy thing. The idea of removing the presidency and trying to elect a kind of national city manager, somehow removed from and above politics, is an illusion and needs to be guarded against. (Thomas Cronin, FSPCT 1982, 4)

. . . the necessity to survive politically results in a real effort to understand and respond effectively to the public's wishes, desires and sensitivities. These are very important to a chief executive in a democracy.

... No matter how wise a reflective handful of people consulting with one another and so-called experts (who often are intimidated by the strength and power of the close leadership group), they are a long way from infallible in their judgments. The process of being responsive to the public, of listening and trying to convince the public, with all of its frustrations and time-consuming as it may be, is I think, a very healthy process—perhaps the essence of the democratic government. Accordingly, I do not support the six year, one term proposition for the President of the United States. . . . (Orville L. Freeman, FSPCT 1982, 5)

Do you think the president is indulging in politics when he campaigns? Today security prevents that. What does he see when he goes out? A cordon of secret service men. Whom does he talk to? Political partisans in that particular area, each with their own ax to grind. National interest is not involved.

To build a budget, to summon the people to a cause, to support a program, to get Congress to act—that takes political skills beyond the capacity of the ordinary man. It takes a kind of political judgment . . . but not the wasteful energy I saw in the presidency of Lyndon Johnson, scrounging for election in 1964. (Jack Valenti, FSPCT 1982, 4)

I do not at all doubt that a single six-year term would add important dimensions of continuity and stability to the conduct of our foreign relations. Seen from the perspective of our friends and allies, as well as from the eyes of our adversaries, we seem to be vulnerable to the vagaries of a foreign policy that is always to some degree affected by the preoccupation with presidential reelection. The result of this is not only a lack of continuity and stability in our dealings abroad, but also affects domestically how we are perceived in conducting our foreign policy . . . (Cyrus Vance, FSPCT 1982, 9-10)

Such a change in our system could definitely introduce an additional note of inflexibility and would restrict the choices available to the American people. A little mathematical exercise illustrates the point.

As our government now works, an effective president has a far better than even chance to serve for eight years [two terms], whereas an ineffective president would probably be retired at the end of four years. The proposed shift would level out the service of both types—decreasing the effective leadership and increasing the ineffective leadership by two years . . . [There is also] the distinct possibility that the single, six-year term would deny the American people the services of a man at a crucial moment when no one else was available. (George Reedy, FSPCT 1982, 3)

from a "self-perpetuating" leader or does it infringe upon their right to choose?

● How has our ideal of a president changed in two hundred years? Is it more important for a president to be a detached and efficient administrator or to be truly one of the people? How many presidents have been both?

● Are the demands on presidents today greater than they were in the early republic? How has the office grown?

References

Cronon, David E., ed. *The Political Thought of Woodrow Wilson*. Indianapolis: Bobbs-Merrill, 1965.

Eisenhower, Milton S. *The President is Calling*. Garden City, N. J.: Doubleday, 1974.

Elliott, Jonathan. *The Debates in the Several State Conventions on the Adoption of the Federal Constitution*. 5 vols. New York: Burt Franklin, 1888.

Foundation for the Study of Presidential and Congressional Terms (FSPCT). *In Their Words: Pros and Cons of the Single Six-Year Term*. Washington, D. C., 1982.

Hamilton, Alexander, John Jay, and James Madison. *The Federalist Papers*. Available in various editions.

Jaworski, Leon. "Can The United States Presidency Survive?" Address to the Philosophical Society of Texas, San Antonio, 6 December 1980.

Jefferson, Thomas. *Autobiography*. 1821.

Tocqueville, Alexis de. *Democracy in America*. New York: Knopf, 1945.

Suggested Readings

Edward S. Corwin. *The President: Office and Powers*. New York: New York University Press, 1957.

Foundation for the Study of Presidential and Congressional Terms. "Term Limitation: The Issue That Never Dies." Washington, D. C., 1980.

Arthur M. Schlesinger, Jr. *The Imperial Presidency*. New York: Popular Library, 1974.

Richard L. Strout. "The 22nd Amendment: A Second Look." *New York Times Magazine*, 28 July 1957.

Edward R. Tufte. *Political Control of the Economy*. Princeton, N. J.: Princeton University Press, 1978.

U. S. Congress. *One Six Year Presidential Term*. Senate Report #34, 80th Cong., 1st sess. U. S. Government Printing Office, 1947.

U. S. Congress. Senate Committee on the Judiciary. *Single Six-Year Term for President*. Hearings, 92d Cong., 1st sess., on S. J. Res 77. U. S. Government Printing Office, 1972.

U. S. Congress. House Committee on the Judiciary. *One Six-Year Presidential Term*. Hearings, 93d Cong., 1st sess. U. S. Government Printing Office, 1974.

4. Terms of Office in the Legislative Branch

"Article— No person who has been elected to the Senate _____ times shall be eligible for election or appointment to the Senate. No person who has been elected to the House of Representatives _____ times shall be eligible for election to the House of Representatives."

"Article— The term of office for Members of the House of Representatives shall be four years."

"Where annual elections end tyranny begins ..." was the rallying cry for many an Anti-Federalist during the Constitution ratification debate. The proposed length of terms in Congress was high on the grievance list of the Anti-Federalists, who suspected they would create a centralized power removed from the people. Fair representation was the right for which the new nation had fought the Revolution. Elections were *the* link between the people and the government; they embodied the very principle of government by and for the people. Debates over term length were therefore prolonged and impassioned at the Constitutional Convention. The debate is still alive today.

Annual elections rarely get serious mention today, but proposals to reform the system to lengthen or limit congressional terms have been introduced in almost every Congress since 1869. While most have suggested four-year House terms, three and six years have been proposed as well. Amendments to limit tenure in the Senate and House generally set from twelve to twenty-four years as the maximum. In recent years amendments combining the two changes have been introduced. The persistence of these proposals shows just how vigilant Americans are when it comes to making the representative system work. In the concept of representative government lies the American commitment to popular sovereignty and one of the founders' major achieve-

by Alice O'Connor and Mary L. Henze

ments. As James Madison said after the Constitution had been ratified and amended with the Bill of Rights:

> A government deriving its energy from the will of the society . . . on the understanding and interest of the society . . . is the government for which philosophy has been searching, and humanity been fighting, from the most remote ages. Such are republican governments which it is the glory of America to have invented, and her unrivalled happiness to possess. (*National Gazette*, 20 February 1792)

By their constant attention to the effectiveness of their representative institutions, Americans have expressed their desire to safeguard their natural rights and freedoms for over two hundred years.

Representation and the Sovereignty of the People

Confidence and Safety

Underlying the creation of the republican system was the question the founders had seen over and over again in the annals of societies since classical civilization: Why do we have government at all? What is it in human nature that requires governing or, more positively, enables people to govern? The founders had enough faith in human nature to believe people capable of governing themselves. For "Publius," writing in *The Federalist Papers* in praise of the proposed Constitution, this meant that republican government was founded in confidence.

> As there is a degree of depravity in mankind which requires a certain degree of circumspection and distrust, so there are other qualities in human nature which justify a certain portion of esteem and confidence. Republican government presupposes the existence of these qualities in a higher degree than any other form. (*Federalist* No. 55)

But even an advocate of popular sovereignty as wholehearted as Thomas Jefferson was aware of the need to temper confidence in human nature with limits on the powers entrusted to government officials.

> . . . It would be a dangerous delusion were a confidence in the men of our choice to silence our fears for the safety of our rights: that confidence is everywhere the parent of despotism—free government is founded in jealousy, and not in confidence; it is jealousy and not confidence which prescribes limited constitutions, to bind down those whom we are obliged to trust with power. . . . (Elliott 1888, 4:543)

In the eighteenth-century debate, optimism about the ability of the people to form their own government never left an awareness of human corruptibility far behind. The founders knew that power could corrupt, and that freedom would be its victim. While the people could be trusted to choose the government, they would need to protect their liberties by institutional "checks" on power.

Actual and Virtual Representation

The founders were not the first to grapple with the question of popular sovereignty or representation. The ancient republics; the philosophic writings of Plato, Aristotle and, more recently, of John Locke and Montesquieu; and their own British constitutional heritage gave them guidance. But some aspects of their task were truly experimental: the idea of a written constitution and the "scheme of representation" among them. As Publius noted:

> The scheme of representation, as a substitute for a meeting of the citizens in person, being at most but very imperfectly known to ancient polity; it is in more modern times only, that we are to expect instructive examples. (*Federalist* No. 52)

The founders did have some "instructive examples" in the representative governments that were set up in each of the original thirteen states. But their examples and eighteenth-century republican theory both pointed to the same maxim: the republican system was meant to govern a small geographic area. A large centralized government would be too distant to be truly representative. Despotism would inevitably result. Governor George Clinton of New York, writing under the name of "Cato," wrote:

> It is natural, says Montesquieu, to a republic to have only a small territory, otherwise it cannot long subsist: in a large one, there are men of large fortunes, and consequently of less moderation; there are too great deposits to trust in the hands of a single subject; an ambitious person soon becomes sensible that he may be happy, great and glorious by oppressing his fellow citizens, and he might raise himself to grandeur, on the ruins of his country. In large republics, the public good is sacrificed to a thousand views; in a small one, the interest of the public is easily perceived, better understood, and more within the reach of every citizen.... (Borden 1965, 37)

The founders were thus taking a chance when they created a republican system to govern a large and diverse geographical area. They drew upon the two kinds of representation they had experienced as British colonists: "actual" representation in the local legislatures and "virtual" representation in the British House of Commons.

In the British representative tradition, the House of Commons was a legitimate sovereign body because it "virtually" represented the people. This idea holds that there is one single homogeneous interest common to all the people and that the role of the representative is to discern and legislate based on that interest. "Actual" representation, on the other hand, meant that the representative body mirrored the population in all its diversity and acted according to the particular wishes of its constituents. Elected delegates were the instruments of the people. There was a premium on accessibility, local ties, and physical proximity to constituents. Power would always be close to the people.

The question of whether a representative should legislate in what he thought to be the "best interest" of the people or whether he should act only according to their instructions had profound implications for the legislative branch. It was not finally decided upon by the Convention, which instead structured the legislature with elements of both.

> The House of Representatives shall be composed of Members chosen every second Year by the People of the several States, and the Electors in each State shall have the Qualifications requisite for electors of the most numerous Branch of the State Legislature.
>
> No Person shall be a Representative who shall not have attained to the age of Twenty five Years, and been seven Years a Citizen of the United States, and who shall not, when elected, be an Inhabitant of that State in which he shall be chosen. (U. S. Const. Art. I, sec. 2)

When electing representatives by district, residence requirements and obtaining the consent of the electorate are part of the actual representation tradition. But federal legislators do not consult the people on every issue. This is because the people give them the power to "virtually" represent their interests. The trust in elected officials necessary to make this type of federal system work made some more uneasy than others.

Terms of Office and Safeguarding Liberties

The Two-Year Term

> As it is essential to liberty that the government in general should have a common interest with the people, so it is particularly essential that the branch of it under consideration [the House] should have an immediate dependence on and intimate sympathy with the people. Frequent elections are unquestionably the only policy by which this dependence and sympathy can be effectually secured. But what particular degree of frequency may be absolutely necessary for the purpose does not appear to be susceptible of any precise calculation, and must depend on a variety of circumstances with which it may be connected. Let us consult experience, the guide that ought always be followed whenever it can be found. (*Federalist* No. 53)

Under the Articles of Confederation, delegates to the Congress were appointed by the state legislature. Their terms varied from state to state, ranging from six months in Connecticut and Rhode Island to two years

A QUESTION OF ARITHMETIC?
THE TWO EXTREMES:
GOVERNMENT BY THE MANY/GOVERNMENT BY ONE

It is not surprising that the founders were watchful of anything that threatened to return to monarchy. Anti-Federalist Patrick Henry saw the danger of monarchy in the shift of power from the states to the federal government:

> The Constitution reflects in the most degrading and mortify-ing manner on the virtue, integrity, and wisdom of the state legislatures; it presupposes that the chosen few who go to Congress will have more upright hearts, and more enlight-ened minds than those who are members of the individual legislatures. To suppose that ten gentlemen shall have more real, substantial merit than one hundred-seventy, is humiliat-ing to the last degree. If ten men be better than one hundred-seventy, it follows of necessity that one is better than ten. . . . (Elliott 1888, 3:167)

But they were equally fearful of the threat from "below": too much democracy would degenerate into government by the mob, or no government at all. Publius responded thus:

> Nothing can be more fallacious than to found our political calculations on arithmetical principles. Sixty or seventy men may be more properly trusted with a given degree of power than six or seven. But it does not follow that six or seven hundred would be proportionately a better depository. And if we carry on the supposition to six or seven thousand, the whole reasoning ought to be reversed. The truth is, that in all cases a certain number at least seems to be necessary to secure the benefits of free consultation and discussion, and to guard against too easy a combination for improper purposes; as, on the other hand, the number ought at most to be kept within a certain limitation in order to avoid the confusion and intem-perance of a multitude. In all very numerous assemblies, of whatever characters composed, the passion never failed to wrest the sceptre from reason. Had every Athenian citizen been a Socrates, every Athenian assembly would still have been a mob. (*Federalist* No. 55)

in South Carolina, with the others adhering to the tradition of annual elections. For Publius, frequent elections were important, but annual elections would cause disruption. Biennial elections were both "necessary and useful" because of the greater amount of knowledge required of federal legislators and the distance they were to travel between their homes and the seat of government.

At the Constitutional Convention, the two-year term emerged as a compromise between annual elections and a proposal for triennial elections supported by James Madison and adopted by the Committee of the Whole until final deliberations on the subject, when Edmund Randolph and George Mason were instrumental in amending the provision to two years. Although the committee recommended the change unanimously, the term length question continued to be one of great controversy throughout the ratification process. The failure to include annual elections was enough to prevent Elbridge Gerry from signing the Constitution:

> When society has thus deputed a certain number of their equals to take care of their personal rights, and the interest of the whole community, it must be considered that responsibility is the great security of integrity and honor; and that annual election is the basis of responsibility—man is not immediately corrupted, but power without limitation, or amenability, may endanger the brightest virtue—whereas a frequent return to the bar of their constituents is the strongest check against the corruption to which men are liable, either from the intrigues of others of more subtle genius, or the propensies of their own hearts. . . . (Ford 1892, 6-17)

For Gerry, as for many Anti-Federalists, the abstract principle of popular sovereignty over government was not enough; more practical safeguards were needed to protect liberty.

Limits on Tenure

The Constitution departed from the Articles of Confederation again by putting no limitation on the number of terms members of Congress could serve. This provision, based on the principle known as "rotation in office," was a check on the accrued power of veteran legislators. Under the Articles, delegates were restricted to serving only three out of six consecutive years. Publius appealed to the principles of the new system to show that rotation or other limitations were unnecessary; the biggest check on power was the Constitution itself, under which no legislator had more power than any other citizen. Beyond that, there was the more practical consideration of the need for experienced legislators and the dangers of too many freshmen congressmen.

> A few of the members, as happens in all such assemblies, will possess superior talents: will, by frequent reelections, become members of long standing, will be thoroughly masters of the public business, and perhaps not unwilling to avail themselves of those advantages. The

THE "FEDERAL CITY"

The House of Representatives was not the only body that spurred debate over term length. The presidential term caused considerable disagreement and the length of senatorial terms caused proponents of states' rights in particular to dissent. Even though senators until 1913 were elected by the state legislatures, what Anti-Federalist writer "Brutus" said about them in 1788 is relevant to the question of terms in general.

> [Senators] should not be so long in office as to be likely to forget the hand that formed them or be insensible of their interest. Men long in office are very apt to feel themselves independent; to form and pursue interests separate from those who appointed them. And this is more likely to be the case with the Senate, as they will for the most part of the time be absent from the state they represent, and association with such company as will possess very little of the feelings of the middling class of people. For it is to be remembered that there is to be a federal city, and the inhabitants of it will be the great and mighty of the earth. For these reasons I would shorten the term of their service to 4 years. Six years is a long period for a man to be absent from his home; it would have a tendency to wean him from his constituents. (*New York Journal*, 10 April 1788)

greater the proportion of new members, and the less information of the bulk of the members, the more apt they will be to fall into the snares that may be laid for them. This remark is no less applicable to the relations which will subsist between the House of Representatives and the Senate. (*Federalist* No. 53)

But in the lack of rotation, Elbridge Gerry found another reason to dissent from the proposed constitution, a reason that outweighed the practical consideration of experience:

> There is no provision for a rotation, nor anything to prevent the perpetuity of office in the same hands for life; which by a little well-timed bribery, will probably be done, to the exclusion of men of the best abilities from their share in the offices of government. By this neglect we lose the advantage of that check to the overbearing insolence of office, which by rendering him ineligible at certain periods, keeps the mind of man in equilibrium, and teaches him the feelings of the governed, and better qualifies him to govern in his turn. (Ford 1892, 6-17)

The Nature of the Legislator

Time and time again, in arguing over the institutional provisions of representative government, the founders returned to the fundamental question of what kind of person made the ideal legislator in a republic. Disagree as they might over the amount of control necessary to prevent tyranny, they did agree that in a republic based on the sovereignty of the people, the most appropriate legislator would be a citizen first. The ideal "citizen legislator" was both well-read in classical republican theory and experienced in the "real world" of his constituents and familiar with their characteristic problems and concerns. The legislature was not a career but a tour of duty, not a life in itself but part of a life devoted to the congressional session and the public good, the rest to private activities.

In the citizen legislator, the founders believed they had found the ideal that could balance the demands of knowledge, legislative experience, and efficiency with those of democracy, accountability, and the need to check the accumulation of power. The tension between those demands is one that has lasted, and part of the impulse to reform Congress is an attempt to retain the eighteenth-century balance in the context of the twentieth century. Some of the same questions faced by the founders as they struggled to implement their ideals have resurfaced as modern Americans contemplate whether change in the legislative branch is advisable.

Congressional Tenure Today

Legislative Demands in the Twentieth Century

> No man can be a competent legislator who does not add to an upright intention and sound judgment a certain degree of knowledge of the subjects on which he is to legislate. A part of this knowledge may be acquired by means of information which lies within the compass of men in private as well as public stations. Another part can only be attained, or at least thoroughly attained, by actual experience in the station which requires the use of it. The period of service ought, therefore, in all cases, to bear some proportion to the extent of practical knowledge requisite to the due performance of the service. (*Federalist* No. 53)

In Publius' opinion, the length of a congressman's term should be directly related to the amount of knowledge he needs to be an effective official of "the great theatre of the United States." When *The Federalist Papers* were written, that knowledge consisted of the commercial and legal affairs of all the states, the "internal circumstances by which the states are distinguished from each other," and treaties and laws of other nations. The modern argument for a three- or four-year House term is similar. But today advocates of a longer term point out that legislators must master a much larger body of knowledge than their eighteenth-century counterparts. Now, they claim, we must add to the list the regulations of a bureaucratic federal government with an expanded role in the lives of its constituents, the trends of a more complex scientific and technological society, and the foreign affairs of a major world power.

In a 1966 message to Congress, President Lyndon Johnson reopened the issue of terms in Congress:

> There was little magic in the number two, even in the year of its adoption. I am convinced that the question of tenure should be reexamined in light of our needs in the 20th century. (Message to the Congress, 20 January 1966)

Johnson thus revived a debate that originated in the Constitutional Convention: Do short terms contribute to the "best interest of democracy" or to "harassed inefficiency and the loss of invaluable experience"? Applied to the realities of a twentieth-century Congress, these questions took on new meaning.

Change in the congressional workload is clearly illustrated in statistics: the first Congress had 144 bills introduced and passed 108 laws; the Ninety-seventh Congress passed 389 laws out of the 10,582 bills introduced. But what to some may seem an obvious case for "modernization" is not so simple to others. The fact that the legislative demands on the first Congress included the "inauguration of the government and the primeval formation of a federal code" should not be overlooked. Nor did the first Congress have the benefit of "past transactions of the government" as a "ready and accurate source of information to new members." It is questionable whether dealing with the huge and complex government of today can even come close to the initial challenge faced by our first legislators.

From Length to Limitation

Another tenure reform has been attracting more attention in recent Congresses than the call for lengthening terms. There is a growing attempt to revive the ideal of the "citizen legislator" by imposing a limit on congressional tenure. While supporters of limitation do believe it would lessen the constant reelection pressure that preoccupies members today, their major goal is to get Congress out of Washington and back among the people. Says Sen. John Danforth, one of the reform's strongest advocates:

POWER WITHIN GOVERNMENT

Two controversial details of the four-year proposal illustrate why other parts of the government would be concerned about the effect of a change in the House term.

1. Should congressmen all run in the presidential election year or should elections be staggered as they are in the Senate? President Johnson proposed that congressional and presidential elections coincide and was accused of trying to subordinate the House to the president by tying its members to his "coattails." Johnson responded:

   If our purpose is to serve the democratic ideal by making the people's House more effective in its performance of the people's business, then we must require that its members be chosen by the largest electorate our democracy can produce. That, assuredly, is the electorate called into being during a presidential year. (Message to Congress, 20 January 1966)

2. Should the proposed amendment require House members to resign their seats if they intend to run for the Senate? Members of the Senate fear a strong challenge from incumbent representatives if they can campaign for Senate seats in the midst of a four-year term. In hearings on the amendment in 1966 and again in 1979, it became clear that a four-year term proposal had no hope of passing the Senate without a clause requiring resignation.

. . . By limiting terms, I hope to change the course of thinking of the people who come to Washington to serve in Congress. The purpose of my proposal is to make certain that each and every Congressman understands that his tenure here is limited, that—however adept a politician he may be, and however skillful he may be in pleasing special interest groups—he will someday have to answer to as well as for the laws he writes. By limiting terms we will remind each Member of Congress that he is not, by virtue of his election, a member of some ruling class, but a citizen on leave to his government—a public servant first, last, and foremost. (Testimony, 14 March 1978)

In Congress, up until the mid-nineteenth century, the tradition was to serve for two terms and then retire; public service was a "sabbatical" in the midst of a private career. By the 1920s, the average stay had doubled, the number of committees had grown, and the seniority system was firmly entrenched; serving in Congress had become a career in itself. To some, this meant a more removed and less responsive body. But to others who oppose the concept of limitation, professionalism is not a bad development and the "citizen legislators" may not be equipped to do the job today. Columnist George F. Will wrote:

> Americans cling to the idea that government in a modern state can be an amateur's avocation. But in government, as in other serious enterprises, knowledge is cumulative. Government is as much a profession as law or teaching; it is a learned activity and an increasingly complicated one.
>
> Politics in our time has been ennobled by the long careers of such Senators as John Stennis, Hubert Humphrey, and Henry Jackson. Granted, long service is only a necessary, not a sufficient, condition of legislative greatness. Granted, greatness is rare, even among those who have long careers. But it should not be made impossible. (*Washington Post*, 30 October 1977)

A growing dissatisfaction with the behavior of Congress has inspired both political scientists and the general public to look at term limitation as a reform that might make a difference. Junior members of Congress continue to be frustrated by the seniority system which they claim is as firmly entrenched and as obstructive of efficient and fair legislation as ever:

> Contrary to popular belief—as fostered in the media—the so-called Watergate class of 1974, of which I am a member, did not destroy the seniority system in the House. Seniority, as we all know, is alive and well, along with its attendant fiefdoms, dominance over legislative priorities, and control of staff and funding in committees. One Senator or one Representative can tie up legislation for months— can, in fact, singlehandedly kill proposals which a majority of his or her committee may favor. A limit on terms would help restrict certain abuses in the committee process. (Rep. Toby Moffett, Testimony, 14 March 1978)

Finally, a major source of support for term limitation comes from internal scrutiny. Members themselves make some of the strongest arguments for limiting themselves. Incumbents are preoccupied with reelection throughout their careers; they never get off the "reelection treadmill." The privileges of being in Congress are constantly abused and the power and perquisites surrounding them in their Washington lives insulate them from the "real world" and seduce them into perpetuating themselves in office indefinitely. In sum, they have seen the future that was predicted by the Anti-Federalist writer Brutus in his criticism of the Senate:

> It is probable that Senators once chosen for a state will, as the system now stands, continue in office for life. The office will be honorable if not lucrative. The persons who occupy it will probably wish to continue in it, and therefore use all their influence and that of their friends to continue in office. Their friends will be numerous and powerful, for they will have it in their power to confer great favors; besides it will before long be considered as disgraceful not to be reelected. It will therefore be considered as a matter of delicacy to the character of the senator not to return him again. Everybody acquainted with public affairs knows how difficult it is to remove from office a person who has long been in it.... (*New York Journal*, 10 April 1778)

Congressional Reform—Other Approaches

Modern attempts to change congressional terms are not only a response to growth and change but are also a part of a larger reform context in the past fifty years. The 1946 Legislative Reorganization Act was perhaps the most significant attempt to make Congress more efficient. Its internal reforms significantly reduced the number of committees, established clear committee jurisdiction, and initiated the congressional staff. More recent procedural reforms during the 1970s were also meant to strengthen the legislative branch from the inside. In the reform impetus created by the Watergate investigations, Congress took steps to open up the system by reducing the powers of committee chairmen and restricting the number of meetings that could be closed to the public. In an attempt to add more cohesion to the Congress, the tools of party discipline were enhanced.

One charge levied by opponents of changes in congressional terms is that the amendments are "solutions in search of a problem." While not denying the existence of problems, these opponents are skeptical of structural changes where internal solutions may be more to the point.

On the other hand, there are critics who say that term changes are not enough; problems in Congress are only a part of more general problems in the structure of government, and there are ways of integrating the electoral process into a broader reform approach. For example:

● Term lengths and the electoral process could be coordinated to promote a more unified and effective national government. Thus the presidential term could be lengthened to six years to match that in the Senate, and the House term would be lengthened to three years. With this arrangement, the way would be open to link congressional and presidential candidates on a single ticket so that voters would be electing officials pledged to work together from the outset. A similar arrangement could be effected with presidential and House terms at four years and the Senate at eight.

- Even though the regularity of elections may seem built into the American political tradition, some argue that "special elections" powers could significantly improve the system by placing the strongest tools of accountability in the executive and legislative branches. The special elections power would allow Congress to pass a vote of "no confidence" in the president and then put the question to the people by calling a special election in which it nominated an opposition candidate. The president would be able to initiate a similar process by dissolving the Congress.

Those who look to nonstructural reforms to solve some of the problems diagnosed by Congress-watchers suggest the following:

- Overcome the perpetual reelection preoccupation by passing laws restricting the length of the campaign season and devising a system of public financing for congressional elections to ease the burden of fund-raising and make the system more equitable.

- Within Congress, pass regulations to lessen the power of incumbency and institute a more stringent oversight of the use of mail and travel privileges that tip the balance toward the incumbent. Exercise sanctions to eliminate absenteeism.

- Prevent individual abuses of the system by strengthening party ties, the role of caucuses, and the emphasis on cooperation. A well-disciplined party machinery could help to ease the campaign burden on individual congressmen and make the committee system work in a more open and equitable way.

Arguments For Lengthening Terms in the House

- A longer term would give representatives more time to develop expertise and sound political judgment. They could devote more time to the issues rather than to running for reelection almost as soon as they start a new term.

- Longer legislative sessions and more responsibility call for adjustment in the system to reflect the fact that being a representative is a full-time job.

- Longer terms would make congressional service more attractive to better quality candidates.

- The need to run less often would lower campaign costs and open the office to more people.

- Longer terms would decrease the number of bills introduced purely for reelection purposes.

- With modern communications and travel, a representative can

CONGRESSIONAL TENURE—
A BRIEF LEGISLATIVE HISTORY

1789   The first congressional tenure reforms proposed rotation in office provisions and annual elections.

1808   Senator Hillhouse called for one-year House terms beginning in 1813.

1869-90   The trend shifted toward lengthening House terms to three, four, or six years, generally with the idea that this would eliminate the need to run for reelection.

1890-1913   While there were more proposals to lengthen House terms, Senate reforms attracted more attention. Proposals to lengthen Senate terms to eight years failed; the Seventeenth Amendment, mandating direct election of the Senate, was ratified in 1913.

1946   The Legislative Reorganization Act was passed.

1951   Harry Truman made a proposal for a four-year House term that was to be repeated by Eisenhower, Johnson, and Nixon. He also called for a twelve-year limit on congressional service.

1966   Lyndon Johnson's Message to the Congress led to hearings but no action.

1972-78   Interest in term limitation gradually surpassed that in lengthening terms. There have consistently been more amendments proposed to limit congressional terms, including twenty-two resolutions in 1977-78.

1981   Gallup polls showed 61 percent of the general public in favor of limiting senators' terms and 59 percent for limiting representatives' terms. Both were up a full 10 percent from surveys a decade earlier. Fifty-one percent of the general public responded favorably to the four-year House term, but that figure, interestingly, was down 10 percent from 1966.

keep in touch with constituents more steadily. The two-year term is not necessary for a representative to keep in touch with constituents.

● A four-year term coincident with the presidential term would strengthen the ties between the branches, and representatives would be elected in years when voter turnout is highest.

● A four-year term with staggered elections would preserve the "mid-term" election while gaining the benefits of giving representatives more time to legislate.

● With a longer term and less constant reelection pressure, representatives would not have to rely so heavily on larger and larger staffs.

● Lengthening the federal term would follow the trend set by the states, where it has worked for better government without a loss of responsiveness.

Arguments Against Lengthening Terms in the House

● Extending terms would remove the "mid-term" election, which is an opportunity for voters to have a say on the performance of the president.

● Reelection every two years keeps Congress in touch with the people and ensures that the House will reflect the changing or unchanging mood of the country. Longer terms will create too much inflexibility.

● Extending terms would not decrease the amount spent on campaigns, only increase the amount spent per campaign.

● Modern communications and travel can be used to lessen the burden of frequent campaigning; they make it easier to do the job in two years.

● Technology is not an adequate replacement for the election process in keeping congressmen truly in touch with constituents.

● The last thing people need today is fewer opportunities to vote. Lengthening terms will only widen the gap between government and the people.

● A four-year term coincident with the president's would create a permanent "coattail effect"; candidates would be too dependent on what happened in the presidential campaign and the president can only weaken the legislative branch.

● A four-year term with staggered elections would be unfair to the congressmen who were always running in an "off" year.

● Congress would be more efficient if it passed internal reforms. The people should not be made to suffer because of representatives' inability to work within the constraints set by the Constitution.

POINTS OF VIEW

On the Four-Year Term

. . . it is easy to examine the attendance record in the second year of every session, the absenteeism created and resulting from the necessity of members to return to their districts for primary elections and for elections—which deprives the people of the productive capacity of the quality of men that they elected to serve them. . . . This retards the progress of our great American democracy, because we should not have one productive year out of every two for the issuance of progressive legislation, for the welfare of the great mass of our people. (Rep. Herbert Tenzer, Testimony, 13 July 1966)

Campaigns are at the center of politics. In a democracy, campaigning is a two-day process: it stimulates and educates the public, and it also stimulates public officials and is an important way for them to learn the views of the people. Campaigning is not a necessary evil, or necessarily a heavy burden that interferes with work of an elected official. It is an important part of his service. What we should aim for is to improve the means for campaigning. (Sen. Eugene McCarthy, Testimony, 14 July 1966)

I believe that a four-year term would give a member of Congress a more secure feeling which, in turn, would give him a freedom which he must have in order to devote himself, heart and soul, to his legislative duties. I do not mean to imply that concern for political success and devotion to legislative duty are necessarily contradictory. They may or may not be. The motivation involved in one is likely to be different from that involved in the other. Elected representatives are not meant to enjoy absolute political security. That would contradict the meaning and efficacy of representative government. But the relative political insecurity and apprehension engendered by too-frequent elections are obstacles, I maintain, to wholehearted devotion to public business. . . . It is my conviction that both the future role of Congress in national affairs and the fundamental interests of constituents would be enhanced by the four-year term for representatives. (Rep. D. R. Matthews, Testimony, July 1966)

. . . we have grown, we certainly have come of age. . . . And to tell you the truth, there is absolutely no comparison—even at the time I came here 22 years ago and today. My district has grown from 273,000 to where I represent over 600,000 people. . . . And yet I have to service those people. And at the end of the day, there are just so many phone calls, so many letters, and so many people that old Frank can see. There are just so many bricks that a bricklayer can lay, there are so many teeth that a dentist can fill, there are so many patients that a doctor can see. So it is with a member of the House of Representatives. There is a limit to what a man can do, unless he starts delegating it, and who wants to delegate the people's representation? . . . (Rep. Frank Chelf, Testimony, 13 July 1966)

If . . . representatives feel the Constitution places upon them an undue burden, I can only answer that they are under no obligation to run. Congress was not created for the benefit of congressmen but rather for the people they represent. Neither, I might add, was Congress created for the benefit of the office of the president. (Sen. Sam Ervin, Testimony, 13 July 1966)

For we do not live in a day when news of congressional action requires weeks to reach our constituents, nor when public opinion is obscured by time and distance. Communications media rush the news to every home and shop within minutes of its occurrence. Public opinion polls, and mountains of mail, leave little doubt about what our people think of the issues most vital to them. I do not fear deafness on the part of those who will take their seats in Congress for a four-year term. (President Lyndon Johnson, Message to the Congress, 20 January 1966)

Public opinion polls and mail are insufficient substitutes for the electoral process. Under the parliamentary system, if the government is challenged on a serious national issue, and it is unable to carry the House, the House is dissolved and elections held. Our comparable institution is the biennial election. (Sen. Eugene McCarthy, Testimony, 14 July 1966)

The reasons for the two-year term are as valid today as they were in 1789. Indeed, today, when travel between home and Washington is much less time consuming, and when ease of communications allows us to be informed immediately and accurately on any problems anywhere in the world, a short term is less of a burden than ever before. (Sen. Sam Ervin, Testimony, 13 July 1966)

Arguments For Limiting Congressional Tenure

● Limiting terms would create a constant influx of new blood and fresh ideas from the citizenry. Congress would be more responsive to what is foremost on the public agenda.

● The advantages of incumbency and seniority would be reduced and merit would play a larger role in determining who has power in Congress.

● The lack of limits on service is a congressman's incentive to perpetuate himself in office and in Washington indefinitely, where members become insulated from what is important to constituents.

● Members might look more closely at legislation they know they will have to live with at the close of a limited tenure.

● Limiting terms would open the job to more people, especially the young or older people who would undertake it as a public service during or after another lifelong career. The reform would revive the "citizen legislator" and eliminate "careerism."

● Limitations on tenure would reduce the constant preoccupation with reelection and encourage more serious attention to issues aside from reelection implications.

● Limitation would help alleviate the cynicism people feel toward government by making Congress more genuinely a branch made up of people like themselves.

● Congressional limitation extends the principle of the Twenty-second Amendment (limiting presidents to two terms in office) to the legislative branch.

Arguments Against Limiting Congressional Tenure

● Congress and the people would lose the valuable expertise of experienced members who become better able to serve as they are there longer.

● The decision about how long is long enough should be left up to the voters, who are the best judges of whether their interests are being served.

● Internal reforms of the seniority system have vastly reduced the advantages of long tenure and made committee positions more open to newer members.

● Limiting terms would reduce the power of the legislative branch vis à vis the executive and create "lame duck" representatives and senators for longer periods and in larger numbers.

● It is undemocratic in any way to limit the right of voters to

POINTS OF VIEW

On Term Limitation

Such an amendment is a recipe for further reducing the power of the legislature relative to the "permanent government," the executive bureaucracy. It would prune deadwood, but also would prevent great legislative careers on the scale of Henry Clay's, Sam Rayburn's, and Robert Taft's—the sort of careers that give continuity, cohesion, and energy to the legislature. Besides, a "fresh face" is by another name a "rookie," with a lot to learn in a town where there is a lot to know. (George Will, *Washington Post*, 30 October 1977)

Skilled and experienced statesmen providing leadership in both houses of the Congress are now more vital than ever to check executive power and bureaucratic excess. This proposed amendment would, in practice, weaken the capability of Congress to perform its historic role of restraining runaway executive power. (Dr. Herbert Garfinkel, Testimony, 14 March 1978)

... By shortening terms I feel that the legislative accountability will be enhanced and the forces which nurture it will be strengthened. This may be another way of saying that I have come to prefer democracy over efficiency. . . .

Two thousand years ago, Plato rejected democracy because he believed the decisions of government should not be made by amateurs. He said we needed philosopher-kings to guide us—divinely anointed experts who clearly saw truth. I reject that view because in the realm of politics there is no truth as such. The best we can do is to seek modes of compromise and accommodation so we can live together peacefully. The legislature is the bar of the people—the forum in which we continue the great experiment in self-government. This is not an exercise that requires any special expertise; it requires commitment to the value of democracy. (Sen. Dennis DeConcini, Testimony, 14 March 1978)

... It really is an infringement on individual liberties, both the liberties of voters and officeholders. Moreover it is essentially anti-democratic. It just does not trust the electorate to decide for itself whether an individual should be returned to office or not. In fact, it substitutes an arbitrary rule for the collective judgment of citizens in this country. (Thomas Mann, American Political Science Association, Testimony, March 1978)

continue electing an effective official—whether the president, senators, or representatives.

● Limited terms would increase the number of "amateurs" in Congress and weaken it drastically in the face of the permanent Washington bureaucracy. We need more competent professional legislators.

● The voters themselves are already likely to turn out a legislator who has genuinely overstayed his welcome.

● Reelection pressure is generally a positive and necessary component of our system which should not be eliminated. Reforming the campaign process would be a more appropriate way of alleviating the problems that reelection can pose.

Questions to Guide Discussion

● Is representative government founded in "confidence" in the people, as Madison said, or in "jealousy"—the need to protect individual rights from the encroachments of those in power? How do these attitudes affect our representative institution?

● How do we justify our system of representation? Does our system give us "actual" representation—a mirror of what the people want—or "virtual" representation—a government in the name of the "national interest"? Would changes in government make ours a more representative system?

● Is the ideal of the "citizen legislator" alive today? Can it work in the modern Congress or do we need to revise our ideal to take modern realities into account?

● Would a longer House term allow congressmen to do a better job? Would there be a loss of accountability? If so, how would that affect performance? Are the demands on a congressman's time more pressing today than in the eighteenth century?

● Would a limit on congressional terms take away the people's right to choose? Would it deprive them of other benefits they are entitled to?

● Have the founders' fears of the corrupting influence of power, the vulnerability of inexperienced legislators to the "intrigues of others" and the seduction threatened by the "federal city" proven justified? How important should a suspicion of human nature be in determining the form government takes today?

References

Borden, Morton, ed. *The Anti-Federalist Papers.* Ann Arbor, Mich.: Michigan State University Press, 1965.

Elliott, Jonathan, ed. *The Debates in the Several State Conventions on the Adoption of the Federal Constitution.* 5 vols. New York: Burt Franklin, 1888.

Ford, Paul Leicester, ed. *Pamphlets on the Constitution of the United States, Published During the Discussion by the People, 1787-1788.* Brooklyn, N.Y.: Historical Printing Club, 1892.

Hamilton, Alexander, John Jay, and James Madison. *The Federalist Papers.* Available in various editions.

Johnson, Lyndon B. "Message to the Congress." 20 January 1966. House Document 264, 89th Cong., 2d sess. U.S. Government Printing Office.

U.S. Congress. *Four Year Term for Representatives.* Hearings before the Subcommittee on Constitutional Amendments of the Committee on the Judiciary, 89th Cong., 2d sess., on S.J. Resolutions 72, 126, and 132, and H.J. Resolution 394, 13 and 14 July 1966. U.S. Government Printing Office, 1967.

U.S. Congress. Senate. *Terms of Office in the Senate and House of Representatives.* Hearings, 95th Cong., 2d sess., on S.J. Resolutions 27 and 28, 14 and 16 March 1978. U.S. Government Printing Office, 1978.

Suggested Readings

Foundation for the Study of Presidential and Congressional Terms. "Term Limitation: The Issue That Never Dies." Washington, D.C., 1980.

Charles O. Jones. *Every Second Year: Congressional Behavior and the Two Year Term.* Washington, D. C.: The Brookings Institution, 1967.

Samuel Kernell. "Toward Understanding 19th Century Congressional Careers: Ambition, Competition, and Rotation." *American Journal of Political Science* 21 (1977): 669-93.

David R. Mayhew. *Congress: The Electoral Connection.* New Haven, Conn.: Yale University Press, 1975.

Robert L. Peabody. "Rebuild the House?" *Johns Hopkins Magazine,* March 1966.

James L. Sundquist. *The Decline and Resurgence of Congress.* Washington, D. C.: The Brookings Institution, 1981.

U.S. Congress. House. *Subcommittee on Constitutional Amendments.* H.J. Resolution 204, 62d Cong., 2d sess. U.S. Government Printing Office, 1912.

U.S. Congress. House. *Committee on Election of President, Vice President, and Representatives in Congress.* Four Year Term for Members of Congress. Hearings, 74th Cong., 1st sess., on H.J. Resolution 32, 21 March 1935. U.S. Government Printing Office, 1935.

Gordon Wood. *The Creation of the American Republic, 1776-1787.* Chapel Hill, N.C.: University of North Carolina Press, 1969.

5. Judicial Independence and Accountability

"Article— The judges, both of the Supreme and inferior courts shall hold their offices for the terms of _____ years, and will be eligible for unlimited reappointment by the President, subject to the reconfirmation by the Senate."

The judicial branch is an American innovation. As the branch founded to uphold the supremacy of the Constitution, it represents what was truly revolutionary about the founding of the American republic. The Constitution is the sovereignty of the people, and no elected government can usurp that fundamental right of self-government as long as the Constitution is preserved as the charter of the country. The Court protects this unique and revolutionary right and symbolizes the continued integrity of the system.

If the Supreme Court inspires pride, it has also provoked opposition throughout its existence, perhaps because it has come to play a much larger role in forming the law of the land than ever anticipated by its creators. One attempt to control the judiciary has been to make it accountable by instituting terms of office.

The Fight Against "Usurpations"

The independence of the Supreme Court stems directly from the colonial experience with the British judicial system. Colonial judges were originally appointed to office during good behavior. But they quickly became dependent on the king when in 1761 the tenure provision was altered to "during the royal pleasure." The judiciary's subordination to the monarch was sealed by 1772, when Massachusetts Superior Court judges were paid from the royal instead of the colonial purse.

Such measures only fueled the revolutionary fires. In the Declaration of Independence Thomas Jefferson accuses the king of "REPEATED injuries and usurpations, ALL HAVING in direct object the establish-

by Alice O'Connor and Mary L. Henze

ment of an absolute tyranny over these states." The king, Jefferson continues,

> ... has obstructed the administration of justice by refusing his assent to laws for establishing judiciary powers. He has made judges dependent on his will alone for tenure of their offices, and the amount and payment of their salaries. (Declaration of Independence)

A "good behavior" term was a feature of most of the revolutionary state constitutions; it was one of the first things to be agreed upon at the Constitutional Convention in Philadelphia in 1787:

> The judicial Power of the United States, shall be vested in one supreme Court, and in such inferior Courts as the Congress may from time to time ordain and establish. The Judges, both of the supreme and inferior Courts, shall hold their offices during good Behaviour, and shall, at stated Times, receive for their Services, a Compensation, which shall not be diminished during their Continuance in Office. (U. S. Const. Art. III, sec. 1)

The Power of Appointment

While there was no argument against a life term for Supreme Court justices, it took months for a decision to be reached on who or what would appoint new judges. The Virginia Plan presented to the Convention on June 6, 1787, proposed that the judiciary be chosen by the "national legislature." James Wilson of Pennsylvania warned that "intrigue, partiality, and concealment" might result from appointments entrusted to a body of people. James Madison proposed removing "appointment by legislature" from the clause and the phrase was left blank, to be filled in upon "maturer reflection." Madison supported appointment by the Senate, which he considered to be "numerous enough to be balanced. Not too numerous to be governed by other motives: stable and independent enough to follow their own judgments."

Throughout the summer most of the framers clung fast to the notion that the legislature, as a representative of the people, should select the judges. By August, however, mistrust of the "mass" decision prevailed and the Committee of Five recommended that the Senate appoint Supreme Court judges. That proposal in turn was rejected for the opposite reason: a majority of senators who represented only a minority of the people could place a judge on the bench.

Not until late in the Convention could the framers agree that the president, as the officer of the people, was an appropriate authority to appoint judges, subject to approval by the Senate. The Constitution provides that the president

> ... shall nominate, and by and with the Advice and Consent of the Senate, shall appoint Ambassadors, other public Ministers and Consuls,

Judges of the supreme Court, and all other Officers of the United States. . . . (U. S. Const. Art. II, sec. 2)

The Paradox of Independence

The widespread agreement on judicial independence may have been in reaction to George III's "usurpations," but it also reflected certain prevailing eighteenth-century beliefs about the effects of power on those who were entrusted to exercise it. As a safeguard for the rights they claimed as an independent nation, the founders fashioned the government with the express purpose of controlling the officers and institutions of power. Concentrations of power were hothouses in which man's evil nature would flourish. The three branches were kept strictly separate to create a natural system of checks and balances that made it impossible for one branch, individual, or scheming faction to wield power independent of the others. The Supreme Court was envisioned as the ultimate check: the purest institution that would remain independent of political pressure and partisan motivations. The Court would protect the rights of the minority against the greed of the majority, restrain the executive from overindulgence in personal power, and demand that all legislation adhere to constitutional principles.

But subsequent generations looking back to the creation of the American judiciary could see a paradox in its independence: the founders did not provide the same powerful checks on the Court as on the other branches. Yet the Court was to be made of mortal men subject to the same temptations as any other. Why wouldn't independence create the danger of the accumulation of too much power?

The "Least Dangerous" Branch

The clue to the paradox of independence can be found in *Federalist* No. 78, without question the finest explanation of the intentions and philosophy of the framers as they created the framework of the judiciary branch. Written by "Publius" in May 1788, it explains the viability of the Court and its role in the complex scheme of the new government. Perhaps the greatest strength of the judiciary, in Publius' argument, was its weakness. It could be independent because it was the "least dangerous" branch:

> Whoever attentively considers the different departments of power must perceive, that in a government in which they are separated from each other, the judiciary, from the nature of its functions, will always be the least dangerous to the political rights of the constitution; because it will be least in a capacity to annoy or injure them. The executive not only dispenses the honors, but holds the sword of the community. The legislature not only commands the purse, but prescribes the rules by which the duties and rights of every citizen are to be regulated. The

> judiciary on the contrary has no influence over either the sword or the purse, no direction either of the strength or of the wealth of the society.... It may truly be said to have neither Force nor Will, but merely judgment.... The judiciary is beyond comparison the weakest of the three departments of power. (*Federalist* No. 78)

The framers' belief in the frailty of the judicial branch stemmed largely from their adherence to the philosophy of Montesquieu who wrote "of the three powers ... the judiciary is next to nothing." It was therefore more important to guard its independence than to check its powers. A real danger would have been created by giving judicial powers to the legislative or executive branches because

> ... liberty can have nothing to fear from the judiciary alone, but would have everything to fear from its union with either of the other departments.... (*Federalist* No. 78)

And the separation of powers had to be constantly reinforced for

> ... as from the natural feebleness of the judiciary, it is in continual jeopardy of being overpowered, awed, or influenced by its coordinate branches.... (*Federalist* No. 78)

"During Good Behavior"

The independence of the judicial branch was provided for in the simple clause "during good behavior." Even though this clause was approved unanimously by the members of the convention, Publius found himself in the position of defending it to the more skeptical public.

> The standard of good behavior for the continuance in office of the judicial magistry is certainly one of the most valuable of the modern improvements in the practice of government. In a monarchy it is an excellent barrier to the despotism of the prince: in a republic it is a no less excellent barrier to the encroachments and oppressions of the representative body. And it is the best expedient which can be devised in any government, to secure a steady, upright and impartial administration of the laws....
>
> ... nothing can contribute so much to [the judiciary's] firmness and independence, as permanency in office, this quality may therefore be justly regarded as an indispensible ingredient in its constitution; and in great measure as the citadel of the public justice and the public security. (*Federalist* No. 78)

Publius and the founders firmly believed that the independence provided by the good behavior clause was crucial to the Court's ability to counteract the naturally power-grasping legislative and executive branches. The Constitution needed constant defense. This, above all, was what the judiciary became identified with.

> If, then, the courts of justice are to be considered as the bulwarks of a limited Constitution against legislative encroachments, this consideration will afford a strong argument for permanent tenure of judicial offices, since nothing will contribute so much as this to the independent spirit in the judges which must be essential to the faithful performances of so arduous a duty. (*Federalist* No. 78)

The Court would also protect individual rights as part of its defense against what the founders saw as the "excesses" of democracy.

> This independence of the judges is equally requisite to guard the Constitution and the rights of individuals from the effects of those ill humors which the acts of designing men, or the influence of particular conjunctures, sometimes disseminate among the people themselves, and which, though they speedily give place to better information, and more deliberate reflection, have a tendency, in the meantime, to occasion dangerous innovations in the government, and serious oppressions of the minor party in the community. (*Federalist* No. 78)

The British Example and Anti-Federalist Opposition

Despite the fervor of revolutionary opposition to the monarchy, American institutions in the formative years were largely patterned on the British examples. Hamilton concludes his argument for the Court by commending the framers for following the example set by the British judicial system:

> Upon the whole, there can be no room to doubt that the convention acted wisely in copying from the models of those constitutions which have established good behavior as the tenure of their judicial offices, in point of duration; and that so far from being blamable on this account, their plan would have been inexcusably defective if it had wanted this important feature of good government. The experience of Great Britain affords an illustrious comment on the excellence of this institution. (*Federalist* No. 78)

But the example of Great Britain also presented the basis for criticism of the proposed Constitution. In a series of essays that appeared in the *New York Journal* during the spring of 1788, the Anti-Federalist writer "Brutus" focused on the good behavior tenure not as the foundation of a fine judiciary, as Publius asserts, but as the source of potentially grave and dangerous consequences. His analysis was based on a comparison between the British and American systems:

> The supreme court under this constitution would be exalted above all other power in the government, and subject to no control . . .
>
> The judges in England are under the control of the legislature, for they are bound to determine according to the laws passed by them. But the judges under this constitution will control the legislature, for the supreme court are authorised in the last resort, to determine what is the

> extent of the powers of the Congress. They are to give the constitution an explanation, and there is no power above them to set aside their judgment . . . they are independent of the people, of the legislature, and of every power under heaven. Men placed in this situation will generally soon feel themselves independent of heaven itself. . . . (*New York Journal*, 20 March 1788; see Kenyon 1966, 350-51)

The British needed to establish a good behavior tenure, Brutus said, because a judiciary without it could not hold its own against the all-powerful monarchy. But no branch of the American government could ever pose the same threat. Why the founders gave the judiciary more independence than the British system was beyond Brutus' comprehension.

Accountability

Brutus was not convinced that the judiciary was the "least dangerous" branch. In his opinion it was potentially the most powerful branch of all and the root of that power was the good behavior tenure. He appealed to the principles of republican government in urging that the Court be made accountable to some authority.

> When great and extraordinary powers are vested in any man, or body of men, which in their exercise, may operate to the oppression of the people, it is of high importance that powerful checks should be formed to prevent the abuse of it.
>
> Perhaps no restraints are more forcible, than such as arise from responsibility to some superior power. Hence it is that the true policy of a republican government is, to frame it in such a manner, that all persons who are concerned in the government, are made accountable to some superior for their conduct in office. This responsibility should ultimately rest with the people. (*New York Journal*, 10 April 1788; see Storing 1981, 2:442)

Brutus did not directly suggest the establishment of terms for judges as a solution to the need for accountability. That suggestion came later. He did say that "the supreme judicial ought to be liable to be called to account, for any misconduct, by some body of men, who depend upon the people for their places." Publius, however, was wary of placing the tools of accountability in the wrong hands, and especially of using the republican institution of renewable terms for that purpose:

> The inflexible and uniform adherence to the rights of the Constitution, and of individuals, which we perceive to be indispensable in the courts of justice, can certainly not be expected from judges who hold their offices by a temporary commission. Periodical appointments, however regulated, or by whomsoever made, would, in some way or other, be fatal to their necessary independence. If the power of making them was committed either to the executive or legislature there would be danger of an improper complaisance to the branch which possessed it; if to

IMPEACHMENT

The only constitutional provision for removal of Supreme
Court justices, as officers of the United States, proclaims
that

> [t]he President, Vice President and all Civil Officers of the
> United States, shall be removed from office on Impeachment
> for, and Conviction of, Treason, Bribery, or other high Crimes,
> and Misdemeanors. (U. S. Const. Art. II, sec. 4)

Brutus, once again foreshadowing criticisms of modern reform-
ists, warned that such a clause did nothing to guard against
routine misconduct and misjudgment. Only if judges could be
proven absolutely "wicked and corrupt" would there be any
hope of impeaching them. In the first years of the Court's
existence it became very clear that bringing impeachment
proceedings to fruition was a long and arduous task. In the past
two hundred years only fifty-five federal judges have been
investigated and of those only eight judges and one Supreme
Court justice have been impeached. Lord Bryce spoke for many
proponents of change when he said:

> Impeachment . . . is the heaviest piece of artillery in the
> congressional arsenal, but because it is so heavy it is unfit for
> ordinary use. It is like a hundred-ton gun which needs
> complex machinery to bring it into position, an enormous
> charge of powder to fire it, and a large mark to aim at. (Bryce
> 1895, 211)

There is some question as to whether the founders intended
impeachment to be the only method of disciplining or removing
federal judges. Controversy stems from varying interpretations
of what the framers meant when they made provisions for
impeachment. Some say they were careful to spell out the
grounds for impeachment because they were afraid it might be
used as a weapon against the judicial branch. They did not go
into detail about other review and removal procedures only
because they expected these would be established as common
administrative practices.

Modern advocates of tenure reform argue that impeachment was always cumbersome, but in today's Congress it is even
more so—its heavy legislative schedule simply does not allow
time for the extended review and deliberation of impeachment
proceedings. Others argue that the founders created a difficult
impeachment process to guard judicial independence and it
should be left that way.

> both there would be an unwillingness to hazard the displeasure of either; if to the people, or to persons chosen by them for the special purpose, there would be too great a disposition to consult popularity to justify a reliance that nothing would be consulted but the Constitution and the laws. (*Federalist* No. 78)

Independence is at the root of Publius' defense of the Court and his resistance to limiting judicial tenure. Accountability is at the root of Brutus' criticisms of the judicial branch just as it is the major argument for the establishment of terms for judges. These two principles of republican government have continued to clash in subsequent attempts to reform the judiciary. Brutus wrote his arguments against the Supreme Court before it went into operation, but his judgments proved remarkably astute over time. He anticipated many of the criticisms that arose within the first decades of the new government and that are still very much alive in today's discussion of the judicial branch in general and the establishment of terms for judges in particular.

Partisanship and the Courts

The founders had intended the judiciary to be weak and nonpartisan; they assumed that it could be. History quickly proved them wrong. Power, partisanship, and the Court became inseparable and controversial issues. Even the men who had supported the theory of an independent judiciary found the reality difficult to live with. For example, Thomas Jefferson spent two terms as president embroiled in battle with John Marshall and his Federalist Court. Jefferson's motivations were blatantly political—he wanted judges who supported his policies and would come to decisions in keeping with his political needs and beliefs.

Unable to weed the Federalist opposition out of the Court through constitutional means—that is, by impeachment—Jefferson and his Republican party attempted to change the system. John Randolph, a Virginia Republican, proposed a constitutional amendment that would allow the president to remove justices from the Supreme Court if both houses of Congress requested their removal. Thomas Jefferson himself was one of the first to propose establishing terms of office for justices as a means of controlling them.

The struggle to control the Court has retained its partisan coloring up into the twentieth century. Any change that would make the judiciary accountable to either the legislative or executive branch—such as terms subject to reappointment—would increase the chance of the Court being shaped for partisan purposes. The more activist stance of the twentieth-century Court in ruling on issues such as reapportionment, busing, school prayer, and abortion has added an extra edge to reform attempts. But the clear link between reforms and current-day legislative issues should not obscure the questions that will be of concern as long as the theory of separated powers remains at the heart of the American republic. Should the Court be more in touch with the political current or would it lose its power to protect the Constitution by being politicized? Is it realistic to assume that the Court can be independent?

Establishing Terms

Attempts to limit and control the judiciary have a history as varied as it is long. Of the methods calling for constitutional amendment, establishing terms of office for the judiciary is the most frequently proposed.

Amendments to establish terms fall into three categories:

1. *Absolute Limits on Tenure*—These proposals would limit all judicial appointments to a single term of a fixed length, subject to the good behavior requirement. Within a lifetime a person could serve one term as an inferior court judge and one term as a Supreme Court justice but never two terms at the same level. A twelve-year term and a fifteen-year term have both been pro- posed.

2. *Limited Term Subject to Popular Election*—These proposals usually call for dividing the United States into nine judicial districts, each of which would elect a single Supreme Court justice and the necessary circuit and district judges. Terms would be six years in length with no limit on reelection eligibility.

3. *Limited Term Subject to Reappointment*—The most popular version of this proposal calls for ten-year terms renewable upon nomina- tion by the president and confirmation by the Senate. Two current variations on this theme call for six- or eight-year terms instead of ten and for reconfirmation by the Senate but no renomination by the president.

Proponents of establishing terms argue that the judiciary is too independent and removed from both the political considerations of the executive and legislative branches and the social considerations of the people. Although Brutus never suggested the establishment of terms for the judiciary, all his fears and arguments are echoed by proponents of the amendment. The judicial branch has too much power; it has too much effect on the legislative process without being answerable to the people or their representatives. Terms are proposed to make the Court accountable for its actions. Those who argue against terms call attention to the carefully crafted separation of powers created by the founders and argue for the continued independence of the judiciary and the need for a removed, nonpartisan check on the other branches.

Periodic reappointment would also provide a way of ridding the judiciary of "problem judges," those unfit for office due to misconduct or physical or mental disability. Supporters of terms point out that impeachment is too cumbersome to be considered a real deterrent in cases of misconduct and that judicial review boards (see "Related Reforms") would expose "dirty laundry" and damage the reputation of the entire branch. Reappointment procedures would provide a quick, painless, and routine way of insuring that only qualified judges remained on the federal bench. Opponents of establishing terms see the damage to the balance of power that would result from reappointment as a far greater danger than a few bad judges. Accountability versus independence and fit versus unfit judges are the two major themes of the debate over terms.

Related Reforms

Establishing terms of office for the judiciary is only one of several proposed solutions to problems arising from too much judicial independence and the life tenure provision. One related proposal would make it easier to remove judges by setting up alternatives to impeachment. Another would institute a mandatory retirement age or at the very least encourage early retirement.

Alternatives to Impeachment. Attempts to change the judiciary began in 1791 with the call for a constitutional amendment to give the president or Congress power to remove judges for misconduct short of impeachable crimes. More recently, judicial reformers have tried to second guess the impeachment clause through legislation rather than by amendment of the Constitution.

The Judicial Tenure Act is a good example of the type of disciplinary mechanism these reforms aim to create. Through a system of special "courts within the Court" the Act would mandate a procedure for retiring disabled judges and removing those who have not committed impeachable offenses but "whose conduct is or has been inconsistent with the good behavior required by Article III, Section 1 of the Constitution." The members of these disciplinary bodies would have the power to review and remove judges of the inferior courts but only to review and recommend action in cases involving Supreme Court justices.

Mandatory or Early Retirement. The other major proposal to change the life tenure clause seeks to reduce the problem of senility on the bench by setting a retirement age. A constitutional amendment calling for mandatory retirement at age seventy has been proposed. Some nonconstitutional solutions have attempted to encourage voluntary retirement. One proposal would permit a judge or justice to retire after eighty years of combined age and service, so that a judge could retire at age sixty-five if he had served fifteen years.

The major argument against retirement is that judges with valuable experience would be forced to retire regardless of their ability to serve. But supporters of retirement claim that retired judges can still contribute by serving when and where they are needed.

Arguments For Establishing Terms

- Judges would be less "removed" and would have to be more responsive to the needs and realities of a changing society.
- A reappointment process would allow for periodic review of a judge's performance.
- Judges who did not perform their duties for reasons such as irresponsibility, disability, or senility could be removed at the end of their term without the stigma of impeachment.
- The Court has taken on a larger role in the legislative process and its power has grown considerably since the eighteenth century. Terms of office would institute a legislative check that is needed in light of this larger role.
- Renewable terms would politicize the Court, which would be a healthy development because it would create more cohesiveness in government policymaking.
- The higher turnover rate and lower average age of justices that would result from the establishment of terms of office would create a more innovative, contemporary Court.
- If the Court is going to rule on issues with immediate social implications, such as abortion and busing, it should be accountable for its actions to the people and their representatives.

Arguments Against Establishing Terms

- Reappointment by any body would create a dependent, biased judiciary, robbing the country of truly equal opportunity under the law.
- Well-qualified and effective judges could be forced from office because they refused to subordinate themselves to the will of the appointing authority.
- Judges might tend to "campaign" when facing the possibility of

---

JUDICIAL TENURE:
A BRIEF LEGISLATIVE HISTORY

1791 A constitutional amendment was proposed that provided for an alternative to removal by impeachment; the first attempt was made to change the Court through constitutional amendment.

1807-12 As a result of the Jefferson/Republican frustration with the Marshall/Federalist Court, nine constitutional amendments relating to judicial tenure were introduced, including the first to propose establishing terms.

1832 The authority of the Court was challenged by Andrew Jackson's administration; a proposed amendment limiting the terms of justices failed to pass the House by a vote of 115-61.

1870 First bill requiring mandatory retirement of federal judges failed enactment.

1936-50 Several bills providing for removal of unfit or problem judges without impeachment were introduced.
For example:

   1936 - A bill was proposed to establish a High Court for Trial of Judicial Officers (except Supreme Court Justices).

   1937 - A bill providing the House of Representatives with the power to initiate hearings and conduct prosecution on behavior of federal judges

---

reappointment, allowing political considerations to influence their decisions.

● Judges might deviate from the letter of the law in order to make decisions in keeping with the desires of the reappointing authority.

● Fixed terms would lead to a higher turnover in the courts, depriving the country of the experience and maturity that is important to fair judgment of the laws.

● The increased opportunity to appoint judges would allow presidents to "stack" the court to suit their political needs.

passed in the House in 1938 but died in the Senate.

1941 - The preceding bill passed in the House but failed to win approval in the Senate.

1967-80 Over a dozen proposals were introduced providing for popular election of federal judiciary.

1969 A bill calling for a "judicial review board" composed of federal judges with power to recommend removal of peers (except for Supreme Court justices) was proposed.

1970 Senate Judiciary Committee Subcommittee on the Separation of Powers concluded that the 1969 proposal was "unconstitutional and a threat to the independence of the judiciary."

1974-78 The Judicial Tenure Act calling for a judicial review board with power to investigate federal and Supreme Court justices was introduced to the Senate three times. It was passed by the Senate in 1978 but not acted on by the House before the close of the Ninety-fifth Congress.

1981 More than twenty-five "court-curbing" bills were introduced in Congress to take away the Court's authority to hear cases on certain issues, such as abortion, desegregation, and school prayer.

1984 Several constitutional amendments to establish judicial terms were proposed in the Ninety-eighth Congress.

● Fixed term lengths might encourage presidents to "give away" seats on the bench as political favors, knowing that it could do no permanent or even long-range damage to the judiciary.

● Making the judiciary accountable to the legislative or executive branches would violate the separation of powers intended by the Constitution and diminish the judiciary's ability to act as a check on the other branches.

● The incidence of truly incompetent or irresponsible judges is so low that it does not warrant jeopardizing the entire judicial system to correct a virtually nonexistent problem.

Arguments For Election by the People

● Election by the people provides a chance for the people to judge the performance of their justices and reconsider their qualifications.
● By making the Court accountable directly to the people, the Court would respond to the needs of society.
● "Judicial restraint" might become a reality.
● The public is more informed and educated than during the eighteenth century and is therefore able to make judgments on candidates for the Court.

Arguments Against Election by the People

● The general public is no more qualified to assess the legal qualifications of candidates than they were in the eighteenth century.
● If elected by the people, the supreme law of the land would be overly affected by the passions of the majority.
● The people are not familiar enough with the complexities of the constitutional system to fully understand the decisions made by the Court and could therefore not fairly assess the performance of each justice.
● Judges might be tempted to make decisions for the wrong reasons, campaigning to the majority rather than protecting the rights of all.

Questions to Guide Discussion

● Are independence and accountability irreconcilable? Can the Court be made more accountable without changing its independent character?
● Is independence necessary to do the job of safeguarding the Constitution and the rights it represents? What does the job of "safeguarding the Constitution" mean? Is it an active or passive role?
● Is the Court still the "least dangerous" branch? If not, what has made it more dangerous?
● Is impeachment a strong enough check on the Court?
● Does "judicial independence" assume infallibility on the part of judges? Is it consistent with the checks on the other branches of government?
● Is it accurate to say that the Court as currently structured is removed from politics? Would it undermine the Court to politicize it?
● Would the creation of judicial terms give the legislative and executive branches a power that does not rightfully belong to them? Does power over the Court rightfully belong to the people?

References

Bryce, James. *The American Commonwealth*. 3d ed. New York: Macmillan and Co., 1895.

Hamilton, Alexander, John Jay, and James Madison. *The Federalist Papers*. Available in various editions.

Kenyon, Cecelia M., ed. *The Antifederalist*. Indianapolis: Bobbs-Merrill, 1966.

Storing, Herbert. *The Complete Anti-Federalist*. 7 vols. Chicago: University of Chicago Press, 1981.

Suggested Readings

American Enterprise Institute Legislative Analyses. *Judicial Discipline and Tenure Proposals*. Washington, D. C.: American Enterprise Institute, 1979.

Raoul Berger. "Impeachment of Judges and 'Good Behavior' Tenure." *Yale Law Journal* 79 (1970).

Morton Borden, ed. *The Anti-Federalist Papers*. (Especially pages 222-40.) East Lansing, Mich.: Michigan State University Press, 1965.

Harry F. Byrd, Jr. "Has Life Tenure Outlived Its Time?" *Judicature* 59 (1976).

Jonathan Elliott, ed. *The Debates in the Several State Conventions on the Adoption of the Federal Constitution*. 5 vols. (Especially Volume III, The Virginia Ratifying Debates.) Philadelphia: J. B. Lippincott, 1859.

Sam J. Ervin, Jr. "Separation of Powers: Judicial Independence." *Law and Contemporary Problems* 35 (1970).

William Jeffrey, Jr. "The Letters of Brutus—A Neglected Element in the Ratification Campaign of 1787-88." (Especially letters XI-XVI.) *University of Cincinnati Law Review* 40 (1963).

Philip Kurland. "The Constitution and the Tenure of Federal Judges: Some Notes from History." *University of Chicago Law Review* 39 (1968-69).

Robert G. McCloskey. *The Supreme Court*. Chicago: University of Chicago Press, 1960.

Page Smith. *The Constitution—A Documentary and Narrative History*. New York: Morrow Quill Paperbacks, 1980.

Preble Stolz. "Disciplining Federal Judges: Is Impeachment Hopeless?" *California Law Review* 57 (1959).

6. The Veto and the Separation of Powers

"Article— The executive powers vested in the President shall include the authority to veto individual items of appropriation within bills submitted by Congress for executive approval."

"Article— The legislative powers vested in the Congress shall include the authority of either house to veto rules and regulations issued by the Executive Department pursuant to laws passed by Congress."

Proposals to revise the veto power of the executive and legislative branches challenge one of the most basic doctrines of American government: the separation of powers. The founders built a representative system confident of man's ability to realize self-government. They created a system of institutional checks and balances because they were equally confident of his ability to abuse power. The accumulation of power could mean the end of freedom; the separation of powers was designed to avoid this.

The executive veto is an example of how the founders sought to separate and check power. "Publius" characterized it as a type of executive "defense":

> The propriety of the thing does not turn upon the supposition of superior wisdom or virtue in the executive. But upon the supposition that the legislature will not be infallible. That the love of power may sometimes betray it into a disposition to encroach upon the rights of the other members of the government; that a spirit of faction may sometimes pervert its deliberations; that impressions of the moment may sometimes hurry it into measures which itself on maturer reflection would condemn. The primary inducement to conferring the power in question upon the executive, is to enable him to defend himself; the secondary one is to increase the chances in favor of the community, against the passing of bad laws, through haste, inadvertence, or design. (*Federalist* No. 72)

by Alice O'Connor and Mary L. Henze

Modern attempts to change the veto come in the context of a continuing reappraisal of the complex system of separated powers. Some claim that free government today is threatened more by its own massive inefficiency than by an imbalance of power. The item and the legislative vetoes are two of many proposed reforms that, by conferring new constitutional powers upon the executive and legislative branches, are meant to make the government less cumbersome and more effective.

The proposed item veto would refine the executive veto power by allowing the president to disapprove part of an appropriations bill without having to veto the entire bill. Instead of "all or nothing," the president could strike out specific items he thought unnecessary while signing the rest of a bill into law. This ability to pick and choose is meant to give the president the opportunity to take the initiative in the budget-cutting process, which critics say the Congress has been unable to do. The item veto would be subject to a congressional override by a two-thirds majority vote. (Sen. Alan Dixon's item veto proposal would allow a simple majority vote override.)

The need for a veto power in the legislative branch was not considered at the Constitutional Convention. Since Congress was to initiate all legislative action, it did not make sense to give it the power to nullify what it had already approved. But the legislative process has diverged a good deal from the framers' original vision, and the "legislative veto" is largely a product of that change.

The expanding size and scope of the government has led Congress to lighten its heavy legislative load by delegating some regulatory duties to specialized executive branch agencies. At the same time, Congress has found a convenient way of keeping control over the agencies by giving itself the right to review and veto any of their proposed regulations or actions. This is the legislative veto, which enables Congress to reject proposed executive branch actions by disapproving them before they become effective. The use of the legislative veto has risen dramatically during the past decade, signaling Congress' increased reliance on the device as a way to delegate power safely.

The legislative veto was declared unconstitutional by the Supreme Court in *Immigration and Naturalization Service vs. Chadha* in June 1983. The Court ruled that it violated the separation of powers doctrine and the "presentment clause" of the Constitution, which says that final legislative approval lies in the hands of the executive. Critics have brought similar charges against the item veto. They say it would give the president too much direct control over the purse, which is rightfully the domain of the legislature. In effect, either one or both of the constitutional amendments to change veto powers would shift governmental powers and make them less separate than the founders intended them to be.

The Formative Debate

"Auxiliary Precautions"

Having only recently won independence from a distant and arbitrary central power, the framers of the Constitution were cautious as they undertook to strengthen the federal government at the Philadelphia Convention. Their caution developed from experience and the examples of history; they were fully aware that giving the people the right to elect their own government was in itself no guarantee against despotism. Publius wrote:

> In framing a government which is to be administered by men over men, the great difficulty lies in this: you must first enable the government to control the governed, and in the next place, oblige it to control itself. A dependence on the people is no doubt the primary control on the government; but experience has taught mankind the necessity of auxiliary precautions. (*Federalist* No. 51)

The founders looked to the writings of the French philosopher Montesquieu for guidance as they considered what type of "auxiliary precautions" they could incorporate into the new American system. The primary lesson, accepted by the Federalists and their opponents alike, was that

> ...the accumulation of all powers, legislative, executive and judiciary in the same branch, whether of one, a few or many, and whether hereditary, self-appointed, or elected, may justly be pronounced the very definition of tyranny. (*Federalist* No. 51)

The way to control power, therefore, was to divide it.

In the system of separated powers, the executive enforces the laws passed by Congress and protects the people from bad laws and "popular or factious injustice." The executive must also protect itself, for

> ...in republican government the legislative authority, necessarily, predominates... As the weight of the legislative authority requires that it should be thus divided the weakness of the executive may require on the other hand, that it should be fortified. (*Federalist* No. 51)

In considering what kind of check to give the executive, the founders had experience as a guide. Alexander Hamilton suggested an absolute veto along with his proposal to elect the president "during good behavior," but both ideas were rejected as too monarchical. At the other extreme, the New Jersey Plan did not provide for a veto of any kind but kept close to the model of the Articles of Confederation and gave the states a stronger hand in checking the federal legislature. The authors of the Virginia Plan used a device found in state constitutions when they proposed a "Council of Revision," consisting of the president and members of the judiciary, who would have the power to review and revise legislation. The "qualified" executive veto, which gave Congress the power to override with a two-thirds majority, was a provision in the Massachusetts state constitution. Publius used all these examples to describe the proposed presidential veto and how it would work:

> The qualified negative of the President differs widely from the absolute negative of the British sovereign; and tallies exactly with the revisionary authority of the Council of revision of [New York], of which the Governor is a constituent part. In this respect, the power of the President would exceed that of the Governor of New York because the former would possess singly what the latter shares with the Chancellor and Judges: But it would be precisely similar with that of the Governor of Massachusetts, whose constitution, as to this article, seems to have been the original from which the Convention have copied. (*Federalist* No. 69)

Like similar provisions in the states, the executive veto had a dual purpose. First, as a negative:

> Every Bill which shall have passed the House of Representatives and the Senate, shall, before it becomes a Law, be presented to the President of the United States; if he approve he shall sign it, but if not, he shall return it, with his Objections, to that House in which it shall have originated, who shall enter the Objections at large on their Journal, and proceed to reconsider it. If after such Reconsideration two thirds of that House shall agree to pass the Bill, it shall be sent, together with the Objections, to the other House, by which it shall likewise be reconsidered, and if approved by two thirds of that House, it shall become Law.... (U.S. Const. Art. I, sec. 7)

And second, as a requirement for approval as contained in the "presentment clause":

> Every Order, Resolution, or Vote, to which the Concurrence of the Senate and the House of Representatives may be necessary (except on a question of Adjournment) shall be presented to the President of the United States; and before the Same shall take Effect, shall be approved by him, or being disapproved by him, shall be repassed by two thirds of the Senate and House of Representatives, according to the Rules and Limitations prescribed in the Case of a Bill. (U.S. Const. Art. I, sec. 7)

The presentment clause is the particular article in the Constitution that is challenged by the legislative veto. By enabling Congress to disapprove of actions taken by the executive branch in carrying out legisla-

TWO USES OF THE SEPARATION OF
POWERS DOCTRINE—1787

The doctrine of separated powers was a universal assumption of all interested in the framing of republican government, whether Federalist or Anti-Federalist. It inspired some of the most memorable prose of the Constitution-making era, including this passage from the famed *Federalist* No. 51, written by James Madison:

> ... the great security against a gradual concentration of the several powers in the same department, consist[s] in giving to those who administer each department, the necessary constitutional means, and personal motives, to resist encroachments of the others. The provision for defense must in these, as in all other cases, be made commensurate to the danger of attack. Ambition must be made to counteract ambition. The interest of the man must be connected with the constitutional rights of the place. It may be a reflection of human nature, that such devices should be necessary to control the abuses of government. But what is government but the greatest of all reflections on human nature?

Another powerful statement, written by an Anti-Federalist who called himself "William Penn," invoked the same principle to oppose the Constitution and, specifically, the executive veto:

> ... I believe that it is universally agreed upon in this enlightened country that all power residing originally in the people, and being derived from them, they ought to be governed by themselves only, or by their immediate representatives ...
>
> The next principle, without which it must be clear that no free government can ever subsist, is the DIVISION OF POWER among those who are charged with the execution of it. It has always been the favorite maxim of princes, to divide the people, in order to govern them. It is now time that the people should avail themselves of the same maxim, and divide powers among their rulers, in order to prevent their abusing it. The application of this great political truth , has long been unknown to the world, and yet it is grounded upon a very plain natural principle. If, says Montesquieu, the same man, or body of men, is possessed both of the legislative and executive power, there is NO LIBERTY, because it may be feared that the same monarch, or the same senate, will enact tyrannical laws, in order to execute them in a tyrannical manner. Nothing can be clearer, and the natural disposition of man to ambition and power makes it probable that such would be the consequence. (*Independent Gazeteer*, 2 and 3 January 1788)

tion, the veto ignores the need for presidential approval and leaves the last word to Congress.

The Power of the Purse

The division of the executive, legislative, and judicial powers of government was more than a question of checks and balances. It was also a question of defining very carefully which branches were to carry on which functions. Tradition and efficiency placed the power of the sword in the hands of the executive. Caution and experience warned against placing the power of the purse in the same hand that held the sword. Entrusting the sole right to initiate money bills to the House of Representatives was a precaution, but it was also the result of a British revolutionary tradition which proudly claimed the emerging sovereignty of the people as its own. The power of the purse symbolized that tradition. Publius argued:

> The House of Representatives can not only refuse, but they alone can propose the supplies requisite for the support of government. They in a word hold the purse, that powerful instrument by which we behold in the history of the British constitution, an infant and humble representation of the people, gradually enlarging the sphere of its activity and importance, and finally reducing, as far as it seems to have wished, all the overgrown prerogatives of the other branches of the government. This power over the purse may in fact be regarded as the most compleat and effectual weapon with which any constitution can arm the immediate representatives of the people for obtaining a redress of every grievance and for carrying into effect every just and salutary measure. (*Federalist* No. 58)

The proposed item veto challenges the House's power over the purse because it gives the president more direct control over what is and what is not in appropriations bills.

Anti-Federalist Response

Despite the precautions taken by the framers, Anti-Federalists still objected to the extent of the power given to Congress in the new Constitution. James Monroe, at the Virginia ratifying convention, challenged

> ... the general power given to them [Congress] to make all laws that will enable them to carry them into effect. There are no limits pointed out. They are not restrained or controlled from making any law, however oppressive in its operation, which they may think necessary to carry their powers into effect ... When, then, will be the check to prevent encroachments on the right of the people? (Elliott 1888, 3:218)

Anti-Federalists shared the Federalist fear of concentrated and unchecked power but found the Federalist remedy inadequate. Separation of powers within the central government was not protection enough. The only check on the legislative branch was in the wrong hands; the power to review and reject proposed congressional legislation belonged not to the executive but to the states.

By giving the executive veto power the framers stopped short of creating totally separate branches of government. They gave the executive a hand in the legislative process as a check on Congress. But some Anti-Federalists saw this check as a further opening for collusion rather than a safeguard against it. The veto raised the specter of the British monarch; separation had to be more absolute. Anti-Federalist "William Penn" argued thus:

> The first and most natural division of the powers of government are into the legislative and executive branches. These two should never be suffered to have the least-share of the other's jurisdiction, or to intermeddle with it in any manner. For whichever of the two divides its power with the other, will certainly be subordinate to it; and if they both have a share of each other's authority, they will be in fact but one body. Their interest as well as their powers will be the same, and they will combine together against the people. It is therefore a political error of the greatest magnitude, to allow the executive power a negative, or in fact any kind of control over the proceedings of the legislature. The people of Great Britain have been so sensible of this truth, that since the days of William III no king of England has dared to exercise the negative over the acts of the two houses of parliament, to which he clearly is entitled by his prerogative. (*Independent Gazeteer*, 3 January 1788; see Storing 1981, 3:168-75)

Liberty or Efficiency?

The framers had one goal as they met in Philadelphia—to create a government that both worked efficiently and protected the liberty of the people. For the sake of efficiency they were not willing to divide powers as absolutely as some Anti-Federalists would have liked. The framework they created was genuinely a balance between the competing demands of power and freedom.

That balance has been called into question many times over the past two centuries, especially by critics frustrated with the inefficiency caused by separation of powers. The search for efficiency is a major force behind item and legislative veto proposals; supporters claim the item veto would streamline the budget process and the legislative veto would make the practical and time-saving delegation of regulatory duties feasible. The desire to safeguard liberty above all else motivates opponents of the vetoes. Chief Justice Warren E. Burger sums up the opposition argument in his majority opinion in the *Chadha* case, declaring the legislative veto unconstitutional:

The choices we discern as having been made in the Constitutional Convention imposed burdens on governmental processes that often seem clumsy, inefficient, even unworkable, but those hard choices were consciously made by men who had lived under a form of government that permitted arbitrary governmental acts to go unchecked. There is no support in the Constitution or decisions of the Court for the proposition that the cumbersomeness and delays often encountered in complying with explicit constitutional standards may be avoided, either by the Congress or by the President ... With all the obvious flaws of delay, untidiness and potential for abuse, we have not found a better way to preserve freedom than by making the exercise of power subject to the carefully crafted restraints spelled out in the Constitution. (Justice Warren E. Burger, opinion on *Chadha*; see Craig 1983, 189-90)

The Debate Continues

The founders regarded the veto primarily as a "negative," a defensive measure against the potential excesses of the legislative branch. But modern use of the veto reveals that, in practice, this instrument of restraint can be a powerful political lever in periods of conflict between the president and Congress.

Two pieces of legislation from the 1970s illustrate the role the veto can play in the struggle between the branches. The War Powers Resolution of 1973 used the legislative veto to check the president's powers as Commander in Chief of the military. In protest over the conduct of the Vietnam War, it gave Congress the power to pass a concurrent resolution ordering the president to withdraw troops from combat areas during peacetime. In 1974 Congress asserted further control over the "imperial presidency" by passing the Budget and Impoundment Control Act to stop President Nixon's practice of impounding funds for programs he thought were unnecessary. In effect, Nixon was using his impoundment powers to do what the item veto would do: cut individual appropriations without vetoing an entire bill. By passing the act, Congress was reclaiming full jurisdiction over the national purse.

The evolution of the veto has gone hand in hand with the changing role and duties of the government. The power of the purse is vastly different and more complex today, if only because there are so many more demands on it. The size and power of the executive branch in the military alone has grown beyond the vision of the founders, to the point where Congress clearly feels the need to assert some control over the traditionally executive functions. Just as the founders hoped, however, the powers originally divided among the branches have been jealously guarded by their owners as usurpation from without threatened.

THE SIZE OF THE REPUBLIC:
FEDERALISM OR DESPOTISM?

The framers were working against precedent when they created a limited republic to govern such a large geographical area, and this put an added burden on them to limit the powers of the central government. Many seriously questioned whether the republican form was suited to any but small geographical areas. Geography would be the downfall of this republican experiment, claimed Anti-Federalists like Mr. Dawson of Virginia:

> If we grant to Congress the power of direct taxation; if we yield to them the sword, and if we also invest them with the Judicial authority, two questions, of the utmost importance, immediately present themselves to our inquiries—whether these powers will not be oppressive in their operations, and, aided by other parts of the system, convert the thirteen confederated states into one consolidated government; and whether any country as extensive as North America, and where climates, dispositions, and interest, are so essentially different, can be governed under one consolidated plan, except by the introduction of despotic principles. (Elliott 1888, 3:607)

James Madison had more confidence in the proposed plan and saw the size and diversity of the country as the key to its success.

> Whilst all authority in [the United States] will be derived from and independent on the society, the society itself will be broken into so many parts, interests and classes of citizens, that the rights of individuals or of the minority, will be in little danger from interested combinations of the majority.
> ... In the extended republic of the United States, and among the great variety of interest, parties and sects which it embraces, a coalition of a majority of the whole society could seldom take place on any other principles than those of justice and the general good ... It is no less certain than it is important, notwithstanding the contrary opinons which have been entertained, that the larger the society, provided it lies within a practicable sphere, the more duly capable it will be of self-government. And happily for the republican cause, the practicable sphere may be carried to a very great extent, by a judicious modification and mixtures of the federal principle. (*Federalist* No. 51)

The Item Veto in Perspective

When President Reagan called for "structural reforms" to help solve the deficit problem in his January, 1984, State of the Union Address, he was proposing a measure supported by almost every president since Grant: the item veto. Formal and informal proposals to enable presidents to weed out only certain items in a bill have been made since the 1830s, with little success. While Congress still weighs in more heavily against the item veto than for it, the proposal has come a long way since 1842, when President John Tyler's attempt to get item veto power resulted in a House Committee charge of "a defacement of the public records and archives." The history of the item veto proposal reflects Congress' determination to keep full power over the purse.

● The Confederate president, who was limited to a single six-year term, was given a line item veto.

● After the Civil War, several states adopted the line item veto; forty-three states give their executives the power today.

● In 1878 President Ulysses S. Grant formally proposed an amendment allowing the president "to approve of so much of any measure passing the two houses of Congress as his judgment may dictate, without approving the whole." The proposal was repeated by President Rutherford B. Hayes in 1879 and Chester A. Arthur in 1882.

● In 1883 and 1884 the item veto amendment gained ground in Congress. It fell just short of the two-thirds majority in the House necessary to approve constitutional amendments, and the Senate Judiciary Committee approved it. No further action was taken, however.

● President Franklin D. Roosevelt submitted a proposal similar to the item veto to Congress in 1938, but the Senate rejected it.

● President Richard Nixon's impoundment of funds for specific items already approved by Congress was halted by the Congressional Budget and Impoundment Act of 1974.

● National opinion polls since 1945 have shown a majority of the general public in favor of the item veto. Support peaked in 1978 with seventy percent in favor, and measured sixty-seven percent in favor in November, 1983.

● President Ronald Reagan proposed the reform in the State of the Union Address on January 23, 1984.

Recent developments have drawn attention to the item veto: support from the balanced budget movement, a number of bills introduced in Congress, and the search for solutions to the growing deficit problem, which has taken top priority on the economic agenda.

In response to those who claim the item veto would enable the president to restore efficiency to the budget process, Sen. Mark O. Hatfield has raised the question of power:

> I believe it is a simple solution on face, full of inherent dangers. I caution my colleagues. . . . it will provide for the transfer of spending power from the legislative to the executive branch of Government. As Members of Congress, we will be giving up one of our most important powers—"the power of the purse." (*Congressional Record*, 5 February 1985, 1004)

Yet others regard the veto more in its original light — as a "negative" and not a dictatorial power:

> The usual argument against the line-item veto—that it would unfairly expand the President's power—is clearly fatuous. Congress in 1974 arrogated to itself responsibility for spending; it has clearly failed. Politics in America most effectively performs its proper role—arbitrating among the competing interests of a huge population of free and informed people—when power is real but rarely used. It's most likely that once a President held the power to veto individual spending items, Congress would sort out for itself what is justifiable spending and what isn't, just as it did before the "budget control act." And if, as now, Congress declined to exercise prudence in managing the people's tax payments, that national constituency that elects a President would surely expect him to use the item veto to restore prudence, regardless of the highly publicised screams of Congress's main constituencies.
>
> That is how the balance of power was intended to work . . . (*Wall Street Journal*, editorial, 14 September 1983)

Similarly, supporters see the item veto as a common sense measure. Sen. Alan Dixon asserted that

> . . . we ought to run the government in a sensible way, so that when the President gets a 1,000 page appropriations bill, or something of that sort, he can turn to page 316, line 14, and take out $11,633,421.16 for the Senate from some place who ought not to have it in the first instance except he made a deal. . . .
>
> These budgets are full of that kind of stuff. Let me tell you something. The Senator from Illinois puts them in, too, and the Senator from Illinois is going to keep on putting them in—I want to put everybody on notice—because I want to stay in this place just like the rest of you.
>
> But we ought to have somebody with an eraser on a pencil downtown that takes it out once in a while. (*Congressional Record*, 29 October 1983, 14934-37)

But to opponents, it is a dangerous way to tamper with the power of the purse, and leaves no protection for the rights of the people:

> . . . who would give instructions on a line item veto? Some budget analyst in OMB, that's who. Do you even know his name? Do you ever

get a chance to vote for him? None of these things. It is a person with an eyeshade and an eraser who would decide whether to cut aid to dependent children by a certain amount of money.

Where does the public get a chance to be heard?

... They came up through the appropriations process and Congress listened. They had a chance to elect the person that makes up the budget ... But to what positive end if it all goes down the drain because of a line item veto triggered in the far-away corners of OBM?

I think that it is the kind of thing that would take away our responsibility and muffle the public voice. (*Congressional Record*, 29 October 1983, 14940-43)

The Legislative Veto in Action

The legislative veto grew from cooperative legislative/executive branch attempts to devise a way of getting around some of the limitations imposed by the Constitution. Since it originally appeared in 1932, the legislative veto has been used to grant the executive branch broad rule-making powers as well as to assert congressional authority over executive branch agencies. It is a measure of convenience that recognizes the fact that the legislative process can be too cumbersome to pass regulations on the technical specialties covered by the agencies.

Today more than two hundred laws contain legislative veto provisions, more than half of which have been passed since 1970, and all of which are called into question by the recent Supreme Court decision.

• The legislative veto was first used in 1932, when President Hoover worked out a deal with Congress. In return for the broad power to reorganize the federal government, he agreed that Congress could overrule his proposed reorganization plans by passing a one-house vote.

• The mechanism initiated by the Hoover administration did not become controversial until the 1970s, when Congress began to employ it to assert more control over the president, such as in the War Powers Resolution of 1973. Presidents have generally opposed the measure since then.

• In foreign affairs and national security areas, the veto was frequently used during the 1970s to increase congressional control over administration policies. In addition to the War Powers Resolution, bills authorizing Congress to block defense contracts, terminate a presidentially-declared national emergency, and disapprove international agreements concerning nuclear technology were passed between 1974-78.

• While handing the responsibility for national energy policy to the executive branch, Congress has required that actions involving export policy, price controls, storage and developing energy alternatives all be subject to congressional approval or disapproval before implemented.

• Similarly, Congress has mandated agency rule-making powers while maintaining the power to reject those rules in the case of the Education Department, the Federal Election Commission, the Department of Health and Human Services (Social Security), the Federal Trade Commission, the Environmental Protection Agency, and others. For instance, the Federal Election Campaign Act amendments of 1979 said that FEC rules and regulations could be disapproved by a one-house resolution. The act creating the Department of Education retained congressional power to disapprove the Department's rules, and in 1980 Congress gained control over Environmental Protection Agency rules governing hazardous substances by use of the legislative veto.

• On June 23, 1983, the Supreme Court declared the legislative veto provision in *Immigration and Naturalization Service vs. Chadha* unconstitutional. That provision was passed in 1952 in response to the many private immigration bills introduced in Congress to allow certain individuals to remain in the United States. Members were allegedly receiving payments for introducing the private bills. Under that law, Congress gave the Attorney General the power to allow immigrants to remain, keeping the right to veto the decision by House or Senate action. The Supreme Court ruled that the veto provision violated the "presentment clause" (Article I, section 7) of the Constitution and the doctrine of separation of powers.

The Legislative Veto Reconsidered

The *Chadha* decision has stimulated fresh discussion of the principles behind the separation of powers. Supporters of the Supreme Court decision herald it as a welcome incentive to return the two branches to the paths intended for them by the founders.

> True the legislative veto was a convenient way for Congress to give authority and retain it at the same time, but it is not indispensable to the effective operation of government.
>
> In the future, legislators will have to be more careful about what functions they delegate: compromises and boundaries will have to be clearly understood before bills are sent to the White House; and special interest groups, which have fought the executive branch with this device, will have to develop new tactics. The lines separating the powers of the three branches of government have been clearly reaffirmed by this decision. That is far more important than the fact that the work of one branch, the legislative, will be more difficult—even more risky—after today. (*Washington Post*, editorial, 24 June 1983)

Proponents of the legislative veto argue that it has evolved as a necessary measure to cope with the demand on today's government and that the Supreme Court decision reflects an unrealistic, unyielding attachment to the founding doctrines:

> The fundamental problem in trying to make the government of the United States work effectively is not to preserve the separation of powers but to overcome it . . . The legislative veto is a device that has served that purpose. Insofar as this device of accommodation is now rendered unavailable, the two branches are condemned that much more often to the confrontation, stalemate and deadlock that so frequently leave the government of the United States impotent to cope with complex problems. (Sundquist, 1984: 222)

> Without the legislative veto, Congress is faced with Hobson's choice: either to refrain from delegating the necessary authority, leaving itself with a hopeless task of writing laws with the requisite specificity to cover endless specific circumstances across the entire policy landscape, or in the alternative, to abdicate its lawmaking function to the executive branch and independent agencies . . . (Justice Byron R. White, dissent in *Chadha*; see Craig 1983, 189-90)

The *Chadha* decision rules that legislative vetoes are flatly unconstitutional. Congress has seen things differently, for a number of bills containing legislative veto provisions have been passed by Congress since June 1983. Whether the executive branch and the judiciary continue to acquiesce in such practices remains to be seen.

Implications of Reform

Interpretation of the actual effects of the item and legislative vetoes varies widely. Would the item veto be a way to lead the country out of the deficit or merely a political tool in the hands of a power-grasping executive? Who will be more restricted by the Supreme Court rejection of the legislative veto? Some claim the executive branch is the loser: Congress will be more reluctant to grant broad powers without the assurance that it can have a check on them. Others think that loss of the legislative veto will put the onus on Congress. Rather than delegating regulatory authority to various agencies, Congress will be responsible for establishing appropriate regulatory legislation.

Debate over these immediate concerns raises more fundamental questions: is adherence to the founding principles more important than enabling government to function? Which alternative, if either, is more true to the spirit of the Constitution? Do these alternatives possess mutually exclusive criteria? For the time being, the Supreme Court has had the last word.

> The fact that a given law or procedure is efficient, convenient, and useful in facilitating functions of government, standing alone, will not save it if it is contrary to the Constitution. Convenience and efficiency are not the primary objectives—or the hallmarks—of democratic government. (Chief Justice Warren E. Burger, Majority Opinion, *Chadha*; see Craig 1983, 189-90)

The Separation of Powers and Government Reform

The item and legislative vetoes are attempts to make government work efficiently while preserving the basic separation and balance of powers. One current proposal combines the vetoes in a single constitutional amendment, in the hopes of gaining efficiency while maintaining an even balance.

Other government reform proposals are direct attempts to overcome the separation of powers. Some would bring our system closer to the parliamentary model, others are simply concerned with encouraging cooperation between the branches. Among the reforms discussed during the recent congressional hearings on the "Political Economy and the Constitution" were measures:

• Enabling members of Congress to serve in the president's Cabinet by altering the "incompatibility clause" (Article I, section 6) of the Constitution and perhaps even requiring a joint executive-legislative cabinet.

• Promoting party government and inter-branch cooperation by linking presidential and congressional candidates on a single ballot in federal elections.

• Giving executive branch officials limited powers in Congress to enable them to introduce legislation, manage floor debate, or otherwise represent administration policy in the legislative branch.

Nonconstitutional reforms to address the problem raised by the veto proposals would:

• Reform the budget process by making it a two-year cycle and otherwise making it more efficient.

• Make use of checks already built into the Constitution and statutary alternatives to the legislative veto such as congressional investigations, passing legislation, and confirmation hearings.

• Establish an informal executive-legislative branch council to facilitate cooperation between the branches.

Arguments For the Item Veto

• An item veto would reduce the number of unnecessary, unrelated provisions which members of Congress tack on to important budget bills. Even though they may not be in the best interest of the country, the president now must accept them or reject the entire bill.

• The item veto would strengthen the ability of the president to eliminate the deficit because it would give him more control over the budget process.

- The item veto has proven effective in the forty-three states where governors are authorized to exercise it.
- Sixty-seven percent of the general public favor the item veto according to the latest Gallup Poll.
- The founders did not discuss the item veto because the appropriations were simple and direct and a yes or no response easily sufficed. Today's omnibus bills are so complex that the president needs to be able to decide on the national priorities from among many competing interests.

Arguments Against the Item Veto

- The item veto tilts the balance of power to the president. By threatening to veto certain items, the president can coerce Congress into capitulating on other issues.
- The veto would take attention away from the deficit, which is the real problem and needs to be addressed more directly.
- The item veto will not help balance the budget because the "add-ons" it seeks to eliminate are an insignificant portion of national expenditures. The "entitlement" programs that would be immune to the item veto are the ones that have been blamed for the deficit increase.
- The item veto puts the power of the purse in the wrong hands: decisions on specific appropriations will be in the hands of anonymous and unelected bureaucrats in the executive branch who are not in touch with the people and do not understand their needs.
- The line item veto reflects the assumption that Congress cannot regulate itself. If Congress agreed to it, members would, in effect, be abdicating their fiscal responsibility to the president.

Arguments For the Legislative Veto

- The legislative veto is a way to make sure that elected officials have an effective voice in important policy decisions which otherwise would be made by appointed executive branch officials who are not accountable to the people.
- The legislative veto enables Congress to be flexible when passing legislation involving technical issues or regulatory functions that cannot be easily anticipated.
- Without the legislative veto, congressional committees will become even more bogged down in the details of technical legislation.
- The veto is the most effective check on presidential war powers.

Arguments Against the Legislative Veto

• Congress has used the legislative veto to avoid important oversight functions. If Congress is doing the job, the legislative veto is unnecessary.

• The Supreme Court challenge will force Congress to be more specific and take a direct role in matters such as agency regulations, foreign affairs, and military appropriations.

• The legislative veto has been used by Congress to satisfy special interest groups seeking a softening of particular agency regulations.

• The veto usurps the president's executing role in the legislative process, violates the separation of powers doctrine, and ignores the presentment clause in the Constitution.

Questions to Guide Discussion

• What does separation of powers mean today? Has experience shown it to be a protection of liberty? Does it cause inefficiency? Are liberty and efficiency in government irreconcilable goals?

• Would changes in veto powers violate the doctrine of separation of powers or would they merely add to the "internal controls" and make the system work better?

• Would the item veto give the president more power over the purse? Would the legislative veto give Congress a larger role in the executive function of government? What does this imply about the way the founders delineated the functions of each branch of government?

• Has the power of the purse been an "effectual weapon" against tyranny in the hands of the House of Representatives?

• Should the branches of government be made more accountable to each other or to the people? Are there sufficient mechanisms for a popular "negative" on federal legislation?

• What has changed since 1787 to cause the reexamination of the separation of powers: The nature of legislation? The size of the unelected bureaucracy? The relative power of the executive and legislative branches? Do these changes warrant reform of veto powers or have the changes perhaps been exaggerated?

References

Craig, Barbara H. *The Legislative Veto.* Boulder, Colo.: Westview Press, 1983.

Elliott, Jonathan. *The Debates in the Several State Conventions on the Adoption of the Federal Constitution.* 5 vols. New York: Burt Franklin, 1888.

Storing, Herbert. *The Complete Anti-Federalist.* 7 vols. Chicago: University of Chicago Press, 1981.

Sundquist, James. "Reaction to *Chadha*" in *Workbook for Constitution System Review.* 2d ed. Washington, D. C.: Committee on the Constitutional System, 1984.

Suggested Readings

Edward S. Corwin. *The President: Office and Powers.* New York: New York University Press, 1957.

Lloyd N. Cutler. "To Form a Government." *Foreign Affairs.* Fall 1980.

Douglas B. Habig. "The Constitutionality of the Legislative Veto." *William and Mary Law Review* 23 (1982).

Alexander Hamilton, John Jay, and James Madison. *The Federalist Papers.* (Especially numbers 47-51.) Available in various editions.

Kevin Phillips. "An American Parliament." *Harper's,* November, 1980.

Nelson W. Polsby. *Congress and the Presidency.* 3d ed. Englewood Cliffs, N. J.: Prentice-Hall, 1976.

James L. Sundquist. *The Decline and Resurgence of Congress.* Washington, D. C.: The Brookings Institution, 1981.

U.S. Congress. Senate. Committee on the Judiciary. *Legislative Veto Proposals.* Hearing. 97th Congress, 1st session on S 890 and S 684, 23 April 1981. Washington D. C.: U.S. Government Printing Office, 1981.

7. Representative Government and Direct Democracy

Introduction

"All legislative Powers herein granted shall be vested in a Congress of the United States, which shall consist of a Senate and House of Representatives."

—Art. I, sec. 1

The opening words of the Declaration of Independence announce the "self-evident" truths "that all men are created equal, that they are endowed by their Creator with certain inalienable Rights, that among these are Life, Liberty and the pursuit of Happiness." The Declaration lists further truths:

> That to secure these rights, Governments are instituted among Men deriving their just powers from the consent of the governed. That whenever any Form of Government becomes destructive of these ends, it is the Right of the People to alter or to abolish it, and to institute new Government, laying its foundation on such principles, and organizing its powers in such form, as to them shall seem most likely to effect their Safety and Happiness.

These ideas were not new in 1776. The great English philosopher John Locke had made similar claims almost a century before. What *was* unique about the American situation at the time of the Revolution was the readiness and ability of Americans to translate these philosophical truths into practical action.

The history of Massachusetts provides a good example of how seriously Americans took the claim that governments were their creations, and that the authority of such governments was derived from the consent of the governed. After the Declaration of Independence was signed, the Massachusetts House of Representatives adopted a reso-

by W. Richard Merriman, Jr.

135

lution announcing its interest in drafting a new state constitution to replace the colonial frame of government, and asked that town meetings be called so that citizens could consider whether such a course of action would be acceptable.

Concord's meeting resolved that a sitting legislature was "by no means a Body proper to form & Establish a Constitution." Governments were not to be created by governments, but by the people. Concord resolved that "it appears to this Town highly necessary & Expedient that a Convention, or Congress be immediately Chosen, to form & establish a Constitution, by the Inhabitants of the Respective Towns in this State, ..." The town meeting of Boston asserted that in making such an important public decision pains must be taken to consult not only the legislature of Massachusetts but all the people in order to "collect the wisest Sentiments" on the subject of a new constitution. Attleborough's town meeting objected to granting the government the right to draft a new form of government because "the right of the Inhabitants of the Said State to negative the Said form, or any Article in it when drawn is not expressly acknowledged. ..."

Undeterred, the state government of Massachusetts drafted the Constitution of 1778. The proposed frame of government was sent to town meetings where approval by two-thirds of votes cast was necessary for adoption. A gathering of citizens in Essex County found much in the proposed constitution that was objectionable. In particular, the assembled citizens asserted

> [t]hat a bill of rights, clearly ascertaining and defining the rights of conscience, and that security of person and property, which every member of the State hath a right to expect from the supreme power thereof, ought to be settled and established, previous to any ratification of any constitution for the State. (Pole 1970, 446)

Other meetings found other aspects of the proposed constitution that were worrisome or objectionable, and it failed to gain the necessary votes for adoption.

In June of 1779 the state government of Massachusetts responded to this defeat by calling for a constitutional convention. This convention, whose delegates were chosen specifically for the task of framing a new state government, drafted a new constitution, the first part of which was a Declaration of the Rights of the Inhabitants of the Commonwealth of Massachusetts. Once again, the town meetings debated, voted, and eventually approved the new constitution. The voters of Massachusetts, acting twice through a popular vote on a proposed course of public action, had exercised their fundamental right to create a government that satisfied them.

The Initiative and Referendum

Even with the establishment of settled representative state govern-ments, Americans have continued to exercise their right to govern themselves directly through the processes of initiative and referendum. The initiative is a process by which citizens may propose laws and constitutional amendments and enact them by a popular vote without the involvement of state legislatures or governors. A *constitutional initiative* allows voters to propose and adopt amendments to their state constitution. *Statutory initiatives* allow voters to enact or amend a law. Initiative measures in states are placed on the ballot for a popular vote when a specified percentage of registered voters has signed a petition calling for such a vote.

The initiative allows popular initiation of constitutional amend-ments and laws; a referendum gives voters an opportunity to express their approval or disapproval of acts taken by their governments. In essence, a referendum allows citizens to approve or repeal an adopted state statute *(statutory referendum)* or approve or reject a legislatively approved change in their state's constitution *(constitutional referendum)*. Referenda in various states may be called by the state legislature or by popular petition, or may simply be required before undertaking certain measures.

In every state except Delaware proposed amendments to state constitutions that have been approved by the state legislature must be submitted to a constitutional referendum of the people. In sixteen states citizens may use the constitutional initiative process to propose and adopt amendments to their state constitutions. In over twenty states citizens may use the statutory initiative to bring proposed statutes to a popular vote. Some states require statutory referenda in certain cases and allow the state legislature to call for a referendum on legislation it has approved. In addition, thousands of local referenda are held each year.

Given the role that initiatives and referenda have played in state and local governance, it is remarkable that there has never been a *national* initiative or referendum. The reason for this is simple: the Constitution of the United States does not provide for direct citizen initiation of, or direct popular vote on, either statutes or constitutional amendments. Americans do not make national law directly through their votes. Instead they choose representatives who determine national policy.

A discussion of why there is no provision in the Constitution for national processes of initiative and referendum and whether there should be such a provision leads inevitably to a discussion of democracy and representation. Does the United States have a representative system of government only because it is impossible for the people to gather to conduct public business (an obstacle that initiatives and referenda seek to eliminate)? Or do we expect that our representatives and our representative form of government will produce better and wiser policies than the people themselves could produce? Are the people of the United States sufficiently well-informed to make wise decisions about public policy issues? Do they have enough regard for the rights and interests of those with minority points of view to avoid damaging those rights and interests? Should the people have the power, ultimately, to make policy directly when they are dissatisfied with the actions, or inaction, of their elected officials?

Democracy and Representation: The Formative Debate

Concerns About Popular Government

In *Federalist* No. 10 James Madison described a "pure Democracy" as "a Society, consisting of a small number of citizens, who assemble and administer Government in person." One argument against creating such a democracy in America was simply that it was impossible to do so given the large territory and widely dispersed population of the United States. But Madison claimed that there were other reasons for avoiding pure democracy: "Democracies have ever been spectacles of turbulence and contention; have ever been found incompatible with personal security, or the rights of property; and have in general been as short in their lives, as they have been violent in their deaths." The reason democracies presented such a sad spectacle, Madison wrote, was that a "common passion or interest" could easily animate a majority of citizens who would find it easy to work together to violate the rights of the "weaker party or an obnoxious individual."

That men were capable of invading the rights of their fellow citizens was an axiom of Anglo-American political thought in the eighteenth century. It was widely assumed that the human appetite for power threatened all political systems, however noble their origins and intentions, with degeneration into tyranny. The men who gathered in Philadelphia were history-minded, and their study of ancient governments and of contemporary European systems taught them that monarchies tended to degenerate into tyrannies of one over all others, that aristocracies degenerated into oligarchies in which a few oppressed the many, and that democracies degenerated into mob rule and anarchy.

Most Americans had no intention of fastening a monarchy on themselves after struggling so hard to cast one off. There existed no formal aristocracy in the United States and Americans were not interested in seeing one created. But the only remaining alternative—a strongly democratic government—was not one that the framers of the Constitution were anxious to establish. Between 1776 and 1787, a number of states had experimented with systems of government in which popularly elected legislatures had dominated weak state executives and judiciaries. The results were alarming to many of the framers.

The democratic nature of various new state constitutions had brought a new kind of man—often a small farmer or person of modest economic background—into government. Many of these men found themselves crushed by debt and taxes in the years following the American War of Independence. To counter this burden, many states issued paper money. In Rhode Island this was accomplished by the adoption of a state law giving landowners loans of new paper money, with their land as security. When this paper money was made legal tender for payment of debts the usual relationship between creditors and debtors was reversed: debtors pursued creditors who wished to avoid being paid with what they regarded as worthless money. In response to this evasion the legislature of Rhode Island made it an offense to refuse paper money and allowed debtors to come to court, declare their debts, and pay them with paper money. Creditors were then informed that the debt had been discharged. Andrew McLaughlin wryly notes that "...seven states entered on the difficult task of legislating their people into financial blessedness by the simple means of making money..." (McLaughlin 1962, 106-107).

Paper money was issued in Massachusetts as well, but continuing economic distress led to calls for yet more relief. When none was forthcoming, a group of armed men attempted to close the courts and disrupt the processes by which mortgage foreclosures and debt collections were carried out. A ragtag army of these hard-pressed and angry men gathered in Worcester, Massachusetts, in 1786, hoping to generate enough pressure on public authorities to receive some relief. Under the "command" of Daniel Shays, they moved against the federal arsenal in Springfield. However, they were met by a force of 4,400 men gathered under the authority of the state of Massachusetts. These troops scattered Shays' men and ended what is now known as Shays' Rebellion.

The Philadelphia Convention

Such events cast a long shadow over the experiment with popularly elected representative state governments and caused great concern among the men who wrote the Constitution. Americans became convinced during the escalation of their conflict with England that they were especially well-suited for republican government, the aim of which was to pursue the "public good" rather than the private interests of any person or group. The design of most state governments reflected this commitment to the public good and the belief that it would be pursued when the public played a role in selecting its representatives.

The framers of the Constitution shared this commitment to government by representation, but disagreed on how representatives were to be chosen and to whom they should be accountable. Should a theory of *actual representation* be translated into a system in which representatives were popularly elected and charged with the task of pursuing the interests of their constituents? Or should a theory of *virtual representation* be translated into a system in which representatives, insulated from public opinion and popular pressure, would seek to identify and pursue the broader "public good"?

Madison's *Notes* record the belief of Roger Sherman that "the people ... immediately should have as little to do as may be about the Government. They [lack] information and are constantly liable to be misled." Elbridge Gerry of Massachusetts, no doubt with the memory of Shay's Rebellion still fresh in his mind, joined Sherman by stating that "the evils we experience flow from an excess of democracy. The people do not [lack] virtue, but are the dupes of pretended patriots."

To these doubts about the character and capability of the people were added the concerns of those, like Charles Pinckney of South Carolina, who wished to maximize the influence of state governments in the work of the national government. Pinckney proposed that each state's legislature choose its representatives to the House of Representatives. Otherwise, Pinckney worried, the state governments will "lose their agency" and "S. Carolina & other States would have but a small share of the benefits of Govt." John Dickinson of Delaware shared these concerns, comparing "the proposed National System to the Solar System, in which the States were the planets, and ought to be left to move freely in their proper orbits." James Wilson replied that while he was not in favor of extinguishing these planets, "neither did he on the other hand, believe that they would warm or enlighten the Sun." Wilson added that selection of members of the House of Representatives by state legislatures was undesirable because state legislatures have "an official sentiment" opposed to the aims and sentiments of a national government "and perhaps to that of the people themselves." Wilson was joined in this view by Alexander Hamilton and other nationalists.

But unlike Hamilton, Wilson opposed state legislative selection of representatives not only because he wanted to avoid undue state influence in the national government but also because he wanted to maximize the influence in the Congress of the people. He urged the popular election of members of both the House of Representatives and the Senate. Wilson invoked the theory of actual representation in arguing that "representation is made necessary only because it is impossible for the people to act collectively." If all citizens could not be gathered to make decisions, then a representative government should possess "not only 1st the *force*, but 2dly the *mind or sense* of the people at large. The Legislature ought to be the most exact transcript of the whole society."

The Convention eventually settled on a plan to have members of the House popularly elected and members of the Senate chosen by state legislatures. As was so often the case during that summer in Philadelphia, opposing views found a compromise. The national legislature was thus subject to both popular influence (in the House) and state influence (in the Senate). This system of election reflected the belief that the people must have some direct influence on government while still allowing for reservations about the people's ability to properly participate in their own governance. In addition to mixing state and popular influence in the national legislature, the Constitution provided for actual representation in the House and virtual representation in the Senate.

But had the Constitution really provided for the actual representation of popular opinion? Was the democratically elected branch of Congress to be easily subject to public opinion?

The Ratification Debate

In describing and defending the Constitution's plan for representative government, Madison harkened back to the problems that arose in the governments of the states, citing complaints that these

> ... governments are too unstable; that the public good is disregarded in the conflicts of rival parties; and that measures are too often decided not according to the rules of justice, and the rights of the minor party; but by the superior force of an interested and over-bearing majority. (*Federalist* No. 10)

A prime advantage of the proposed constitution's representative form of government, Madison asserted, was that a great number of citizens from a large extent of territory would be brought together in an *extended republic*. This republic would contain a variety of groups and interests. The principle of majority rule in the legislature, however, would curb the pursuit of narrow interests by minority factions. And the multiplicity and geographic distance of interest groups from one another would discourage the effective operation of a majority faction that might threaten the rights of the numerical minority.

The Constitution's plan for representation had, Madison wrote, an additional advantage: because members of the House of Representatives would be chosen in large districts with large constituencies,

> ...it will be more difficult for unworthy candidates to practise with success the vicious arts, by which elections are too often carried; and the suffrages of the people being more free, will be more likely to centre on men who possess the most attractive merit, and the most diffusive and established characters. (*Federalist* No. 10)

Madison believed that the popular election of members of the House of Representatives would bring to office men of considerable prominence. These men would "refine" the views of the public and pursue policies that showed a proper regard for the public good and a proper disdain for the political projects of special interests.

To all of these checks against "factious" influence in the House, the framers of the Constitution added additional checks against the threat of popular factions in the national government. A Senate, not chosen by popular election, had to approve any legislation passed by the House before it could go to the president; the president, also not chosen by popular election, had the power to veto it; and the Supreme Court, chosen by the president with the consent of the Senate, would judge the constitutionality of legislation.

Not surprisingly, some of the most cogent complaints raised against the proposed Constitution focused on the alleged absence of democratic processes and on its overall "aristocratic tendency." Melancton Smith of New York, speaking to the New York ratifying convention about the Constitution's system of representation, expressed this view:

> The idea that naturally suggests itself to our minds, when we speak of representatives, is, that they resemble those they represent. They should be a true picture of the people, possess a knowledge of their circumstances and their wants, sympathize in all their distresses, and be disposed to seek their true interests. The knowledge necessary for the representative of a free people not only comprehends extensive political and commercial information, such as is acquired by men of refined education, who have leisure to attain to high degrees of improvement, but it should also comprehend that kind of acquaintance with the common concerns and occupations of the people, which men of the middling class of life are, in general, more competent to than those of a superior class. (Kenyon 1966, 382)

Smith wanted representatives to be attentive to the special concerns of their constituents. He also believed that a large number of representatives should be chosen in smaller districts: "... the number of representatives should be so large, as that, while it embraces the men of the first class, it should admit those of the middling class of life."

Many opponents of the Constitution concluded, like Smith, that a small number of representatives serving large constituencies would prevent the common American from being elected to the House of Representatives. This would preclude a desirable resemblance between the representative and the represented. The likely effect of this system, said opponents of the Constitution, would be diminished power of the people within the only part of government they directly selected. This "aristocratic" bias in the House was intolerable given what opponents of the Constitution regarded as the flatly undemocratic character of the remainder of the government.

Opponents of the Constitution argued for the establishment of an advisory council to limit the power of the president, shorter terms and/or rotation of office for both senators and the president, a provision allowing states to recall senators, and a bill of rights to safeguard the rights of the individual. The Constitution was eventually ratified as written, though only after its supporters agreed to propose amendments forming a bill of rights once the government was in operation.

The Democratic Impulse

Under the original Constitution, the power of voters only reached directly as far as the House of Representatives. But as the national government increasingly asserted its supremacy over state governments and began to make policies on taxes, banking, international commerce, transportation, the opening and settlement of western lands, and a variety of other issues that directly affected the welfare of millions of citizens, Americans began to demand a larger voice.

Manhood Suffrage

One of the changes demanded in the early 1800s was an expansion of the electorate by the removal of property qualifications for voting. "Manhood suffrage"—voting by free white men—was common in the new states of the west, and by 1850 Virginia and North Carolina had joined the other original thirteen states in adopting it. Article I, section 2 of the Constitution specifies that a state's members of the U.S. House of Representatives are to be designated by the electorate that chooses the most numerous branch of that state's legislature; thus manhood suffrage in the states brought manhood suffrage to the elections to the House of Representatives.

Choosing the President

By the time John Adams was elected to the presidency in 1796, serious conflicts over national government policies had divided the nation's leaders into groups that would eventually become political parties. As these parties sought to attract popular support they democratized the presidential selection process. By 1832 party conventions had replaced congressional caucuses as the mechanism for nominating presidential candidates. These conventions, at least in theory, gave the parties' rank and file membership a greater voice in choosing candidates.

As parties became more prominent in nominating presidential candidates they transformed the operation of the electoral college. Candidates for selection to the electoral college were frequently pledged to a particular party and its presidential nominee. By 1832 every state but South Carolina had shifted the selection of these electoral college electors from state legislators to voters. The popular election of pledged electors retained the form of the electoral college's mediation between voters and presidential candidates, but the discretion of electors was substantially reduced in favor of greater public influence in the selection of a president.

The Expanding Electorate

The demand for broader public participation in government has led to a significant expansion of the electorate. The Fifteenth Amendment, ratified in 1870, forbade denying the vote on "account of race, color, or previous condition of servitude." In 1848 the Woman's Rights Convention in Seneca Falls, New York, echoed the Declaration of Independence in asserting that "all men and women are created equal" and that the history of mankind "is a history of repeated injuries and usurpations on the part of man toward woman, having in direct object the establishment of an absolute tyranny over her." Seventy years of pressure for women's suffrage eventually led to the ratification in 1920 of the Nineteenth Amendment, which gave women the vote in national elections. The Twenty-third Amendment, ratified in 1961, brought the voters of the District of Columbia into the presidential electorate; in 1964 the Twenty-fourth Amendment banned the poll tax, which had been used to deprive many blacks of their votes; and the Twenty-sixth Amendment, ratified in 1971, extended the right to vote to eighteen-year-olds.

Populists and Progressives

From 1890 to 1916 a strong upsurge of public pressure to democratize reform in American politics occurred. The rapid development of American industry during and after the Civil War had brought into existence large and powerful corporations whose activities were not regulated to any great extent by government. Many Americans were economically powerless against these large organizations and complained that government was increasingly dominated by them.

The 1892 platform of the new Populist Party dramatically voiced the complaints of its members against the domination of American society by business interests:

> The newspapers are largely subsidized or muzzled, public opinion silenced, business prostrated, homes covered with mortgages, labor impoverished, and the land concentrating in the hands of capitalists. . . . The fruits of the toil of millions are boldly stolen to build up colossal fortunes for a few, unprecedented in the history of mankind; and the possessors of these, in turn, despise the Republic and endanger liberty. From the same prolific womb of governmental injustice we breed the two great classes—tramps and millionaires. (Levy 1982, 293)

These economic wrongs would not be righted by the Democratic or Republican parties, the Populists argued, because both were servants of business interests:

> We have witnessed for more than a quarter of a century the struggles of the two great political parties for power and plunder, while grievous wrongs have been inflicted upon suffering people. We charge that the controlling influences dominating both these parties have permitted the existing dreadful conditions to develop without serious effort to prevent or restrain them. . . . They propose to sacrifice our homes, lives, and children on the altar of mammon; to destroy the multitude in order to secure corruption funds from the millionaires. (Levy 1982, 293)

The Populists claimed that the answer to this political problem was more democracy. They favored the secret ballot, which would shield voters from intimidation; direct popular election of senators; and the use of the initative and referendum.

While the economic analyses and rhetoric of the Populists received a cold reception from most Americans, their complaints about the domination of political processes by special interests and corrupt parties found a large and responsive audience. The Progressive Movement, which succeeded the Populists, pursued a number of the Populists' reforms. Its greatest achievement at the national level was the adoption of the Seventeenth Amendment, which provided for popular election of senators. Progressives successfully pressed for use of secret ballots, regulation of political parties, and use of nonpartisan elections at the local level. They also led the fight for direct democracy in the states, urging state adoption of the initiative and referendum processes.

The Progressive Movement was extremely diverse, claiming both Democratic and Republican adherents. But the Progressive Movement's greatest concern was over the growth of large and powerful organizations—corporations, organized labor, and party political machines—and their influence on American society and politics. Progressives feared that such organizations undermined the role of the "unorganized individual" in American life and American politics. Against the power of these groups, which wielded money, votes, and patronage to pursue their special political aims, the Progressives hoped to muster the power and the votes of the average citizen.

Progressives and the Case for Initiative and Referendum

Progressives viewed the processes of initiative and referendum as ideal ways of reinstating the political power of the average American who was not part of an organized interest group. The Progressives' argument made several key claims. First, through the processes of initiative and referendum any issue of real concern to voters could be discussed and voted on. While both interest groups and political parties might wish to keep certain issues off the political agenda, the people would have the opportunity to place key issues squarely before the voters. Second, the initiative and referendum would bring public decisions close to the people instead of leaving them to be shaped by the interests of parties, legislators, and lobbyists. Third, they would ensure that public decisions were made publicly instead of in smoke-filled rooms. Fourth, initiatives and referenda would accurately reflect the public will without the distorting influence of parties, legislators, and interest groups. Fifth, they would diminish citizen apathy and reverse the alienation that had increased with the domination of governments by interest groups, legislators, and boss-controlled parties. Finally, the Progressives asserted that the *true* public interest could best be perceived and pursued by the average "Man of Good Will" who participated in initiatives and referenda (Butler and Ranney 1978, 24-33).

Between 1898 and 1914 the push for direct democracy won the amendment of state constitutions allowing initiatives and referenda in South Dakota, Utah, Oregon, Montana, Oklahoma, Maine, Missouri, Arkansas, Colorado, Arizona, California, Idaho, Nebraska, Nevada, Ohio, and Washington. The pioneering spirit of many relatively new states was reflected in their early adoption of the initiative and referendum.

National Initiative and Referendum

Americans have made changes in their political system at both the state and national levels that would, no doubt, astound the framers of the Constitution. In the national government only the federal judiciary has not been made substantially more dependent on the will of the people. Limits on political participation based on property, race, sex, and age have all been eliminated. In the states the initiative and referendum have greatly extended the power of Americans to act directly to make and repeal laws and to change their state constitutions. Americans, apparently, have become more confident of their ability to participate in government and more assertive, often in the face of considerable resistance, in their demand to be allowed this participation.

Some Americans believe that amending the Constitution to allow direct popular votes on statutory and constitutional issues is the logical and desirable next step in the ongoing process by which our national government has been democratized. Others think such amendments would be a fundamental and ill-advised departure from the principle and practice of a democratically elected but nevertheless representative government.

The push for direct democracy moved from the state level to the national level in 1907, when Rep. Elmer Fulton of Oklahoma introduced House Joint Resolution 44. This resolution, which was eventually unsuccessful, would have amended the Constitution to provide for national initiatives on both proposed statutes and constitutional amendments.

In the 1916 presidential campaign the supporters of President Woodrow Wilson advised voters that, while war raged in Europe:

> You are working, not fighting!
> Alive and happy, not cannon fodder!
> Wilson and peace with honor?
>   or
> Hughes with Roosevelt and war.

Many Americans were not convinced that this would long remain the case because of loan arrangements that led to the shipment of U.S. munitions to Britain. Such notable reformers as William Jennings Bryan, Robert LaFollette, and Jane Addams supported a proposal that required a national referendum on any declaration of war. After Wilson's reelection this proposal was the subject of congressional hearings in February, 1917. By March of 1917 American merchant seamen were arming themselves against anticipated attacks by German submarines. On April 6, 1917, German attacks on American shipping prompted a U.S. declaration of war.

Disillusioned by America's involvement in World War I and chagrined by the harsh peace that followed, Americans turned again to the war referendum proposal in the late 1930s as war menaced Europe once more. Rep. Louis Ludlow's "Ludlow Amendment" calling for a war referendum went further in the legislative process than any national referendum proposal before or since. The proposed amendment came to the floor of the House in December, 1937. President Franklin Roosevelt lobbied for the defeat of the proposal. A House vote of 188-209 fell well short of the two-thirds vote needed for further advancement.

The most recent significant proposals for a national initiative were advanced in 1977. These proposals were in response to a perceived loss of effective popular contact with and control over national policymakers. An unpopular war in Vietnam, the resignation of a president in disgrace, and scandals in Congress all contributed to a low level of public confidence in national leadership. In December, 1977, the Subcommittee on the Constitution of the Senate Committee on the Judiciary held hearings on two national initiative proposals.

In introducing Senate Joint Resolution 67, 95th Congress, 1st session, sponsored by Sen. James Abourezk and Sen. Mark Hatfield, Senator Abourezk stated that

> [t]he last few years have seen a growing dissatisfaction, and in many cases a serious distrust, of Government by the very people who are its source of power and who elect its leaders. People stay home on election day not because they are lazy or do not care but because they have decided that meaningful communication with their leaders is no longer possible or effective.

Echoing an earlier Progressive theme, Abourezk continued:

> ... much of the alienation and helplessness that citizens experience can be mitigated if avenues for constructive participation exist. The initiative procedure is one means to provide direct citizen access to our governmental decision-making process through a legal and democratic method. (Hearings on Voter Initiative Constitutional Amendment)

Among the key features of the Abourezk-Hatfield proposal were the following:

● The people of the United States would have the power to propose and enact laws, except with respect to carrying out the powers granted to Congress in clauses 11 and 15 of Article I, section 8, of the Constitution.

● The proposal did not grant the people of the United States the power to propose amendments to the Constitution.

● A law could be proposed by presenting to the Attorney General of the United States a petition containing the text of the proposed law and signatures, collected within the eighteen months prior to the presentation of the petition, of registered voters equal in number to three percent of the ballots cast in the last general election for president, including the signatures of registered voters in each of ten states equal in number to three percent of the ballots cast in the last general election for president in each of the ten states.

● Within ninety days of receiving such petitions, the Attorney General would determine the validity of the signatures on the petitions through consultation with the appropriate states. Upon a determination that the petitions contain the required number of valid signatures, the petition would be certified and the proposed law would be placed on the ballot at the next general election held for choosing members of the House of Representatives occurring at least one hundred and twenty days after such certification.

● A proposed law would be enacted upon approval by a majority of the people casting votes, and would take effect thirty days after approval.

● Any law enacted in this way would be a law the same as any other law of the United States, and could be held unconstitutional by the Supreme Court.

● A law enacted through the initiative and referendum process could be repealed by Congress by a two-thirds vote in each house.

In an interesting departure from earlier proposals that were particularly concerned with war powers, S. J. Res. 67 specifically precluded intiatives touching on the declaration of war (clause 11, Article I, section 8) and the calling of state militia (clause 15, Article I, section 8). And unlike Fulton's 1907 proposal, S. J. Res. 67 specifically avoided giving the people the power to use the initiative to propose amendments to the Constitution. Statutes initiated under S. J. Res. 67 would be liable, just as are all other statutes, to being judged unconstitutional by the national judiciary.

Also introduced during the first session of the Ninety-fifth Congress was House Joint Resolution 544, whose prime sponsor was Rep. Guy Vander Jagt. There are two key differences between this proposal and the Abourezk-Hatfield proposal. First, a successful initiative would require not a simple majority of all voters but a majority of votes cast in each of three-fourths (thirty-eight) of the states. Second, a three-fourths vote of both houses of Congress rather than a two-thirds vote would be necessary for Congress to reverse the action of the people. The same majority of votes in three-fourths of the states would be needed for the repeal of a law or a provision of a law.

The amendments proposed in 1977 did not involve proposals for national constitutional initiative or referendum processes. A constitutional initiative process would allow voters to propose amendments and put them to a national popular vote by gathering a specified number of signatures on a petition. Such a process would supplement, or could conceivably replace, the current amending process, which requires both houses of Congress to pass a proposed amendment by a two-thirds vote before sending the proposal to the states where approval by three-fourths of the states (expressed either by state legislature or special convention) is required for ratification. A constitutional referendum process would require a popular vote on constitutional amendments approved by Congress.

Another option not discussed during the 1977 hearings is the statutory referendum, a process that could work in several ways. Congress and the president could be required to submit certain types of legislation to a popular vote before it could become law. Or Congress and the president may be given the option of referring some legislation to a popular vote. Finally, a process could be established that would employ a popular petition to require that a statute approved by Congress and the president be submitted to a popular vote.

Obviously, some of these alternatives are more sweeping than others and hence would be more controversial. Statutory initiatives and referenda would be subject to repeal by Congress and invalidation by the Supreme Court. Constitutional changes enacted by popular vote would become part of the nation's fundamental charter and could only be changed or removed by subsequent amendment. Debate about all proposals for direct democracy, though, would focus on arguments about the comparative merits of democratic and representative forms of government.

Arguments For a National Initiative and Referendum Process

● The use of initiatives and referenda would be an exercise by the people of their sovereign power to govern themselves. This is the logical next step in democratizing American national government.

● Initiatives and referenda actualize Americans' First Amendment right "to petition the Government for redress of grievances" by allowing them to act for themselves when elected representatives fail to do so.

● A national initiative/referendum process would lessen both alienation and apathy of millions of Americans by providing for more direct participation in the making of public policy.

● A national initiative/referendum process is a natural complement to our system of representative government because it would correct that system when it loses touch with the wishes of the majority.

● The initiative and referendum would free our nation's policy-making process from the undue influence of special interest groups.

● Initiatives and referenda would enhance the accountability of government. They can be avoided as long as representatives pursue the policy preferences of the majority.

● National initiatives and referenda would produce an open, educational debate about problems and issues that might otherwise be inadequately discussed or not acted upon.

Arguments Against a National Initiative and Referendum Process

● Initiatives and referenda will not enhance citizen participation because many citizens—particularly those who are alienated and apathetic—are unlikely to make the effort needed to acquire information about ballot issues.

● If the chance to cast one vote out of hundreds of thousands in congressional elections does not bring the apathetic voter to the polls, the chance to cast one vote out of millions on a ballot question will not do so either.

● Initiatives and referenda complicate the ballot by adding issues that are too technical and complicated for many voters to understand. They discourage voting.

● The process of placing initiative and referendum questions on the ballot and then winning the election is so complicated and expensive that only already mobilized and well-financed constituencies will succeed in putting their concerns before voters. Rather than decreasing the influence of special interest groups, initiatives and referenda will increase their impact.

● A national initiative/referendum process could be used for regressive purposes and attacks on the rights and interests of minority groups. In 1964, for instance, California voters used the process to repeal that state's fair housing law.

● A national initiative/referendum process will have a polarizing and fragmenting effect on American society by bringing highly divisive issues to a yes or no vote. For the good of the country, such issues are better handled through a legislative process that encourages discussion, moderation, compromise, and consensus.

The truth about the likely impact of national initiative and referendum processes is less tidy than one would gather from the claims of

POINTS OF VIEW

Abourezk says six of the last 10 constitutional amendments "have in some way extended voting rights," so the initiative would be just "a further step in this evolutionary process." But the initiative would be decisively different; it would not expand the electorate, it would alter the function of the electorate. Only the 17th Amendment—popular election of senators—did that. And the initiative would do so at the expense of the principle of representation.

Advocates of the initiative say representative government is "government by elites": the representative and the "interests" who lobby them. But any national initiative would be dominated by an intense, unelected minority using direct mail, television commercials and other techniques of mass persuasion. (George Will, *Washington Post*, 28 July 1977)

Will believes people should not govern or decide issues, but are supposed "to decide who will decide." he states that public policy "is best given shape by representative institutions, which, unlike 'the people,' are deliberative bodies." Those of us who favor the initiative process believe that an educated and well-informed public, operating in an atmosphere of unrestrained First Amendment rights, is fully capable of acting as a deliberative body.

Contrary to Will's suggestion that it would undermine our representative form of government, the initiative process would provide a much-needed complement to the system. To an electorate frustrated by a Congress unwilling to act, it provides another democratic means to bring about change. To the federal government itself, the initiative process would provide another check in our system of checks and balances, a dilution of centralized power. (James Abourezk, *Washington Post*, 10 August 1977)

their advocates or detractors. It is true, for instance, that the referendum process has been used in ways that damaged the interests of minority groups. But the same results have been produced by representative governments at both the state and national levels. It is true that the initiative/referendum process could heighten citizen awareness of and interest in political questions. It is also true that this heightened awareness could bring increased emotion and acrimony to political life.

The education value and politicization potential from a national initiative could be substantial. Thousands of people would be involved in any national initiative campaign on one side or the other. Furthermore, the public's attention would be focused on debate and discussion of the merits or demerits of public policy issues rather than just on style, looks, image, and other similar aspects of many modern campaigns. Furthermore, the debate would be in public and in the open. . . . The initiative process will provide one more way for the vox populi to speak and, more importantly, it will permit them to act rather than simply react to actions taken by others. (Larry Berg, Testimony on Voter Initiative Constitutional Amendment, 13 and 14 December 1977)

The political arena which [the initiative process] creates will be preempted by groups that have money, that have organization, that have political skill, and that have power. (Peter Bachrach, Testimony on Voter Initiative Constitutional Amendment, 13 and 14 December 1977)

In the end, in fact, the real issue . . . is whether or not America believes in democracy, and believes it can afford the risks that go with democratic life. All of the objections to it are so many different ways of saying "the people are not to be trusted"—a skepticism which, it is perfectly true, can be traced back to the "realism" and cynical elitism of a significant group of constitutional fathers. . . . If Americans sometimes seem unfit to legislate, it may be because they have for so long been passive observers of government. The remedy is not to continue to exclude them from governing, but to provide practical and active forms of civic education that will make them more fit than they were. Initiative and referendum processes are ideal instruments of civic education. . . . (Benjamin Barber, Testimony on Voter Initiative Constitutional Amendment, 13 and 14 December 1977)

Questions about the capabilities of citizen voters do not admit of pat answers. It is undeniable that many citizens lack information about public issues and do not participate widely in the nation's political life. The question is whether widespread citizen apathy and lack of information is a normal state of affairs or whether it is a product of a representative system that leaves us to *decide who decides* on policy issues instead of deciding for ourselves.

References

Bailyn, Bernard. *The Ideological Origins of the American Revolution.* Cambridge, Mass.: Harvard University Press, 1967.

Butler, David, and Austin Ranney. *Referendums: A Comparative Study of Practice and Theory.* Washington, D. C.: American Enterprise Institute, 1978.

Hamilton, Alexander, John Jay, and James Madison. *The Federalist Papers.* Available in various editions.

Kenyon, Cecelia M., ed. *The Antifederalists.* Indianapolis: Bobbs-Merrill, 1966.

Levy, Michael B., ed. *Political Thought in America.* Homewood, Ill.: Dorsey Press, 1982.

Madison, James. *Notes of Debates in the Federal Convention of 1787.* New York: W. W. Norton, 1969; copyright 1966, The Ohio University Press.

McLaughlin, Andrew C. *The Confederation and the Constitution 1783-1789.* New York: Collier Books, 1962.

Pole, J. R., ed. *The Revolution in America, 1754-1788.* Stanford, Calif.: Stanford University Press, 1970.

U. S. Congress. Senate. Subcommittee on the Constitution of the Committee on the Judiciary. Hearings on Voter Initiative Constitutional Amendment, 95th Cong., 1st sess., S. J. Res. 67, 13 and 14 December 1977.

Wood, Gordon. *The Creation of the American Republic, 1776-1787.* Chapel Hill, N. C.: University of North Carolina Press, 1969.

Suggested Readings

Thomas M. Durban. *Initiative, Referendum, and Recall: A Resume of State Provisions.* Washington, D. C.: Congressional Research Service, 1981.

Richard Hofstadter, ed. *The Progressive Movement, 1900-1915.* Englewood Cliffs, N. J.: Prentice-Hall, 1963.

Michael J. Malbin. "Framing a Congress to Channel Ambition" in *this Constitution.* Project '87, American Political Science Association and American Historical Association. Washington, D. C.: Congressional Quarterly, 1986.

8. Campaigns, Money, and the Public Good

Elections, and lots of them, are a central feature of American political life. All seats in the U.S. House of Representatives are contested every two years, as are one-third of those in the Senate. The rigors of modern campaigns mean that one presidential election is hardly ended before campaigning for the next begins. Add in primaries, elections in about eighty thousand state and local jurisdictions, and popular votes on matters of public policy, and the number of elections held every year in this country is staggering. So is the expense of campaigning.

In 1972 the Nixon presidential campaign spent over $61 million in defeating George McGovern, whose campaign spent $30 million. The cost of all elections in 1972 was $425 million. This figure increased "modestly" to $540 million in 1976, but jumped to $1.2 billion in 1980. While this is undeniably a huge sum of money, political scientist Robert Lineberry helps put it in perspective by noting that Americans spend about $1 billion each year for power lawn mowers and over $1.5 billion for the combined purchase of microwave ovens and beauty shop services. Lineberry concludes that, all things considered, our elections are a "bargain" (Lineberry 1981, 235).

Elections are important, and many Americans would sooner live with an uncut lawn than without the opportunity to learn about and choose between candidates for public office. But the matter of whether we spend too much on election campaigns is only one of the key questions raised by the increasing cost of campaigns and elections. Who contributes the money that is spent in political campaigns? Why do individuals and groups contribute to campaigns and what do they expect in return? How do candidates raise money and for what purposes do they spend it? What do candidates think they must do in return for campaign contributions? Most importantly, how does modern campaigning, its expense, and the need for campaign funds affect the quality of our national government?

by W. Richard Merriman, Jr.

Republican Government and the Public Good

It has often been remarked that the men who designed the Constitution could not have foreseen many of the changes that have occurred in American society and politics. Certainly the framers did not anticipate the development of a political system characterized by frequent popular elections that pit candidates from political parties against each other. As a consequence, it could be argued that the intentions of the framers are not particularly relevant to a discussion of issues of modern campaigns and campaign spending. But the American political thought of the 1770s and 1780s has one particularly important idea to contribute: the idea of "the public good."

Time has made the term "republican government" almost synonymous with the idea of government by elected representatives. To the Americans of 1776, creating new representative state governments was certainly part of the work of creating republican governments; but it was only one part. In 1776 a republican government was not defined simply in terms of institutional forms or processes. Rather, a republican government was one in which the "public good" was the only objective.

The substance of the public good was difficult to define, but as Gordon Wood writes, it

> ... was not, as we might today think of it, simply the sum or consensus
> of the particular interests that made up the community. It was rather an
> entity in itself, prior to and distinct from the various private interests of
> groups and individuals. (Wood 1969, 58)

The public good was considered to be morally superior to the narrower interests that exist in any society, and it could be discerned only by citizens who would consider what was best for the whole society rather than what was best only for themselves.

The American colonists immersed themselves in political writings that extolled the glories of republican government. While these writings celebrated English liberty, some of them also complained of governmental encroachments on that liberty. This literature, and the history of monarchical government in Europe, convinced many Americans that in society two distinct interests exist: that of the government and that of the governed. While the governed seek liberty, governments seek power. And power preys on liberty. As relations with England worsened throughout the 1760s and 1770s, Americans increasingly became convinced that the government of Great Britain intended to extinguish their liberties and impose a tyranny over all British subjects. Given this view Americans felt the need to sever relations with the government of Great Britain. Once done, they could exercise their right, proclaimed in the words of the Declaration of Independence, to "institute new government, laying its foundation on such principles, and organizing its powers in such form, as to them shall seem most likely to effect their safety and happiness."

When Americans turned to creating new state governments, it became clear that most hoped to erect governments on the "republican principle." A poet of the period expressed this intention:

> Here Governments their last perfection take.
> Erected only for the People's sake:
> Founded no more on Conquest or in blood,
> But on the basis of the Public Good.
> No contests then shall mad ambition raise,
> No chieftains quarrel for a sprig of praise,
> No thrones shall rise, provoking lawless sway,
> And not a King to cloud the blissful day.
> (Quoted in Wood 1969, 55)

How did Americans expect to create governments that would pursue the public good? Part of the answer was to create governments in which most power was lodged in the branch of government—the legislative—where popular election would encourage shared interests and goals between governors and governed. Another part of the answer was to minimize the power of the executive and the judiciary. Concern over the power of the executive was a natural residue of the American experience with both the king and his colonial officers. It was generally conceded that judges could not properly be elected; consequently, neither could they be trusted with great power.

But proper design of the new governments was not in itself sufficient to guarantee republican policies. Much depended on the character of the people and whether they possessed "republican virtue." The French philosopher-historian Montesquieu described the spirit that animated different systems of government in his book, *The Spirit of the Laws.* He wrote of monarchies and despotisms that "there is no great share of probity necessary to support" them. The threat of legal punishment in a monarchy and the threat of "the prince's arm" in a despotism were sufficient to maintain obedience and order. But in a popular republic, Montesquieu wrote, "one spring more is necessary, namely, virtue."

Republican virtue was a sentiment or passion that moved individuals to put the good of society before their private interests. George Washington, who left the comforts of his home to lead the nation in war and to launch its new government, was hailed as an example of the purest republican virtue. A republic's survival, however, required more than the timely appearance of a virtuous leader. The people must

157

themselves be virtuous and seek the public good when choosing those who will govern or when chosen to govern.

The expectation of Americans that they could create and sustain republican systems of government in which the prime motive in making policy would be love of the public good may today seem naive, even utopian. But the political literature of the 1770s and the popular state governments designed after the Declaration of Independence make it clear that Americans were determined to try.

The Constitution, Factions, and the Public Good: The Theory

A decade after Americans began their experiment with popular republican government James Madison expressed his conviction that the states' efforts had not been very successful, his chagrin that the national government of the Articles of Confederation had not been an effective counter to this lack of success, and his belief that a properly designed national government might yet produce national policy for the public good. In *Federalist* No. 10 Madison wrote that "complaints are every where heard from our most considerate and virtuous citizens . . . that the public good is disregarded in the conflicts of rival parties." He continued: "However anxiously we may wish that these complaints had no foundation, the evidence of known facts will not permit us to deny that they are in some degree true." Madison concluded that "a factious spirit has tainted our public administrations." Madison saw that factious spirit at work both in clashes within state governments and in the unwillingness of the states to confer on the government of the Articles of Confederation the power it needed to pursue the best interest of the whole country.

Where was Americans' regard for the public good? Madison believed it had given way to the "mischiefs of faction." He defined a faction as

> a number of citizens, whether amounting to a majority or a minority of the whole, who are united and actuated by some common impulse of passion, or of interest, adverse to the rights of other citizens, or to the permanent and aggregate interests of the community. (*Federalist* No. 10)

In pursuing any interest other than the "permanent and aggregate interests of the community," factions worked against the public good. In general, Madison believed that humans are intellectually incapable of knowing with real certainty what is true or what course of action is best and so end up disagreeing with one another. This tendency to disagree is so pronounced in some people "that where no substantial occasion presents itself, the most fanciful distinctions have been sufficient to kindle ... unfriendly passions, and excite ... violent conflicts." Moreover, the partiality of human reasoning inclines almost everyone to confuse judgments about their own self-interest with assertions about what is best for the society as a whole. Madison concluded that these facts make the existence of factions virtually inescapable:

> ... a landed interest, a manufacturing interest, a mercantile interest, a monied interest, with many lesser interests, grow up of necessity in civilized nations, and divide them into different classes, actuated by different sentiments and views. (*Federalist* No. 10)

But while Madison believed factions were inevitable he did not believe that this precluded the creation and maintenance of a government that would both pursue the public good and be accountable to the public. Indeed, *Federalist* No. 10 was intended to convince Americans that the proposed constitution would create just such a government. Madison claimed that an "extended republic," encompassing a large and diverse populace, would harbor such a multiplicity of factions and interests that no particular interest or combination of interests would come to dominate the councils of the national government. The proposed constitution would create just such an extended republic. All factions would be rendered relatively ineffectual by their small size and by the difficulty of working in concert. Breaking the power of factions would free society's governors to pursue the public good. But only if the right type of people governed.

Only one part (the House of Representatives) of one branch (the Congress) of the proposed government would be directly subject to the votes of a factious public. And the members of this body would be chosen from large districts, enhancing the chance that men with broad reputations for virtue and good character would be elected instead of men of parochial and factious tempers. If a particular representative with a narrow point of view was elected to the House, this individual would quickly learn to join with others to craft policies for the public good that could attract a legislative majority. To these curbs on factious influence were added the checks of the Senate and the presidency.

Factions and Politics: The Reality

Madison's literary and theoretical brilliance are displayed unmistakably in *Federalist* No. 10. So too is his genuine concern for preserving both virtue and the pursuit of the public good in government. By the time of his own presidency (1809-17), however, the realities of American politics and society bore almost no resemblance to Madison's somewhat genteel vision of government by virtuous men, untainted by factious impulses.

As soon as the Constitution's new government began to operate, disagreements over fiscal and economic policy issues quickly pitted Secretary of the Treasury Alexander Hamilton against both Madison, then a member of the House of Representatives, and Secretary of State Thomas Jefferson. The rancor of these disagreements is evident in a letter from Jefferson to President George Washington:

> That I have utterly, in my private conversations, disapproved of the system of the Secretary of the Treasury, I acknowledge and avow: and this was not merely a speculative difference. His system flowed from principles adverse to liberty, and was calculated to undermine and demolish the republic, by creating an influence of his department over the members of the legislature. I saw this influence actually produced, and its first fruits to be the establishment of the great outlines of his project by the votes of the very persons who, having swallowed his bait were laying themselves out to profit by his plans: ... These were no longer the votes then of the representatives of the people, but of deserters of the rights and interests of the people ... (Peterson 1975, 456)

The seeds of the country's first political parties—the Federalists and the Republicans—were sown early in the conflict over Hamilton's financial plan. Under Hamilton's leadership the Federalists began publishing (with public money) the *Gazette of the United States* to express their views. In response, Jefferson gave a clerkship at the State Department to Philip Freneau, who undertook the editorship of the anti-Federalist *National Gazette*.

As the parties sought to advance their policy preferences they naturally turned to the people for support. The American people, in turn, were becoming increasingly insistent on playing a larger role in their national government. The development of political parties and the democratization of American politics thus went hand in hand.

By the early 1800s many Americans were calling for the elimination of property qualifications for voting. As the states heeded this call they expanded their electorates for state and local elections *and* for the U.S. House of Representatives. By 1832 every state but one had moved the power to select electoral college electors from state legislatures to voters. Candidates for election to the electoral college pledged themselves to vote in the college for a particular party and presidential candidate. The practice of popular election of pledged electors greatly democratized the selection of the president. In the years since the early 1800s the Constitution has been amended to expand the American electorate by including, in turn, black men, women, and eighteen-year-olds. The Seventeenth Amendment to the Constitution gave the choice of U.S. senators to the voters. The democratization of our national politics has created an arena—electoral politics—in which the American people choose who will govern. Writing of the change that has occurred in American politics since 1787, Garry Wills writes:

> In that world, the concept of public virtue had a hard and clear meaning, a heft and weightiness of the real, no longer apparent to us. We do not even pretend that we choose our politicians for their virtue. That kind of talk would look sappy or insincere in our political discourse. (Wills 1981, 268)

If Wills is correct in claiming that we do not choose our public officials for their ability to discern and pursue the public good, we need to ask then what do we expect from them and how do we try to make them meet our expectations? It is in elections and, increasingly, through campaign contributions, that Americans reveal these expectations.

Money and Elections

The sixth president of the United States, John Quincy Adams, wrote of the presidency that "to pay money for securing it directly or indirectly" was "incorrect in principle." Such a view of public service was becoming quaint by the time of Adams' presidency, and Adams himself was swept from office by the insurgent democracy of Andrew Jackson.

The rise of popular democracy in America made it imperative for candidates to communicate with voters. In 1860, for example,

> Abraham Lincoln secretly bought a small German weekly in Illinois for $400 and turned it over to an editor who agreed to follow the policies of the Republican party and to publish in both English and German. (Alexander 1984, 6)

The Republican and Democratic parties spent a combined total of $150 thousand in the presidential campaign of 1860. The cost of subsequent presidential campaigns gradually increased until the divisive and controverted Hayes-Tilden contest of 1876. Spending in that campaign approached $2 million. Twenty years later William McKinley spent over $3 million against $675 thousand spent by William Jennings Bryan. McKinley won, at least in part because of Republican fund-raiser Mark Hanna, who specified for banks and other businesses their expected "quota" of contributions to the McKinley campaign. No presidential contest topped this $3 million mark until 1920.

The next spending peak came in 1936. Alf Landon, the Republican presidential nominee in 1936, proved that there was more to winning an election than raising and spending money: he spent almost $9 million and still lost by a landslide. The first $20 million presidential campaign took place in 1960. This was followed by a $24 million campaign in 1964, a $37 million campaign in 1968, and a record-smashing $91 million campaign in 1972.

Spending large amounts of money in campaigns is not confined to presidential contests. In 1972 a little over $26 million was spent in Senate campaigns. In 1982 the figure was $139 million. House races in 1972 cost $40 million. In 1982 they cost over $200 million.

The reasons for the increasing cost of political campaigns are not mysterious. The American electorate has grown considerably, and it now chooses the president (via the electoral college), the Senate, and the House of Representatives. The electorate expects to be courted by candidates, and courting costs money. The advent of radio and television has greatly expanded the capacity of candidates to reach voters, but use of these media is expensive. Combined spending for radio and television time by the 1980 Carter and Reagan campaigns topped $30 million, over half the total combined spending of these campaigns.

Competition also escalates campaign costs. Opponents in political campaigns bid campaign costs up as they compete for votes. If one candidate has $1 million to spend in a campaign, his or her opponent is likely to try and meet or exceed that figure. The other candidate knows this and will raise and spend accordingly. Escalating expenditures take on momentum of their own.

Regulating Elections and Money

The need to gather money to mount effective campaigns has raised concerns that campaign contributions may give some individuals and groups improper influence on the selection of public officials and the making of public policy. Part of this concern stems from the doctrine of political equality in America: each voter has only one vote, so all are equal. Americans are not naive. They know there are other ways besides voting to exercise political influence. But Americans become concerned when campaign contributions by individuals and groups give these donors more political clout than is wielded by the individual voter. Another, related concern, one that goes back to the idea of the public good as the primary concern of lawmakers, is the worry that attention to the policy interests of campaign contributors distracts public officials from proper attentiveness to the broader public good.

These concerns have prompted numerous laws that regulate campaign contributions and spending. The first federal campaign contribution law, passed in 1907, prohibited contributions by corporations to candidates for federal office. A law requiring disclosure of campaign funds was enacted in 1910. The next major enactment was the Federal Corrupt Practices Act of 1925, which sought to limit campaign expenditures. The Hatch Act of 1940 limited any individual's contribution to a federal candidate to five thousand dollars. But individuals could make additional contributions to various campaign committees, thus avoiding contribution limits. In 1947 the Taft-Hartley Act extended the ban on corporate campaign contributions to labor unions.

More recently a series of laws and amendments established new rules on campaign contributions and spending. The Federal Election Campaign Act of 1971 limited contributions by candidates (or their own immediate families) to their own campaigns to $50 thousand for presidential or vice-presidential campaigns, $35 thousand for senatorial races, and $25 thousand for House contests. The bill also sought to curb campaign spending in federal elections by restricting spending for communications media: a ten cent per eligible voter or $50 thousand limit, whichever was greater. The bill also required public disclosure of campaign contributions of one hundred dollars or more and prohibited contributions by one person given in the name of another.

The Revenue Act of 1971 instituted a policy of public financing of presidential campaigns, which first operated in 1976. Under the bill the Presidential Election Campaign Fund gave each major party's presidential nominee a sum of money in the amount of fifteen cents for each U.S. resident over eighteen years of age. Candidates who accepted these public funds were prohibited from accepting campaign contributions from any other source. The bill allowed taxpayers to contribute one dollar of their annual income tax to the fund. The bill also sought to encourage more political contributions by allowing a tax credit or tax deduction for small contributions to candidates for local, state, and federal office.

The Watergate scandal, which was intimately linked to campaign activities, focused considerable attention on campaign financing. A few individuals had made whopping contributions to the campaigns of Nixon and McGovern: W. Clement Stone contributed over $2 million to Nixon's 1972 campaign and Richard Mellon Scaife gave $1 million. Stewart Mott gave $400 thousand to McGovern's war chest. The Watergate special prosecutor discovered that a number of U.S. corporations had made illegal contributions during the 1972 campaign. The twenty-one companies that pleaded guilty gave almost $1 million, with over 80 percent of that total going to the Nixon campaign.

Passage of the Federal Election Campaign Act Amendments of 1974 reflected post-Watergate concern about campaign financing. The amendments curbed large contributions by individuals by setting a one thousand dollar limit on individual contributions to a candidate for each primary, runoff, or general election. The bill also set a $25 thousand annual aggregate limit on individual contributions to federal candidates. Contributions from organizations, political committees, and national and state party organizations to a federal candidate were limited to five thousand dollars in each election. Cash contributions of more than one hundred dollars were outlawed. The 1974 amendments also established the Federal Election Commission, which is responsible for administering laws on campaign finance.

The 1974 amendments set spending limits of $10 million per candidate in the presidential primary process and $20 million per candidate in the presidential general election. In Senate primaries candidates were limited to spending $100 thousand or eight cents per eligible voter, whichever was greater. During senatorial general elections, campaign spending by candidates could not exceed $150 thousand or twelve cents per eligible voter, whichever was greater. A limit of $70 thousand was set for each candidate in a House primary, and the same limit was set for expenditures during House general election contests.

Political Action Committees

As the campaign finance legislation of the 1970s clarified which types of campaign contributions and expenditures were legal, political action committees (PACs) became more numerous and more prominent in campaigns. PACs come in two varieties. *Separate, segregated funds* are PACs established by labor unions, corporations, membership organizations, and trade associations. These organizations maintain separate funds that are supported by voluntary contributions made by members and contribute these funds to candidates. *Nonconnected* political committees are not affiliated with any other organization. They raise and spend money to try and influence the outcomes of election campaigns.

The first political action committee was created by the Congress of Industrial Organizations in 1943. Businesses and associations were slow in creating PACs. The American Medical Association created AMPAC in 1961. The National Association of Manufacturers created the Business-Industry PAC (BIPAC) in 1963. Corporations were particularly cautious about creating PACs because of questions about their legality. The Federal Election Campaign Act of 1971 authorized use of separate, segregated funds by corporations and unions, but doubts about whether government contractors could form PACs held some groups back. Mary

Stone reports that the "watershed event that legitimized corporate PAC activity" was an advisory opinion from the newly created Federal Election Commission that made it clear that corporations and unions that were government contractors could solicit voluntary contributions from their employers and contribute money to federal candidates (Stone 1984, 5).

One hundred thirteen PACs existed when the 1971 Federal Election Campaign Act went into effect. By December 1983 the number was 3,525. Corporate PACs now greatly outnumber both labor PACs and association/membership group PACs. The amount of money given to candidates by PACs also has increased dramatically. In 1975 about $12 million was given to congressional candidates. The advent of public funding of presidential candidates in the mid-1970s coincided with a surge in the number of PACs. The result has been a shift of PAC money to congressional candidates. Over $87 million was given by PACs to congressional candidates in 1982. PAC contributions made up over 25 percent of total congressional campaign receipts in 1982.

Nonconnected political action committees have attracted a good deal of attention because they often make "independent" campaign expenditures. Instead of contributing to a particular candidate, groups making independent expenditures simply spend money themselves, often for advertising, to influence election outcomes. These efforts frequently focus on the defeat of an incumbent and, consequently, tend to convey negative messages to voters. The National Conservative Political Action Committee, for example, spent over $3 million in 1980-81 to advocate the defeat of certain candidates.

Buckley v. Valeo

In 1976 the U.S. Supreme Court's ruling in *Buckley v. Valeo* had an important impact on campaign finance law. The case arose because of a challenge to the constitutionality of the 1974 Federal Election Campaign Act. The Court ruled that the 1974 Act's limits on contributions by candidates to their own campaigns, limits on independent PAC expenditures, and limits on campaign expenditures were unconstitutional. The Court ruled that these limits restricted the First Amendment rights to free speech and association.

The Court noted that any limitation on campaign contributions and expenditures restricts freedom of expression. But the Court distinguished between the degree of restriction involved in limiting contributions and the degree of restriction involved in limiting expenditures. In essence, the Court ruled that expenditure limits have a more severe impact on free expression than limits on contributions. Contributions to a candidate, which, in the Court's view, are intended to facilitate free expression by someone else (the candidate), may be limited. The Court accepted the claim that government has a legitimate interest in the prevention of corruption and therefore upheld limits designed to prevent the kinds of large contributions that raise the specter of corruption. The Court upheld the one thousand dollar limit on individual contributions to candidates and the five thousand dollar limit on PAC contributions.

In the Court's opinion, expenditures have to be treated differently. Any restriction on expenditures is a direct restriction on the "speaker's" ability to communicate with voters. The Court therefore ruled that limitations on campaign expenditures, independent expenditures, and candidates' contributions to their own campaigns are unconstitutional restrictions of free expression.

The Court rejected the claim that government had a legitimate interest in limiting the skyrocketing costs of political campaigns. It did, however, uphold the legality of restricting contributions to and spending by presidential candidates who accept public campaign funds. This ruling left the door open for those who advocate public funding of congressional elections as a way of limiting contributions and spending in congressional races.

A New View of Finding the Public Good

What the Contribution Buys

In a book on money and politics Elizabeth Drew asks questions about campaign finance: "Why is all this money floating about? What do the investors expect?" Drew's study concludes that contributions can bring an individual or group "access." One lobbyist reports:

> We are in such a retail business that for a hundred and fifty dollars you can get access. There are some senior members of Congress whose fund-raisers I've gone to, giving a hundred and fifty dollars, and when I call I can get through. I think if I hadn't given the money it would have been harder.... I can imagine how someone who gives a thousand dollars or directs a five-thousand-dollar PAC contribution to someone is treated. (Drew 1983, 77)

"Access" means a chance to inform a public official or candidate about one's stake or interest in public policy issues and to provide information and a point of view. Access is not necessarily influence. But access is an important prerequisite of influence.

Political action committees and other contributors use money to cultivate access, encourage their friends on Capitol Hill, and oppose those who are not friendly. Drew reports that the National Association of Realtors asks congressional candidates to answer a questionnaire on issues about which it is particularly concerned. The Realtors Political Action Committee contributed over $2 million to federal candidates between the beginning of 1981 and the end of 1982. Says Richard Thaxton, vice president for political affairs of the National Association of Realtors, "We go to an awful lot of receptions. We look at that as access money: 'We know you're there and casting votes, and we'd like to be able to talk to you.'" Thaxton continues:

> Thirty percent of our money will go to Democrats and seventy percent to Republicans. But in terms of the numbers we give to, it's fifty-fifty, because the Democrats control the House and we go to a lot of two-hundred-and-fifty-dollar receptions. I can legitimately say to my Democratic friends that fifty percent of our giving is to Democrats, and I can legitimately say to my Republican friends that seventy percent of our money goes to Republicans.... (Drew 1983, 93)

That PACs focus their contributions on policy-makers who deal with certain issues of particular interest is evident from two 1986 reports:

> Sixty-five political action committees (PACs) which advocate strong U. S. support of Israel gave congressional candidates a combined total of $853,520 during 1985.... [N]early half of the 1985 contributions from these PACs—$397,625—went to 34 members of Congress serving on key committees with significant jurisdiction over questions of U. S. policy toward Israel. (Common Cause 1986b)

> Political action committees ... gave $6,693,915 to the 56 members of the Senate Finance and House Ways and Means Committees during 1985— when both committees were considering comprehensive tax reform legislation.... (Common Cause 1986a)

This amount was nearly two and a half times more than these members of Congress received in 1983.

Pluralism and the Public Good

The Madison of *Federalist* No. 10 would take a dim view of a political system in which so many groups—he would call them factions—work so hard to influence the content of public policy by giving campaign funds and cultivating access. But is Madison's standard the only one by which we can judge contemporary politics?

The political theory of pluralism claims to give an accurate description of how our political system works and finds much in its operation to commend. Pluralist theory emphasizes the primacy of groups in American politics: Americans relate to the political system primarily through their perception of themselves as members of groups with group interests. Americans, then, ask two questions about any particular public policy issue: Does this issue affect me? What is the interest that I, and others like me, have at stake in this issue?

Each person, in the pluralist view, is really a bundle of interests. One individual may be concerned about teachers' salaries, environmental issues, and property taxes. Another might be interested in civil rights issues and the problems of small businesses. Most such interests are already represented by interest groups. To a group of people who have a shared interest and want to pursue it in the political process pluralist theory offers a simple directive: get involved with a relevant interest group and if there isn't such a group organize it.

Pluralist theory portrays American politics as an ongoing competition among interest groups for influence on public policy. On almost every issue one group or coalition of interest groups will find itself pitted against another group or coalition that desires a different policy outcome. Some groups compete for access by contributing money to candidates. Others can deliver significant numbers of votes to a particular candidate. Some groups compete by providing information on issues. Others rely on litigation to shape policy. Many groups do all these things.

Pluralist theory maintains that every group that has an interest and that is willing to compete by the accepted rules of the game can have some influence on public policy. Of course, each group will win some and lose some, but every group that tries can get a hearing for its views—and it won't lose all the time.

Out of the pluralist theory comes the claim that the "public good," in the old republican sense, does not exist in any meaningful way in American society. Ours is a complex society that is fragmented into thousands of groups with specific interests. In such a society it becomes pointless to try and discern a public good that transcends these divisions. For instance, most Americans are concerned about the size of the federal government's deficit. Would the public good be realized by the elimination of the deficit? Many Americans would answer yes, though some economists would dispute that answer. But at the level of practical politics debate about balancing the budget quickly turns to the question of who must lose some government benefits and who is going to pay more in taxes. At this practical level interests of all sorts come into the political process to press their claims, and the high-minded search for the public good ends.

Instead of seeking a *substantive* public good, pluralism argues, we should focus on perfecting *procedural* guarantees that every group can make itself heard on issues it really cares about. Out of the welter of interest group pressure and counter-pressure comes policy that roughly approximates the "public interest." No group will get all it wants, but no organized group will get left out either.

The pluralist point of view almost completely reverses Madison's views on factions; we need factions, and lots of them, if every interest in society is going to be adequately organized and spoken for. Campaign contributions also look different. If we wish to encourage wide-open interest group competition it is important to protect the First Amendment right of people to associate in groups and express their opinions through campaign contributions. While it is important, as the Supreme Court ruled in *Buckley v. Valeo,* to avoid the possibility of untoward and corrupt group influence, it is also crucial, in the pluralist view, to allow groups to use campaign contributions to get access to policy-makers and make their views known.

Proposed Constitutional Amendments

The key issue at the heart of current debates over amending the Constitution to allow limitations on campaign contributions and spending is whether the old republican view of factions or the pluralist view of groups is valid.

Advocates of limitations on campaign spending see a link between campaign contributions and campaign spending that the Supreme Court did not emphasize in its *Buckley* decision. Drew describes this linkage when she comments:

> It is often said that what is driving the chase for money on the part of candidates for Congress is the ever-increasing cost of campaigning, but that gets it backward. What is driving the chase for money is its own momentum. It is the domestic equivalent of the arms race. A candidate feels compelled to spend so much money because his opponent is spending so much, or might spend so much, or groups intent on his defeat are spending so much. . . . And the quest for money has distended and distorted the political system to the point where it bears little resemblance to what was supposed to be. (Drew 1983, 94)

In 1982 Rep. Jonathan Bingham, along with twelve other sponsors, introduced House Joint Resolution 628. The text of the proposed amendment to the Constitution follows:

> *"Article—*
> *Section 1. The Congress may enact laws regulating the amounts of contributions and expenditures intended to affect elections to Federal offices.*
> *Section 2. The several States may enact laws regulating the amounts of contributions and expenditures intended to affect election to State and local offices."*

If added to the Constitution, the amendment would reinstate the government's ability to regulate campaign contributions and expenditures that was denied it in *Buckley*. A similar amendment, Senate Joint Resolution 110, was introduced by Sen. Ted Stevens in 1983.

In presenting his proposed amendment Representative Bingham asserted that with current campaign financing practices,

> [t]he political process is distorted, and public confidence in our domestic system is undermined, as high offices are perceived to be for sale to the highest bidder. The need to raise large sums for their campaigns puts incumbents and challengers under intolerable pressures and obligations that may well influence their conduct in office. (*Congressional Record*, 8 December 1982, 9205)

Bingham adds that Congress had sought, through the 1971 and 1974 legislation and in subsequent laws, to control campaign spending. But the Court's *Buckley* ruling effectively took from the government the authority to make laws limiting campaign spending.

A restoration of that authority would allow Congress to enact laws that would limit total campaign spending by candidates for federal office. Such limits, presumably, would prevent candidates from falling into the cycle of escalating expenditures and would leave them much less dependent on interest group contributions.

Legislative limits could also be set on the amount of money a candidate could give to his or her own congressional campaign. In 1978 a total of fifty-eight candidates for Congress gave at least $100 thousand or more to their own campaigns. In 1982 Frank Lautenberg of New Jersey gave or lent $5.1 million to his own Senate campaign. Mark Dayton of Minnesota spent $6.9 million of his own money in an unsuccessful 1982 bid for a seat in the Senate. Justice Marshall, in a dissent from the Court's *Buckley* opinion, wrote:

> ... the perception that personal wealth wins elections may not only discourage potential candidates without significant personal wealth from entering the political arena, but also undermines public confidence in the electoral process. (Quoted in *Congressional Record*, 8 December 1982, 9206)

A third likely target for limitations is independent campaign spending. In *Buckley* the Supreme Court ruled that independent expenditures could not be limited. In *Common Cause v. Schmitt* the Court made it clear that this freedom to spend extends to presidential contests in which the major party's candidates have accepted public funding. In the 1980 presidential election campaign groups spent $14 million independently, most of it on behalf of Ronald Reagan. Independent spending in both presidential and congressional campaigns could be limited if the proposed amendment were adopted.

The proposed amendment would only set the stage for congressional action, and, because members of Congress consult their own self-interest before legislating, there are concerns over what they would do with the authority given them by the proposed amendment. A particular concern centers on the problem of how high spending limits for congressional elections should be. Research indicates that members of Congress benefit in elections from an "incumbency effect." That is, they are generally well-known in their districts or states and are in a position to provide a number of services and benefits to constituents that challengers cannot provide. Challengers must spend a good deal of money to overcome the name-recognition advantage enjoyed by incumbents. In fact, challengers often must outspend incumbents to overcome incumbents' advantages. Setting a ceiling on spending in congressional campaigns could, in normal political circumstances, go a long way toward guaranteeing that incumbents will win.

Representative Bingham states: "I do not accept the argument that Congress, being always composed of incumbents, will never treat challengers fairly" (*Congressional Record*, 8 December 1982, 9206). Political scientist Jacobson has reached a different conclusion, asserting that as long as members of Congress "remain free to make campaign finance policy as it suits their individual and partisan interests . . . [they] will no doubt continue to do so" (Jacobson 1980, 226).

Leaving aside the debate over the likely motives of incumbent members of Congress who would, under the proposed constitutional amendment, make the new rules on campaign expenditures, there are other concerns about efforts to limit campaign spending. In making "The Case for PACs" Herbert Alexander concedes that while "competing interests may . . . cause what Madison calls 'the mischiefs of faction,' they also may bring to society ideas and values of great worth." Alexander adds that

> the ability of groups and interests in society to articulate their demands, to coalesce and to oppose government with the resources they command, is the only reliable guarantee against dominance by either the government or the media. (Alexander 1983, 15)

If limits on campaign spending are imposed, then so, too, are opportunities for groups to convey to candidates, through campaign contributions, their concerns and policy preferences.

Campaigns and the Public Good: Two Views

It seems inevitable that, in the absence of restraint, campaign costs will continue to rise. The cost of communicating with voters continues to increase, and competition between opponents exerts constant upward pressure on campaign expenditures. As candidates have confronted the need to raise more money, Americans have become more concerned about the sources of these funds and the influence that individual and group contributors may exercise on the content of public policy. Two solutions to this problem have been proposed.

Every Citizen a Faction?

Alexander suggests that campaign spending "should be considered the tuition the American people must spend for their education on the issues." As he notes,

> ... many campaigns are not edifying, but, through all the political verbiage, issues are brought forward, and the nation determines its agenda. The people elected to office then determine public policies that affect all of us—an educational, if not always pleasing, process. (Alexander 1984, 196)

The problem, Alexander claims, is that "Americans are willing to spend only sparingly for politics." Jacobson concurs that "most of the public is contented to enjoy a free ride."

Such attitudes work against any effort to institute public financing of congressional elections. Jacobson writes:

> It is very doubtful that the public would tolerate subsidies anywhere near that size that would permit it effective competition in most congressional constituencies ... (Jacobson 1980, 226)

These attitudes also work against an alternative suggested by Alexander: an increase in small, individual contributions.

> The value of contributing small sums for political activity is neither taught in schools nor widely understood as an act of good citizenship, although voting is both honored and respected, at least in principle. The challenge is to associate contributing with voting as an act of good citizenship, to upgrade and dignify political giving, and to gain for the popular financing of politics the public approval accorded voting. (Alexander 1984, 198)

In the 1930s Huey Long promised to make "Every Man a King." Alexander proposes, in effect, to make every citizen a faction. This might appear to be a prescription for pluralism run rampant. But careful consideration of Alexander's proposal makes it clear that, in a sense, he is proposing a solution that Madison might embrace. If campaigns are waged with small contributions given by numerous individual "factions," would not all these factions become relatively ineffectual at exerting pressure on the policy-making process?

Absent a dramatic increase in the amount of small contributions, Alexander's pluralist viewpoint calls for all interests to become organized and involved in campaigns. While the "public good" may not be found in such a situation, the "public interest," in which every group gets some of what it wants, can be. Increased citizen involvement in politics through interest group competition will, at least, work to head off the domination of policy-making by any particular group or coalition of groups. It will also work to ensure that policy-makers in government are attentive to the various concerns of America's myriad groups.

A Constitutional Remedy?

Proponents of a constitutional amendment allowing Congress to limit campaign spending, and by extension campaign contributions, believe that the clamor of interest groups in American society is already so deafening that public officials have little chance to think about—and little incentive to pursue—the public good. More interest groups contributing more money would only raise the noise level. Supporters claim that easing the pressure on federal candidates to raise campaign funds will curtail opportunities for interest groups to cultivate access to elected officials and a feeling among them of indebtedness to certain interests.

Certainly, amending the Constitution to allow limits on campaign spending will not be a sufficient step toward ushering in a "golden age" of virtue and regard for the public good. But such a goal, even if it seems difficult, is worth pursuing, and limiting campaign spending and contributions is a necessary step toward that goal.

Arguments For an Amendment that Would Allow Limits on Campaign Expenditures

- The founders focused on creating republican governments that would pursue the public good. That goal is still valid.
- The skyrocketing costs of political campaigns put candidates under tremendous pressure to raise campaign funds. Interest groups are all too willing to make their contributions, but they use these contributions to cultivate access to and influence on policy-makers that work against the pursuit of the public good.
- While the Supreme Court allows limitations on campaign contributions as a way of avoiding the reality or appearance of corruption, its failure to limit spending invites more groups to become involved in making contributions. While the recipients of these contributions may avoid corruption, the ability of our government to pursue the public good is, nonetheless, corroded.

• The pluralist theory of American politics overlooks the fact that some groups have tremendous resources to use in influencing public policy while others have almost none. There are no "Poor PACs" or "Food Stamp PACs." How can a public official keep the needs of such unorganized people in mind when he or she must legislate in an environment that is dominated by well-organized and well-financed interest groups?

• The charge that members of Congress will not use equitably new authority given under the proposed amendment to the Constitution is not valid. Congress has already made rules to limit the use by members of their free mail privilege during campaign seasons.

• The Court's ruling that campaign spending is constitutionally protected speech calls for a constitutional remedy. The alternative solution, public financing of congressional campaigns, would be extremely expensive, especially if challengers are to be given funds sufficient to offset the advantages of incumbents.

• An amendment to limit expenditures would help control the negative campaigns funded by independent PACs.

• An amendment to limit expenditures would help keep the wealthy from dominating congressional elections.

Arguments Against an Amendment that Would Allow Limits on Campaign Expenditures

• As much as we might like to live in a society where there is some discernible public good to be pursued by elected officials, we don't. In a pluralistic society like ours there are so many divergent interests that it is probably impossible to identify and pursue a transcendent public good.

• The best thing to do in a pluralistic society with a myriad of different interests is to encourage groups of all kinds to become involved—through campaign contributions and in other ways—in the political process.

• A constitutional amendment limiting campaign spending would inevitably limit opportunities for groups and individuals to make campaign contributions. This would limit citizens' ability to influence the content of public policy.

• Rather than curbing citizens' ability to make their policy preferences known, we should encourage the development of more interest groups. The more points of view that are represented the better the chance that every citizen will feel that his or her voice has been heard.

• The goal of political campaigns is to let as many voters as possible learn about the candidates and their positions on public issues. If campaign spending is restricted this will limit the voter-education potential of campaigns.

• Congress may use new authority in the area of campaign spending to set spending limits that will virtually ensure, given their advantage, that incumbents will be reelected.

• The right of free speech is essential to the maintenance of a free society. Actions that limit the ability of candidates and citizens to publicly express their opinions about public issues are inherently dangerous to freedom.

• It is not a good idea to get into the practice of amending the Constitution to overturn decisions of the Supreme Court.

References

Alexander, Herbert E. *Financing Politics: Money, Politics, and Political Reform.* 3d ed. Washington, D. C.: Congressional Quarterly, 1984.

Common Cause. "Gimme a Break." *Common Cause News.* 11 February 1986. Washington, D. C.: Common Cause, 1986a.

———. *Common Cause News.* 28 February 1986. Washington, D. C.: Common Cause, 1986b.

Congressional Research Service. *"Buckley v. Valeo":* The Opinion of the United States Supreme Court in the Election Campaign Case: Summary and Commentary. Washington, D. C.: Congressional Research Service, 1976.

Drew, Elizabeth. *Politics and Money: The New Road to Corruption.* New York: Collier Books, 1983.

Hamilton, Alexander, John Jay, and James Madison. *The Federalist Papers.* Available in various editions.

Jacobson, Gary C. *Money in Congressional Elections.* New Haven, Conn.: Yale University Press, 1980.

Lineberry, Robert L. *Government in America: People, Politics, and Policy.* Boston: Little, Brown, 1981.

Montesquieu, Baron de. *The Spirit of the Laws.* New York: Hafner Press, 1949.

Peterson, Merrill D., ed. *The Portable Thomas Jefferson.* New York: Viking Press, 1975.

Public Affairs Council. *The Case for PACs.* Washington, D. C.: Public Affairs Council, 1983.

Stone, Mary N. *Facts on PACs: Political Action Committees and American Campaign Finance.* Washington, D. C.: League of Women Voters Education Fund, 1984.

Wills, Garry. *Explaining America: The Federalist.* New York: Doubleday, 1981.

Wood, Gordon S. *The Creation of the American Republic, 1776-1787.* New York: W. W. Norton, 1969.

Appendix A

The Jefferson Meeting on the Constitution

Two hundred years ago a small group of Americans gathered in Philadelphia to design a new government. The government they created reflected their beliefs about human nature, their learning—from historical study and personal experience—about the strengths and weaknesses of different kinds of governments, and their preferences about the kind of society and political system that should be "constituted" by a new constitution. They tried to design governmental institutions that would give continuing life to their political values.

It is appropriate, indeed necessary, that Americans should periodically assess how well the government created in Philadelphia in 1787 is working. Thomas Jefferson wrote in 1816 that "I am certainly not an advocate for frequent and untried changes in laws and constitutions. But ... laws and institutions must go hand in hand with the progress of the human mind." Americans have taken Jefferson's belief to heart, and have amended the Constitution twenty-six times.

The Jefferson Meeting on the Constitution was developed as a way to promote, in the Jeffersonian spirit of informed and rational discussion, understanding of the fundamentals of the American constitutional system and evaluation of the contemporary performance of American government. The preceding chapters were initially written for use by participants in Jefferson Meetings on the Constitution. While the substance of these chapters makes interesting reading, it is in public discussion and debate of the issues discussed in these chapters that the issues really come to life.

On the following pages are presented two guides to organizing a Jefferson Meeting that will bring citizens together for discussion of constitutional change. The first guide discusses how to organize a community Jefferson Meeting for adults. The second discusses ways of organizing classroom Jefferson Meetings for students in high schools and colleges.

The Jefferson Meeting
in the Community:
A Guide for Planners

Why Have a Community Jefferson Meeting?

There are many good reasons to have a Jefferson Meeting in your community. Jefferson Meetings are stimulating educational experiences. Delegates take from a Meeting a fuller understanding of how the Constitution was designed and how its design shapes our contemporary government and politics.

A Jefferson Meeting is also an exercise in civic participation. The citizens of your community will organize and carry out their Jefferson Meeting. By running their own Jefferson Meeting delegates exercise their right to assemble and discuss their government. Moreover, effective Jefferson Meetings emphasize the value in political life of procedures that allow for open debate. Meetings also emphasize the importance of tolerance and respect for persons with differing views and opinions.

A Jefferson Meeting can play an important role in building a stronger sense of community in your town. By bringing together a diverse group of citizens for a serious discussion of important issues, a Jefferson Meeting can kindle a stronger sense of shared life and purpose.

Finally, Jefferson Meetings are fun. While a Jefferson Meeting requires careful planning and involves discussion of important issues, the feeling of an overwhelming number of participants in such Meetings is that they are exciting, interesting, and fun.

Planning

Leadership

Organizing a community Jefferson Meeting is not a one-person job, and even if it were possible for one person to successfully take on such a job, it is preferable to involve a number of people in planning the Meeting. One approach to leadership and planning that has worked well is the creation of a "Council," for example "The Smithville Jefferson Meeting Council." Your Council should be made up of ten to fifteen community members who are interested in holding a Jefferson Meeting and willing to devote some time and effort to making the Meeting happen.

Your Council should reflect the diversity of your community as fully as possible. This means involving persons from the business community, labor unions, churches, the news media, schools, neighborhoods, and government. A good Council sends important messages to your community. It tells community members that your Jefferson Meeting is nonpartisan, that all kinds of people are welcome to participate, and that a number of important people in your town think a Jefferson Meeting is a worthwhile activity.

Once a Council is in place, the various aspects of organizing a Jefferson Meeting can be assigned to different members. You may want to create small groups to take care of raising funds, publicizing the Meeting, recruiting and selecting delegates, printing and mailing materials, arranging facilities, finding a keynote speaker and discussion leaders, and so forth. A person on your Council who is an effective fund-raiser can make the whole process of putting on a Meeting much easier. Look for people who have experience with writing grants, who have good connections with the business community, and who know how to make a "pitch" for your Meeting.

Spreading the Word

When the time and place of your Meeting have been set you will want to publicize the Meeting throughout the community. Some ways of doing this are obvious. For instance, you can prepare news releases on your Meeting and attempt to publicize the Meeting through newspapers, radio, and television. Having a member of the news media on your Council will be useful for this purpose. Probably just as important is to get the word about the Meeting out into all the little networks and grapevines that move information in your town: the Lions Club, the PTA, the union locals, neighborhood associations, the local Y, and so on.

To reach people and give them the concrete opportunity to express an interest in becoming a delegate to your Jefferson Meeting, you will need to print and distribute a brochure that describes the purpose, date, and place of the Meeting. Include in this brochure an application form that can be detached and returned to the Council by persons who wish to become delegates to the Meeting.

Delegate Selection

Members of the Council will make final decisions about who will be selected as delegates to the Meeting. In general, you can count on including all comers. But it is important to be sensitive to the fact that some potential delegates have agendas of their own for your Meeting, and theirs may not mesh well with yours. It should be made clear that your Meeting is concerned with certain issues related to the *structure* and *performance* of our government. You simply must not allow digressions into abortion, school prayer, and other such controversial issues. If a potential delegate seems unlikely to play by those rules, think carefully about his or her acceptance for participation.

Facilities

A Jefferson Meeting can be held in a variety of settings, but there are some general requirements to keep in mind. Issue committees need separate rooms for their meetings, and ideally pro and con groups within committees will have their own meeting rooms. If that many rooms are not easily available, try to find committee meeting rooms that will allow pro and con groups to separate and work without distracting each other. The plenary session should be held in an area that will comfortably accommodate all Meeting delegates. Keep in mind that many delegates will be getting up to speak during the plenary. The chairperson should probably have a podium and a microphone. Unless the plenary meeting room has exceptional acoustics at least one other microphone will be needed for delegates who will be speaking. Additional microphones will allow delegates to exchange ideas without having to climb over other delegates to reach a single microphone.

Program

Prepare a program that provides delegates with a schedule and agenda of the Meeting. You may want to supplement this information with a brief summary of the Meeting's rules of procedure, a list of your Council's members, an acknowledgment of persons and organizations who contributed to the Meeting, a list of discussion leaders, and a list of all the delegates.

Expenses

You can exercise a good deal of control over the expense of your Jefferson Meeting with the decisions you make about meals, facilities, and other things. Some items, though, are indispensable. Probably foremost among these necessary items are Jefferson Foundation Issue Discussion Guides, the individual texts of which are combined in this book. The guides are available in quantity, at seventy-five cents each, from The Jefferson Foundation, 1529 18th Street, N.W., Washington, D.C. 20036. These guides should be distributed to delegates a few weeks in advance of the Meeting, and ideally each delegate should receive discussion guides on all the issues to be discussed at the Meeting. This assures that each delegate has an opportunity for knowledgeable participation in discussion of his or her committee's issue *and* the other issues discussed during the plenary session.

Other expenses to budget for are the printing of Meeting brochures and programs, postage for mailing, rent (if necessary) for Meeting facilities and public address equipment, honoraria (if necessary) for the keynote speaker and discussion leaders, and any meals to be provided.

Fund Raising

There are a number of ways to raise the money needed to meet expenses. Delegates to community Jefferson Meetings have been asked, in some cases, to pay a registration fee of five dollars. Before establishing such a fee, consider its likely impact on your pool of potential delegates. If it seems likely that such a fee will prevent some persons from participating, you may want to avoid a fee or make a contribution optional.

Another fund-raising route is simply to ask individuals, organizations, and businesses to contribute to the Meeting. A Jefferson Meeting is a worthwhile community undertaking, and you can sell the idea to your state humanities council, local civic organizations, businesses, and foundations. Don't overlook the possibility of "in kind" rather than money support. Perhaps a local school building can be made available for your Meeting, or a public address system donated, or access to a copying machine provided.

It is in this area of fund-raising and finding "in kind" support that a good Council can be a real plus. That is a good thing to keep in mind when approaching members of the community about becoming members of your Council. If the "right" individuals become interested in organizing a Jefferson Meeting, they can make the Meeting much easier to organize and execute.

Step-by-Step Guide to the Community Jefferson Meeting

Roles in the Jefferson Meeting

There are a number of key roles to be played in a Jefferson Meeting. You should take care that the right people are chosen for them. Some of these roles are played by nondelegates whom you will recruit to help lead the Meeting. Others are played by persons who also participate as delegates.

Plenary Chairperson. The plenary chairperson calls the plenary session to order, presides over the debate, calls on speakers in turn, fields questions from the floor, and enforces time limits on speakers. This job calls for a firm hand, a sense of humor, tact, and poise. The chairperson must stand above the issues being discussed and should not express opinions about the issues. It is not important that the chairperson be a master of parliamentary procedure—the Meeting's rules of procedure are simple—but the chairperson must be consistent and fair. You may want to designate a secretary or timekeeper to assist the chairperson.

Discussion Leaders.   The work of the Jefferson Meeting begins in issue committees, and the work of the issue committees begins with a good discussion leader. Delegates to your Jefferson Meeting will be assigned to a particular issue committee—for instance, the committee on the president's term of office—on the basis of their expressed interest. When the members of each committee meet for their committee meetings, the discussion leader gets the work started by presenting a brief overview of the issue at hand, stimulates discussion, and answers questions about both the issue and the procedure for debating it. The objective at this stage of the issue committee meeting is to help delegates decide whether they favor or oppose the proposed change in the Constitution they are considering. These delegates then divide into "pro" and "con" groups within the committee and prepare presentations for the plenary session.

Experience has taught that humanities scholars, such as political scientists, historians, and philosophers, make good discussion leaders. You may want to contact qualified scholars such as these at a local college or university to enlist their help. If you decide to find discussion leaders elsewhere, you should look for persons who have, or will work to develop, real expertise about the issue to be discussed. Moreover, you should look for discussion leaders who have no axes to grind on the issues being considered, because the discussion leader must help both the pro and con groups in fashioning their arguments for the plenary session. In sum, discussion leaders need to be well-prepared, helpful, and neutral.

Floor Managers.   Once issue committees have divided into pro and con groups, each group needs the leadership of a floor manager. Your Council may select such managers ahead of time or let each pro and con group on each issue committee select their own floor manager from their own ranks. The floor manager coordinates the preparation of his or her group's delegates for the plenary session. This entails helping select delegates who will speak during the plenary, working with these speakers on the ideas and arguments to be presented in the plenary, and drawing up a "speakers list." This list will be given to the plenary chairperson so he or she can call on appropriate speakers during plenary debates on each committee's issue.

Delegates. The Jefferson Meeting is unlike other conferences because the delegates themselves are responsible for familiarizing themselves with the issues and organizing and presenting a coherent debate. It is a unique opportunity for citizens to exchange ideas and learn from each other. The interaction between people from different backgrounds adds enormously to the intellectual stimulation of the Meeting and enhances its role as a community builder.

Attracting a diverse group of delegates is the biggest challenge in organizing your Jefferson Meeting, but the basic strategy is simple: you should let as many people as possible know about the Meeting and the opportunity to participate. Over and over again, participants in Jefferson Meetings have commented on how an interesting mixture of delegates really *made* the Meeting they attended. So don't hesitate to beat the bushes, and give special attention to attracting participants who either doubt (mistakenly) their ability to participate or might feel they would not be welcome.

Basic Steps in the Jefferson Meeting

Setting the Agenda. The Jefferson Foundation has prepared Issue Discussion Guides on a number of issues and, because five or six issues is the maximum number that can be discussed at a Jefferson Meeting, a decision will need to be made about which issues to include. The planners of the Meeting can either set the agenda or ask potential delegates to choose from a list of potential topics those they find most interesting. Each approach has its strengths and drawbacks. If the Meeting's agenda is set by its planners, you avoid the work of soliciting and tabulating the issue preferences of delegates. This approach is simpler, but it runs the risk of narrowing the pool of potential delegates by ruling out an issue that some might find especially interesting. Presenting a list of possible issues and asking delegates to specify which they want to discuss makes it certain that the agenda reflects their interests. Since you will need to know the issue preferences of delegates to assign them to issue committees, this approach has much to commend it.

The Opening Session. The opening session of your Jefferson Meeting gets things rolling. The entire delegation meets for a brief welcoming speech and a keynote address. The welcoming address should give delegates a preview of what lies ahead. This is a good opportunity to summarize the schedule of the Meeting. The keynote address should touch on constitutional themes and help set the tone for the Meeting.

Issue Committee Meetings. Following the opening session, delegates meet in their various issue committees. Each committee should have about twenty-five or thirty members. Committee meetings begin with a presentation by the discussion leader of an overview of the issue being considered. This is followed by a discussion of the committee's issue. Committee members should use this discussion to explore their issue thoroughly and to decide whether they favor or oppose the constitutional change their committee is examining. For example, a committee on judicial tenure and accountability would probably discuss how accountable a judge should be to public opinion. Should a judge do what the public wants when there is strong public opinion? Or should a judge do what he or she believes is just, despite public opinion? Should a judge serve for life "during good behavior" in order for society to benefit from his or her growing experience? Or should a judge serve a fixed term in order to assure the entry of fresh ideas and perspectives into the judiciary?

After committee members have had such a discussion they will be ready to divide into pro and con groups. It is desirable to have pro and con groups of equal size, but that won't always happen. At this point each pro and con group is led by a floor manager. The floor manager helps his or her group prepare for the plenary session. Assume that each pro and con group will be allowed to present eight speakers in the plenary session. The floor manager helps his or her group decide who will speak and what each speaker will say. It is important for each group to orchestrate its plenary presentation so all the key points in their argument are presented with a minimum of repetition. Each committee's discussion leader will "float" back and forth between the pro and con groups, answering questions and helping with the development of ideas and arguments.

An issue committee meeting should last about three hours. This allows for the discussion leader's presentation, discussion by the whole committee, division into pro and con groups, and preparation for the plenary session. At the end of the committee meetings, floor managers should give the plenary chairperson a list of group members chosen to present their group's arguments in the plenary.

The Plenary Session. The plenary session is the focal point of the Meeting. At the beginning of the plenary session the plenary chairperson should briefly review the schedule of the plenary session and summarize the rules of procedure for presentations by committees and for general debate. Each issue is then called to the floor in turn, with initial presentations by the designated pro and con speakers from the relevant committee. Designated speakers should be called, using the speakers lists, in an alternating pattern: pro then con, pro then con, and so on. These speakers are followed by discussion among all delegates. Each issue should be given a maximum of seventy-five minutes for presentation and discussion. This time should be allotted as follows:

3 minutes each for eight pro speakers = 24 minutes
3 minutes each for eight con speakers = 24 minutes
Open discussion by all delegates,
2 minutes for each speaker   = 25 minutes

Pro and con speakers may yield to questions. Time spent answering a question is counted as part of the three minutes given to the speaker. Speakers should be careful not to yield to too many questions because this can disrupt the flow of their presentations.

The amount of time given to each issue could be shortened by allowing for either fewer speakers or giving each speaker less time. Sixty minutes is probably the minimum that should be allotted to the discussion on an issue.

The plenary chairperson presides over the Meeting and recognizes speakers, first from the speakers list and then from the floor. The chair should be tactful but firm in holding speakers to their time limits. The atmosphere of the plenary, however, should be kept as informal as possible in order to encourage the free exchange of ideas. It is not a good idea to take votes on any of the issues being discussed. While a Jefferson Meeting looks superficially like a debate, it is, in reality, a cooperative venture in which citizens learn about the Constitution through discussing it. Anything that raises the idea of "winners" and "losers," such as voting, is likely to undermine a desirable spirit of cooperation.

Schedules

A good schedule for your Meeting is one that gives most members of your community a chance to participate. That means scheduling around typical work hours and avoiding conflicts with other important events. A typical schedule would be as follows:

Friday

4:30 to 6:30 —Registration
6:00 —Potluck, served dinner, or snack (cheese, crackers, and so forth)
6:30 —Welcome and Keynote Speech
7:00 to 10:00 —Issue Committee Meetings

Saturday

9:00 —Plenary Session Begins

9:00 to 10:15 —Discussion of Issue 1
10:15 to 11:30 —Discussion of Issue 2
11:30 to 12:45 —Discussion of Issue 3
12:45 to 1:30 —Lunch
 1:30 to 2:45 —Discussion of Issue 4
 2:45 to 4:00 —Discussion of Issue 5
 4:00 to 5:15 —Discussion of Issue 6
 5:15 —Plenary adjourns, reception and conversation

This Saturday schedule is a rather demanding one. You may decide to consider fewer than six issues, have lunch earlier, schedule ten-minute breaks, and so forth. A good community Meeting can be held in one day, if you limit the agenda to two or three issues. In a one-day format, issue committees meet in the morning and the plenary is held in the afternoon. A good rule of thumb for making decisions about the number of issues to be discussed, and in what format, is to maintain a ratio of one issue for every twenty-five or thirty delegates.

The Jefferson Meeting in the Classroom: A Guide for Teachers

Why Have a Classroom Jefferson Meeting?

In his "Report of the Commissioners for the University of Virginia" (1818), Thomas Jefferson listed among his goals for the student the following:

> To know his rights; to exercise with order and justice those he retains; to choose with discretion the fiduciary of those he delegates; and to notice their conduct with diligence, with candor, and judgment. . . .

Among Jefferson's goals for educators were

> . . . to develop the reasoning faculties of our youth, enlarge their minds, cultivate their morals and instill into them the precepts of value and order.

The Jefferson Meeting seeks to reflect these educational principles. Its emphasis on participation in self-regulating committees, a critical awareness of governmental institutions and their history, and on forming and articulating opinions on important current issues makes it an exercise in citizenship skills as well as a learning device.

Participation in a Jefferson Meeting gives students the opportunity to develop and apply important analytical skills. During committee meetings and debates, students must select, research, and defend a position on a constitutional issue. They must identify and clarify issues, ask appropriate and searching questions, and evaluate the consequences of alternative positions. Working in groups develops interpersonal skills such as cooperating with others, giving and receiving constructive criticism, and respecting the opinions of peers.

Planning

When to Have a Jefferson Meeting

The Jefferson Meeting should be used as a supplement to course work on constitutional history and American government. While the timing of the Meeting is best left up to the teacher, it will be most effective after students have developed a knowledge of the Constitution itself, the structure of American government, and the events and circumstances surrounding the Philadelphia Convention of 1787.

To get a preliminary idea of the steps and days involved in a classroom Jefferson Meeting, review the timetable below. There is nothing hard and fast about this timetable. It can be adjusted according to the abilities of students, schedule constraints, and other factors.

Timetable for the Jefferson Meeting in the Classroom

Days 1 and 2:

An opinion poll is used to stimulate thinking about issues.
Issues raised by the poll are identified and discussed.
The concept of the Jefferson Meeting is introduced.
Issues to be placed on the Meeting's agenda are selected.
Students choose the issue they wish to explore and are placed on appropriate committees.

Days 2 and 3:

Issue committees meet, discuss their respective issues, and begin research.

Day 4:

Each issue committee divides into a "pro" group that favors a particular proposal for constitutional change and a "con" group that opposes such a proposal.
Pro and con groups continue research.

Days 5 and 6:

Pro and con groups prepare their presentations for the plenary session and prepare a list of committee members that will speak during the plenary session.

Plenary Days:

Plenary sessions occur during which each issue on the agenda is discussed in turn, with pro and con groups making presentations, followed by questions and comments from other students.

Wrap Up:

Arguments presented in the plenary session are summarized and discussed.

Preparing Students for the Jefferson Meeting

One good way to introduce constitutional issues to the class and stimulate student interest in the Jefferson Meeting is to duplicate the opinion poll on page 189 and distribute it to the students. The issues raised in the opinion poll items are the ones presented in the preceding chapters and in Jefferson Foundation Issue Discussion Guides (each guide contains the text of one of the preceding chapters), which may be purchased for seventy-five cents each from The Jefferson Foundation, 1529 18th Street, N.W., Washington, D.C. 20036. Discussion of proposals for constitutional change should be easy to stimulate once students have been asked to express opinions about such issues as lengthening the president's term of office, abolishing the electoral college, setting constitutional limits on the length of service of senators and representatives, curbing the expenses of political campaigns, and other issues.

Once student interest in constitutional change has been created, either through the use of the opinion poll or another approach, students should be introduced to the concept of the Jefferson Meeting. Explain that the Meeting is an opportunity for them to debate constitutional issues in the way the framers of the Constitution did. Students should also be told that these issues are currently under consideration in the nation. This will help them see that a Jefferson Meeting is not merely an exercise in studying history but also a chance to participate in a national debate about current problems and proposed solutions.

In explaining to students how the Meeting will work, it is a good idea to tell them how they will be evaluated, what each phase of the Meeting will require of them, and what writing assignments, if any, will follow the Meeting. Students should also be told that they are expected to participate, to research issues carefully, and to respect and closely follow the contributions of their fellow student-delegates.

OPINION POLL
CONSTITUTIONAL ISSUES: WHAT IS YOUR OPINION?

Give your opinion about each statement by checking the appropriate box.

1. The electoral college should be abolished so voters can elect the president directly.
   Agree _____ Disagree _____ No opinion _____

2. A single six-year term would make the president more effective.
   Agree _____ Disagree _____ No opinion _____

3. Longer terms for members of the House of Representatives would make Congress more effective.
   Agree _____ Disagree _____ No opinion _____

4. The Constitution should set a retirement age for all federal judges, including justices of the U.S. Supreme Court.
   Agree _____ Disagree _____ No opinion _____

5. Rather than being appointed by the president and approved by the U.S. Senate, federal judges, including justices of the U.S. Supreme Court, should be elected by voters.
   Agree _____ Disagree _____ No opinion _____

6. The president should be able to veto specific parts of a bill and sign the rest of it into law, instead of having to veto the entire bill.
   Agree _____ Disagree _____ No opinion _____

7. Congress should be able to exercise its own veto over the executive branch when it disapproves of the way the executive branch is implementing the provisions of a law.
   Agree _____ Disagree _____ No opinion _____

8. There should be some limit placed on the number of terms a member of Congress may serve.
   Agree _____ Disagree _____ No opinion _____

9. Citizens should be able to enact laws and/or amend the Constitution by a direct popular vote.
   Agree _____ Disagree _____ No opinion _____

10. The Constitution should be amended to allow Congress to put limits on campaign spending and contributions.
    Agree _____ Disagree _____ No opinion _____

11. A constitutional convention should be called for the purpose of proposing amendments to the Constitution.
    Agree _____ Disagree _____ No opinion _____

Step-by-Step Guide to the Jefferson Meeting in the Classroom

Student Roles in the Jefferson Meeting

Students play the key roles in the classroom Jefferson Meeting, so care should be taken to see that the right students play them. Students can be chosen to play these roles by vote of the class, volunteering, or appointment by the teacher. Some of the roles require advance preparation and will have to be assigned in advance. Others cannot be assigned until the agenda has been set and issue committees have begun their work.

Plenary Chairperson. This job calls for a firm hand, a sense of humor, and poise. The plenary chair presides over the debate, calls on designated speakers in turn, fields questions from the floor, and keeps time (with the help of a secretary or timekeeper). The chairperson has to be somewhat removed from the debate and should not express opinions. This role presents a challenge that is appropriate for a student. It may be better played, however, by the teacher or a guest.

Discussion Leader/Reporter. Each issue committee needs a discussion leader. This is a very important job. Each discussion leader is responsible for introducing the committee's issue to his or her committee and explaining to them how it relates to the larger philosophical principles of our government. Discussion leaders should be worked closely with to make sure they understand the concepts to be conveyed.

The first meeting of each issue committee will be directed by its discussion leader, who will present a summary of the history and significance of the issue. He or she will then lead a discussion and answer questions about the issue. After this first committee meeting, the other committee members will be deciding whether they want to argue for or against a proposed change in the Constitution and dividing into pro and con groups. After pro and con groups have formed, the discussion leader should "float" between the pro and con groups, offering help to each group in the preparation of its plenary presentation.

During the plenary session, discussion leaders become reporters. The job of each reporter is to closely follow plenary debate about his or her issue committee's topic and prepare a presentation about that debate for the wrap-up session. This presentation will review the arguments presented, give an account of how the pros and cons interacted, and put the debate into a larger perspective by relating it to history or current events.

Floor Manager. There will be two floor managers in each issue committee: one for the pro side and one for the con side. The floor managers may be elected by their fellow pro and con members within an issue committee. Each floor manager is responsible for lining up five speakers (or another number chosen by the teacher) to present the views of his or her group during the plenary session. Each speaker is limited to three minutes, so the floor manager should organize the speakers and their presentations in such a way that all the main points in the argument are effectively presented with a minimum of repetition. Each floor manager prepares a speakers list containing the names of the group members who will speak during the plenary. This list is given to the plenary chairperson before the plenary session begins. Floor managers may also be speakers.

Student Role Descriptions. "Student Role Descriptions" for the plenary chairperson, discussion leaders/reporters, floor managers, and delegates are given at the end of this discussion. These descriptions should be distributed to the students.

Four Basic Steps of the Jefferson Meeting

Setting the Agenda. The agenda is the list of issues the class will study and debate. The teacher may set the agenda or have students set the agenda after the class opinion poll has been conducted. The number of issues to be discussed is up to the teacher. Generally speaking, a plenary session discussion of one issue will require one class period (assuming a fifty to sixty minute period). After the agenda is set, the students should be asked to list, in order of preference, two issues on the agenda they most want to consider in depth. Based on their choices, issue committees of equal size may be formed, trying to balance personalities and viewpoints as much as possible.

Issue Committee Meetings. Once the agenda has been set and students have been assigned to issue committees, students meet in their respective issue committees to prepare for the debate in the plenary session. Each issue committee will complete the following tasks:

1. Discuss the assigned issue under the leadership of the committee discussion leader.
2. Read the appropriate Issue Discussion Guide and/or do other research on the topic.

3. After members of each committee have formed individual opinions about their issues, the committee will divide into pro and con groups, with the pro group favoring a proposed change in the Constitution and the con group opposing the change.

4. Under the leadership of its floor manager, each pro and each con group within each issue committee prepares speeches for the plenary. Each floor manager prepares a speakers list and submits it to the plenary chairperson.

The Plenary Session. The plenary session is the main event of the Jefferson Meeting. For the plenary session the classroom/auditorium should be arranged in theater style with a podium and chairs for the speakers at the front. The plenary will be called to order by the chairperson. Using the speakers lists submitted by the floor managers, the chairperson will call all speakers for the issue under consideration to the front, seating the pro group on one side of the podium and the con group on the other. Starting with the pro side, the chairperson will call each speaker to the podium for his or her three minute speech, alternating between pro and con speakers until the speakers list has been exhausted. The timekeeper and/or clock should be in full view of both the chairperson and speakers. When the speakers list has been exhausted, the chairperson will invite questions and comments from the floor. Everyone can participate in this portion of the plenary session. All comments and questions must be kept to two minutes. The chairperson should try to create an informal, spontaneous atmosphere to encourage students from every part of the room to get involved in the discussion. A typical plenary debate on one issue would last fifty minutes, with five pro and five con speeches, each lasting three minutes (total of thirty minutes), followed by twenty minutes of comments and questions from the floor.

It is important to establish the procedure for the plenary debate ahead of time. A summary of plenary rules is provided at the end of this discussion.

Wrap-Up Activities. The wrap-up session is a chance for students to summarize and synthesize the debate of the plenary session. Begin with reporters for each issue reviewing the arguments presented in the plenary. These reports should be limited to about five minutes each. These presentations can be followed by a discussion of how the Meeting was similar to and unlike the original Constitutional Convention, discussion of other constitutional issues, and so forth. Having students complete the opinion poll again will stimulate discussion of how participating in a Jefferson Meeting changed students' opinions about certain issues. The teacher may also want to talk about the format and rules of the Jefferson Meeting, for it conveys important implicit lessons about the importance to a free society of discussions in which all sides of an issue may be examined in a setting in which differing points of view are respected and tolerated.

Alternative Settings. The most obvious setting for a Jefferson Meeting for students is within the confines of one classroom. Some other alternatives that have been tried and worked well include a multi-class Meeting (bringing together several classes), a multi-school Meeting (now an annual event in some areas), and a school-community Meeting. The last option is especially worthy of consideration. Students who have become acquainted with the Jefferson Meeting in their classrooms can definitely hold their own with adults in such a Meeting.

Student Role Descriptions

Plenary Chairperson

The plenary chairperson will:

1. Preside over the plenary session debate.
2. Call on designated speakers in turn.
3. Recognize speakers from the floor.
4. Hold speakers to time limits.

Discussion Leader/Reporter

During issue committee meetings the discussion leader/reporter will:

1. Act as a committee coordinator by leading the initial discussion and answering questions about the committee's issue.
2. Help to coordinate research and division of the committee into pro and con groups.
3. Float between the pro and con groups, making sure delegates are covering the essentials in preparing the plenary presentations.
4. Coordinate the whole committee's presentation for the plenary.

During the plenary session the discussion leader/reporter will:

1. Observe the plenary debate and prepare a presentation on his or her committee's issue for the wrap-up session.

During the wrap-up session the discussion leader/reporter will:

1. Summarize the debate of his or her committee's issue, give an account of how the pros and cons interacted and, where possible, relate the debate to current issues in the news.

Floor Manager

Each floor manager will:

1. Lead a group (pro or con) in developing arguments to be presented in the plenary session.
2. Help a group develop its plenary presentation, with special attention given to arranging the group's presentation in such a way that the group's views are presented effectively.
3. Prepare the speakers list for a group. A list of speakers (the teacher will specify the number of speakers) should be given to the plenary chairperson before the plenary discussion of the issue.

Floor managers are also delegates, and need to read the delegate description too.

Delegate

Student delegates will:

1. Choose or be assigned to an issue committee.

During issue committee meetings delegates will:

1. Take part in an initial discussion and do preliminary research about the constitutional issue under consideration.
2. Choose a position (pro or con) on the issue being discussed.
3. Help set debate strategy within pro or con group by listing arguments to use in the plenary session and helping determine the order of speeches and speakers.
4. Go over the rules for the plenary session.

During the plenary session delegates will:

1. Be speaking, listening, and asking questions. In sum, keeping an open mind and learning.

Rules for the Plenary Session

Time Rules

1. Each speaker from a pro or con group has ____ minutes to present his or her argument to the delegates.
2. If a speaker yields to questions from the floor, time will not be counted while the question is being asked. The answer will be counted as part of his or her three minutes.
3. Following the pro and con speeches for each issue, all delegates

may speak. Questions and comments will be limited to _____ minutes for each delegate.

Procedure

1. The plenary session is called to order by the chairperson.
2. Speakers for the first issue are called to the front and seated.
3. Starting with the pro side, the chairperson will call each speaker to the podium for his or her presentation. Speakers are called in the order provided by the speakers lists, alternating between pro and con.
4. After the speakers list for an issue has been exhausted, the floor is opened for questions and discussion.

Steps 1-4 are repeated for each issue.

5. The chairperson keeps order, enforces time limits, and recognizes speakers.

The Constitution of the United States of America

The Preamble

We the People of the United States, in Order to form a more perfect Union, establish Justice, insure domestic Tranquility, provide for the common defence, promote the general Welfare, and secure the Blessings of Liberty to ourselves and our Posterity, do ordain and establish this Constitution for the United States of America.

Article I

Section 1

All legislative Powers herein granted shall be vested in a Congress of the United States, which shall consist of a Senate and House of Representatives.

Section 2

1. The House of Representatives shall be composed of Members chosen every second Year by the People of the Several States, and the Electors in each State shall have the Qualifications requisite for Electors of the most numerous Branch of the State Legislature.

2. No Person shall be a Representative who shall not have attained to the age of twenty five Years, and been seven Years a Citizen of the United States, and who shall not, when elected, be an Inhabitant of that State in which he shall be chosen.

3. [Representatives and direct Taxes shall be apportioned among the several States which may be included within this Union, according to their respective Numbers, which shall be determined by adding to the whole Number of free Persons, including those bound to Service for a Term of Years, and excluding Indians not taxed, three fifths of all other Persons.][1] The actual Enumeration shall be made within three Years after the first Meeting of the Congress of the United States, and within

every subsequent Term of ten Years, in such Manner as they shall by Law direct. The Number of Representatives shall not exceed one for every thirty Thousand, but each State shall have at Least one Representative; and until such enumeration shall be made, the State of New Hampshire shall be entitled to chuse three, Massachusetts eight, Rhode-Island and Providence Plantations one, Connecticut five, New-York six, New Jersey four, Pennsylvania eight, Delaware one, Maryland six, Virginia ten, North Carolina five, South Carolina five, and Georgia three.

4. When vacancies happen in the Representation from any State, the Executive Authority thereof shall issue Writs of Election to fill such Vacancies.

5. The House of Representatives shall chuse their Speaker and other Officers; and shall have the sole Power of Impeachment.

Section 3

1. The Senate of the United States shall be composed of two Senators from each State, [chosen by the Legislature thereof,] [2] for six Years; and each Senator shall have one Vote.

2. Immediately after they shall be assembled in Consequence of the first Election, they shall be divided as equally as may be into three Classes. The Seats of the Senators of the first Class shall be vacated at the Expiration of the second Year, of the second Class at the Expiration of the fourth Year, and of the third Class at the Expiration of the sixth Year, so that one third may be chosen every second Year; [and if Vacancies happen by Resignation, or otherwise, during the Recess of the Legislature of any State, the Executive thereof may make temporary Appointments until the next Meeting of the Legislature, which shall then fill such Vacancies.] [3]

3. No Person shall be a Senator who shall not have attained to the Age of thirty Years, and been nine Years a Citizen of the United States, and who shall not, when elected, be an Inhabitant of the State for which he shall be chosen.

4. The Vice President of the United States shall be President of the Senate, but shall have no Vote, unless they be equally divided.

5. The Senate shall chuse their other Officers, and also a President pro tempore, in the Absence of the Vice President, or when he shall exercise the Office of President of the United States.

6. The Senate shall have the sole Power to try all Impeachments. When sitting for that Purpose, they shall be on Oath or Affirmation. When the President of the United States is tried the Chief Justice shall preside: And no Person shall be convicted without the Concurrence of two thirds of the Members present.

7. Judgment in Cases of Impeachment shall not extend further than to removal from Office, and disqualification to hold and enjoy any Office of honor, Trust or Profit under the United States: but the Party convicted shall nevertheless be liable and subject to Indictment, Trial, Judgment and Punishment, according to Law.

Section 4

1. The Times, Places and Manner of holding Elections for Senators and Representatives, shall be prescribed in each State by the Legislature thereof; but the Congress may at any time by Law make or alter such Regulations, except as to the Places of chusing Senators.

2. The Congress shall assemble at least once in every Year, and such Meeting shall [be on the first Monday in December],[4] unless they shall by Law appoint a different Day.

Section 5

1. Each House shall be the Judge of the Elections, Returns and Qualifications of its own Members, and a Majority of each shall constitute a Quorum to do Business; but a smaller Number may adjourn from day to day, and may be authorized to compel the Attendance of absent Members, in such Manner, and under such Penalties as each House may provide.

2. Each House may determine the Rules of its Proceedings, punish its Members for disorderly Behaviour, and, with the Concurrence of two thirds, expel a Member.

3. Each House shall keep a Journal of its Proceedings, and from time to time publish the same, excepting such Parts as may in their Judgment require Secrecy; and the Yeas and Nays of the Members of either House on any question shall, at the Desire of one fifth of those Present, be entered on the Journal.

4. Neither House, during the Session of Congress, shall, without the Consent of the other, adjourn for more than three days, nor to any other Place than that in which the two Houses shall be sitting.

Section 6

1. The Senators and Representatives shall receive a Compensation for their Services, to be ascertained by Law, and paid out of the Treasury of the United States. They shall in all Cases, except Treason, Felony and Breach of the Peace, be privileged from Arrest during their Attendance at the Session of their respective Houses, and in going to and returning from the same; and for any Speech or Debate in either House, they shall not be questioned in any other Place.

2. No Senator or Representative shall, during the Time for which he was elected, be appointed to any civil Office under the Authority of the United States, which shall have been encreased during such time; and no Person holding any Office under the United States, shall be a Member of either House during his Continuance in Office.

Section 7

1. All Bills for raising Revenue shall originate in the House of Representatives; but the Senate may propose or concur with amendments as on other Bills.

2. Every Bill which shall have passed the House of Representatives and the Senate, shall, before it become a Law, be presented to the President of the United States; If he approve he shall sign it, but if not he shall return it, with his Objections to that House in which it shall have originated, who shall enter the Objections at large on their Journal, and proceed to reconsider it. If after such Reconsideration two thirds of that House shall agree to pass the Bill, it shall be sent, together with the Objections, to the other House, by which it shall likewise be reconsidered, and if approved by two thirds of that House, it shall become a Law. But in all such Cases the Votes of both Houses shall be determined by yeas and Nays, and the Names of the Persons voting for and against the Bill shall be entered on the Journal of each House respectively. If any Bill shall not be returned by the President within ten Days (Sunday excepted) after it shall have been presented to him, the Same shall be a Law, in like Manner as if he had signed it, unless the Congress by their Adjournment prevent its Return, in which Case it shall not be a Law.

3. Every Order, Resolution, or Vote to which the Concurrence of the Senate and House of Representatives may be necessary (except on a question of Adjournment) shall be presented to the President of the United States; and before the Same shall take Effect, shall be approved by him, or being disapproved by him, shall be repassed by two thirds of the Senate and House of Representatives, according to the Rules and Limitations prescribed in the Case of a Bill.

Section 8

1. The Congress shall have Power To lay and collect Taxes, Duties, Imposts and Excises, to pay the Debts and provide for the common Defence and general Welfare of the United States; but all Duties, Imposts and Excises shall be uniform throughout the United States;

2. To borrow Money on the credit of the United States;

3. To regulate Commerce with foreign Nations, and among the several States, and with the Indian Tribes;

4. To establish an uniform Rule of Naturalization, and uniform Laws on the subject of Bankruptcies throughout the United States;

5. To coin Money, regulate the Value thereof, and of foreign Coin, and fix the Standard of Weights and Measures;

6. To provide for the Punishment of counterfeiting the Securities and current Coin of the United States;

7. To establish Post Offices and post Roads;

8. To promote the Progress of Science and useful Arts, by securing for limited Times to Authors and Inventors the exclusive Right to their respective Writings and Discoveries;

9. To constitute Tribunals inferior to the supreme Court;

10. To define and punish Piracies and Felonies committed on the high Seas, and Offences against the Law of Nations;

11. To declare War, grant Letters of Marque and Reprisal, and make Rules concerning Captures on Land and Water;

12. To Raise and Support Armies, but no Appropriation of Money to that Use shall be for a longer Term than two Years;

13. To provide and maintain a Navy;

14. To make Rules for the Government and Regulation of the land and naval Forces;

15. To provide for calling forth the Militia to execute the Laws of the Union, suppress Insurrections and repel Invasions;

16. To provide for organizing, arming, and disciplining, the Militia, and for governing such Part of them as may be employed in the Service of the United States, reserving to the States respectively, the Appointment of the Officers, and the Authority of training the Militia according to the discipline prescribed by Congress;

17. To exercise exclusive Legislation in all Cases whatsoever, over such District (not exceeding ten Miles square) as may, by Cession of Particular States, and the Acceptance of Congress, become the Seat of the Government of the United States, and to exercise like Authority over all Places purchased by the Consent of the Legislature of the State in which the Same shall be, for the Erection of Forts, Magazines, Arsenals, dock-Yards, and other needful Buildings;—and

18. To make all Laws which shall be necessary and proper for carrying into Execution the foregoing Powers, and all other Powers vested by this Constitution in the Government of the United States, or in any Department or Officer thereof.

Section 9

1. The Migration or Importation of such Persons as any of the States now existing shall think proper to admit, shall not be prohibited by the Congress prior to the Year one thousand eight hundred and eight, but a

Tax or duty may be imposed on such Importation, not exceeding ten dollars for each Person.

2. The Privilege of the Writ of Habeas Corpus shall not be suspended, unless when in Cases of Rebellion or Invasion the public Safety may require it.

3. No Bill of Attainder or ex post facto Law shall be passed.

4. No capitation, or other direct, Tax shall be laid, unless in Proportion to the Census of Enumeration herein before directed to be taken.[5]

5. No Tax or Duty shall be laid on Articles exported from any State.

6. No Preference shall be given by any Regulation of Commerce or Revenue to the Ports of one State over those of another; nor shall Vessels bound to, or from, one State, be obliged to enter, clear or pay Duties in another.

7. No Money shall be drawn from the Treasury, but in Consequence of Appropriations made by Law; and a regular Statement and Account of the Receipts and Expenditures of all public Money shall be published from time to time.

8. No Title of Nobility shall be granted by the United States: And no Person holding any Office of Profit or Trust under them, shall, without the Consent of the Congress, accept of any present, Emolument, Office, or Title, of any kind whatever, from any King, Prince or foreign State.

Section 10

1. No State shall enter into any Treaty, Alliance, or Confederation; grant Letters of Marque and Reprisal; coin Money; emit Bills of Credit; make any Thing but gold and silver Coin a Tender in Payment of Debts; pass any Bill of Attainder, ex post facto Law, or Law impairing the Obligation of Contracts, or grant any Title of Nobility.

2. No State shall, without the Consent of the Congress, lay any Imposts or Duties on Imports or Exports, except what may be absolutely necessary for executing its inspection Laws: and the net Produce of all Duties and Imposts, laid by any State on Imports or Exports, shall be for the Use of the Treasury of the United States; and all such Laws shall be subject to the Revision and Controul of the Congress.

3. No State shall, without the Consent of Congress, lay any Duty of Tonnage, keep Troops, or Ships of War in time of Peace, enter into any Agreement or Compact with another State, or with a foreign Power, or engage in War, unless actually invaded, or in such imminent Danger as will not admit of delay.

Article II

Section 1

1. The executive Power shall be vested in a President of the United States of America. He shall hold his Office during the Term of four Years, and together with the Vice President, chosen for the same Term, be elected, as follows.

2. Each State shall appoint, in such Manner as the Legislature thereof may direct, a Number of Electors, equal to the whole Number of Senators and Representatives to which the State may be entitled in the Congress: but no Senator or Representative, or Person holding an Office of Trust or Profit under the United States, shall be appointed an Elector.

3. [The Electors shall meet in their respective States, and vote by Ballot for two Persons, of whom one at least shall not be an Inhabitant of the same State with themselves. And they shall make a List of all the Persons voted for, and of the Number of Votes for each; which List they shall sign and certify, and transmit sealed to the Seat of the Government of the United States, directed to the President of the Senate. The President of the Senate shall, in the Presence of the Senate and House of Representatives, open all the Certificates, and the Votes shall then be counted. The Person having the greatest Number of Votes shall be the President, if such Number be a Majority of the whole Number of Electors appointed; and if there be more than one who have such Majority, and have an equal Number of Votes, then the House of Representatives shall Immediately chuse by Ballot one of them for President; and if no Person have a Majority, then from the five highest on the list the said House shall in like Manner chuse the President. But in chusing the President, the Votes shall be taken by States, the Representation from each State having one Vote; a quorum for this Purpose shall consist of a Member or Members from two thirds of the States, and a Majority of all the States shall be necessary to a Choice. In every Case, after the Choice of the President, the Person having the greatest Number of Votes of the Electors shall be the Vice President. But if there should remain two or more who have equal Votes, the Senate shall chuse from them by Ballot the Vice President.][6]

4. The Congress may determine the Time of chusing the Electors, and the Day on which they shall give their Votes; which Day shall be the same throughout the United States.

5. No Person except a natural born Citizen, or a Citizen of the United States, at the time of the Adoption of this Constitution, shall be eligible to the Office of President; neither shall any Person be eligible to

that Office who shall not have attained to the Age of thirty five Years, and been fourteen Years a Resident within the United States.

6. In Case of the Removal of the President from Office, or of his Death, Resignation, or Inability to discharge the Powers and Duties of the said Office,[7] the Same shall devolve on the Vice President, and the Congress may by Law provide for the Case of Removal, Death, Resignation or Inability, both of the President and Vice President, declaring what Officer shall then act as President, and such Officer shall act accordingly, until the Disability be removed, or a President shall be elected.

7. The President shall, at stated Times, receive for his Services, a Compensation, which shall neither be encreased nor diminished during the Period for which he shall have been elected, and he shall not receive within that Period any other Emolument from the United States, or any of them.

8. Before he enter on the Execution of his Office, he shall take the following Oath or Affirmation:—"I do solemnly swear (or affirm) that I will faithfully execute the Office of President of the United States, and will to the best of my Ability, preserve, protect and defend the Constitution of the United States."

Section 2

1. The President shall be Commander in Chief of the Army and Navy of the United States, and of the Militia of the several States, when called into the actual Service of the United States; he may require the Opinion, in writing, of the principal Officer in each of the executive Departments, upon any Subject relating to the Duties of their respective Offices, and he shall have Power to grant Reprieves and Pardons for Offenses against the United States, except in Cases of Impeachment.

2. He shall have Power, by and with the Advice and Consent of the Senate, to make Treaties, provided two thirds of the Senators present concur; and he shall nominate, and by and with the Advice and Consent of the Senate, shall appoint Ambassadors, other public Ministers and Consuls, Judges of the supreme Court, and all other Officers of the United States, whose Appointments are not herein otherwise provided for, and which shall be established by Law: but the Congress may by Law vest the Appointment of such inferior Officers, as they think proper, in the President alone, in the Courts of Law, or in the Heads of Departments.

3. The President shall have Power to fill up all Vacancies that may happen during the Recess of the Senate, by granting Commissions which shall expire at the End of their next Session.

The Constitution of the United States of America

Section 3

He shall from time to time give to the Congress Information of the State of the Union, and recommend to their Consideration such Measures as he shall judge necessary and expedient; he may, on extraordinary Occasions, convene both Houses, or either of them, and in Case of Disagreement between them, with Respect to the Time of Adjournment, he may adjourn them to such Time as he shall think proper; he shall receive Ambassadors and other public Ministers; he shall take Care that the Laws be faithfully executed, and shall Commission all the Officers of the United States.

Section 4

The President, Vice President and all Civil Officers of the United States, shall be removed from office on Impeachment for, and Conviction of, Treason, Bribery, or other high Crimes and Misdemeanors.

Article III

Section 1

The judicial Power of the United States, shall be vested in one supreme Court, and in such inferior Courts as the Congress may from time to time ordain and establish. The Judges, both of the supreme and inferior Courts, shall hold their Offices during good Behaviour, and shall, at stated Times, receive for their Services, a Compensation, which shall not be diminished during their Continuance in Office.

Section 2

1. The judicial Power shall extend to all Cases, in Law and Equity, arising under this Constitution, the Laws of the United States, and Treaties made, or which shall be made, under their Authority; — to all Cases affecting Ambassadors, other public Ministers and Consuls; — to all Cases of admiralty and maritime Jurisdiction; — to Controversies to which the United States shall be a Party; — to Controversies between two or more States; — between a State and Citizens of another State;[8] — between Citizens of different States; — between Citizens of the same State claiming Lands under Grants of different States, and between a State, or the Citizens thereof, and foreign States, Citizens or Subjects.[8]

2. In all Cases affecting Ambassadors, other public Ministers and Consuls, and those in which a State shall be Party, the supreme Court shall have original Jurisdiction. In all the other Cases before mentioned, the supreme Court shall have appellate Jurisdiction, both as to Law and

205

Fact, with such Exceptions, and under such Regulations as the Congress shall make.

3. The Trial of all Crimes, except in cases of Impeachment, shall be by Jury; and such Trial shall be held in the State where the said Crimes shall have been committed; but when not committed within any State, the Trial shall be at such Place or Places as the Congress may by Law have directed.

Section 3

1. Treason against the United States, shall consist only in levying War against them, or in adhering to their Enemies, giving them Aid and Comfort. No Person shall be convicted of Treason unless on the Testimony of two Witnesses to the same overt Act, or on Confession in open Court.

2. The Congress shall have Power to declare the Punishment of Treason, but no Attainder of Treason shall work Corruption of Blood, or Forfeiture except during the Life of the Person attainted.

Article IV

Section 1

Full Faith and Credit shall be given in each State to the public Acts, Records, and judicial Proceedings of every other State. And the Congress may by general Laws prescribe the Manner in which such Acts, Records and Proceedings shall be proved, and the Effect thereof.

Section 2

1. The Citizens of each State shall be entitled to all Privileges and Immunities of Citizens in the several States.

2. A Person charged in any State with Treason, Felony, or other Crime, who shall flee from Justice, and be found in another State, shall on Demand of the executive Authority of the State from which he fled, be delivered up, to be removed to the State having Jurisdiction of the Crime.

3. [No Person held to Service or Labour in one State, under the Laws thereof, escaping into another, shall, in Consequence of any Law or Regulation therein, be discharged from such Service or Labour, but shall be delivered up on Claim of the Party to whom such Service or Labour may be due.] [9]

Section 3

1. New States may be admitted by the Congress into this Union; but

no new State shall be formed or erected within the Jurisdiction of any other State; nor any State be formed by the Junction of two or more States, or Parts of States, without the Consent of the Legislatures of the States concerned as well as of the Congress.

2. The Congress shall have Power to dispose of and make all needful Rules and Regulations respecting the Territory or other Property belonging to the United States; and nothing in this Constitution shall be so construed as to Prejudice any Claims of the United States, or of any particular State.

Section 4

The United States shall guarantee to every State in this Union a Republican Form of Government, and shall protect each of them against Invasion; and on Application of the Legislature, or of the Executive (when the Legislature cannot be convened) against domestic Violence.

Article V

The Congress, whenever two thirds of both Houses shall deem it necessary, shall propose Amendments to this Constitution, or, on the Application of the Legislatures of two thirds of the several States, shall call a Convention for proposing Amendments, which, in either Case, shall be valid to all Intents and Purposes, as Part of this Constitution, when ratified by the Legislatures of three fourths of the several States, or by Conventions in three fourths thereof, as the one or the other Mode of Ratification may be proposed by the Congress; Provided [that no Amendment which may be made prior to the Year One thousand eight hundred and eight shall in any Manner affect the first and fourth Clauses in the Ninth Section of the first Article; and] [10] that no State, without its Consent, shall be deprived of its equal Suffrage in the Senate.

Article VI

1. All Debts contracted and Engagements entered into, before the Adoption of this Constitution, shall be as valid against the United States under this Constitution, as under the Confederation.

2. This Constitution, and the Laws of the United States which shall be made in Pursuance thereof; and all Treaties made, or which shall be made, under the Authority of the United States, shall be the supreme Law of the Land; and the Judges in every State shall be bound thereby, any Thing in the Constitution or Laws of any State to the Contrary notwithstanding.

3. The Senators and Representatives before mentioned, and the Members of the several State Legislatures, and all executive and judicial Officers, both of the United States and of the several States, shall be bound by Oath or Affirmation, to support this Constitution; but no religious Test shall ever be required as a Qualification to any Office or public Trust under the United States.

Article VII

The Ratification of the Conventions of nine States, shall be sufficient for the Establishment of this Constitution between the States so ratifying the Same. Done in Convention by the Unanimous Consent of the States present the Seventeenth Day of September in the Year of our Lord one thousand seven hundred and Eighty seven and of the Independence of the United States of America the Twelfth In witness whereof We have hereunto subscribed our Names, George Washington, President and deputy from Virginia.

New Hampshire:	John Langdon, Nicholas Gilman.
Massachusetts:	Nathaniel Gorham, Rufus King.
Connecticut:	William Samuel Johnson, Roger Sherman.
New York:	Alexander Hamilton
New Jersey:	William Livingston, David Brearley, William Paterson, Jonathan Dayton.
Pennsylvania:	Benjamin Franklin, Thomas Mifflin, Robert Morris, George Clymer, Thomas FitzSimons, Jared Ingersoll, James Wilson, Gouverneur Morris.
Delaware:	George Read, Gunning Bedford Jr., John Dickinson,

Richard Bassett,
Jacob Broom.

Maryland:

James McHenry,
Daniel of St. Thomas Jenifer,
Daniel Carroll.

Virginia:

John Blair,
James Madison Jr.

North Carolina:

William Blount,
Richard Dobbs Spaight,
Hugh Williamson.

South Carolina:

John Rutledge,
Charles Cotesworth Pinckney,
Charles Pinckney,
Pierce Butler.

Georgia:

William Few,
Abraham Baldwin.

[The language of the original Constitution, not including the Amendments, was adopted by a convention of the states on Sept. 17, 1787, and was subsequently ratified by the states on the following dates: Delaware, Dec. 7, 1787; Pennsylvania, Dec. 12, 1787; New Jersey, Dec. 18, 1787; Georgia, Jan. 2, 1788; Connecticut, Jan. 9, 1788; Massachusetts, Feb. 6, 1788; Maryland, April 28, 1788; South Carolina, May 23, 1788; New Hampshire, June 21, 1788.

Ratification was completed on June 21, 1788.

The Constitution subsequently was ratified by Virginia, June 25, 1788; New York, July 26, 1788; North Carolina, Nov. 21, 1789; Rhode Island, May 29, 1790; and Vermont, Jan. 10, 1791.]

Amendment I

Congress shall make no law respecting an establishment of religion, or prohibiting the free exercise thereof; or abridging the freedom of speech, or of the press; or the right of the people peaceably to assemble, and to petition the Government for a redress of grievances.

Amendment II

A well regulated Militia, being necessary to the security of a free State, the right of the people to keep and bear Arms, shall not be infringed.

Amendment III

No Soldier shall, in time of peace be quartered in any house, without the consent of the Owner, nor in time of war, but in a manner to be prescribed by law.

Amendment IV

The right of the people to be secure in their persons, houses, papers, and effects, against unreasonable searches and seizures, shall not be violated, and no Warrants shall issue, but upon probable cause, supported by Oath or affirmation, and particularly describing the place to be searched, and the persons or things to be seized.

Amendment V

No person shall be held to answer for a capital, or otherwise infamous crime, unless on a presentment or indictment of a Grand Jury, except in cases arising in the land or naval forces, or in the Militia, when in actual service in time of War or public danger; nor shall any person be subject for the same offence to be twice put in jeopardy of life or limb; nor shall be compelled in any criminal case to be a witness against himself, nor be deprived of life, liberty, or property, without due process of law; nor shall private property be taken for public use, without just compensation.

Amendment VI

In all criminal prosecutions, the accused shall enjoy the right to a speedy and public trial, by an impartial jury of the State and district wherein the crime shall have been committed, which district shall have been previously ascertained by law, and to be informed of the nature and cause of the accusation; to be confronted with the witnesses against him; to have compulsory process for obtaining witnesses in his favor, and to have the Assistance of Counsel for his defence.

Amendment VII

In Suits at common law, where the value in controversy shall exceed twenty dollars, the right of trial by jury shall be preserved, and no fact tried by a jury, shall be otherwise re-examined in any Court of the United States, than according to the rules of the common law.

Amendment VIII

Excessive bail shall not be required, nor excessive fines imposed, nor cruel and unusual punishments inflicted.

Amendment IX

The enumeration in the Constitution, of certain rights, shall not be construed to deny or disparage others retained by the people.

Amendment X

The powers not delegated to the United States by the Constitution, nor prohibited by it to the States, are reserved to the States respectively, or to the people.

Amendment XI

The Judicial power of the United States shall not be construed to extend to any suit in law or equity, commenced or prosecuted against one of the United States by Citizens of another State, or by Citizens or Subjects of any Foreign State.

Amendment XII

The Electors shall meet in their respective states and vote by ballot for President and Vice-President, one of whom, at least, shall not be an inhabitant of the same state with themselves; they shall name in their ballots the person voted for as President, and in distinct ballots the person voted for as Vice-President, and they shall make distinct lists of all persons voted for as President, and of all persons voted for as Vice-President, and of the number of votes for each, which lists they shall sign and certify, and transmit sealed to the seat of the government of the United States, directed to the President of the Senate; — The President of the Senate shall, in the presence of the Senate and House of Representatives, open all the certificates and the votes shall then be counted; — The person having the greatest number of votes for President, shall be the President, if such number be a majority of the whole number of Electors appointed; and if no person have such majority, then from the persons having the highest numbers not exceeding three on the list of those voted for as President, the House of Representatives shall choose immediately, by ballot, the President. But in choosing the President, the votes shall be taken by states, the representation from each state having one vote; a quorum for this purpose shall consist of a member or members from two-thirds of the states, and a majority of all the states shall be necessary to a choice. [And if the House of Representatives shall not choose a President whenever the right of choice shall devolve upon them, before the fourth day of March next following, then the Vice-President shall act as President, as in the case of the death or other constitutional disability of the President —][11] The person having the greatest number of votes as Vice-President, shall be the Vice-President, if such number be a majority of the whole number of Electors appointed, and if no person have a majority, then from the two highest numbers on the list, the Senate shall choose the Vice-President; a quorum for the purpose shall consist of two-thirds of the whole number of Senators, and a majority of the whole number shall be necessary to a choice. But no person constitutionally ineligible to the office of President shall be eligible to that of Vice-President of the United States.

Amendment XIII

Section 1

Neither slavery nor involuntary servitude, except as a punishment for crime whereof the party shall have been duly convicted, shall exist within the United States, or any place subject to their jurisdiction.

Section 2

Congress shall have power to enforce this article by appropriate legislation.

Amendment XIV

Section 1

All persons born or naturalized in the United States and subject to the jurisdiction thereof, are citizens of the United States and of the State wherein they reside. No State shall make or enforce any law which shall abridge the privileges or immunities of citizens of the United States; nor shall any State deprive any person of life, liberty, or property, without due process of law; nor deny to any person within its jurisdiction the equal protection of the laws.

Section 2

Representatives shall be apportioned among the several States according to their respective numbers, counting the whole number of persons in each State, excluding Indians not taxed. But when the right to vote at any election for the choice of electors for President and Vice President of the United States, Representatives in Congress, the Executive and Judicial officers of a State, or the members of the Legislature thereof, is denied to any of the male inhabitants of such State, being twenty-one years of age,[12] and citizens of the United States, or in any way abridged, except for participation in rebellion, or other crime, the basis of representation therein shall be reduced in the proportion which the number of such male citizens shall bear to the whole number of male citizens twenty-one years of age in such State.

Section 3

No person shall be a Senator or Representative in Congress, or elector of President and Vice President, or hold any office, civil or military, under the United States, or under any State, who, having previously taken an oath, as a member of Congress, or as an officer of the United States, or as a member of any State legislature, or as an executive or judicial officer of any State, to support the Constitution of the United States, shall have engaged in insurrection or rebellion against the same, or given aid or comfort to the enemies thereof. But Congress may by a vote of two-thirds of each House, remove such disability.

Section 4

The validity of the public debt of the United States, authorized by law, including debts incurred for payment of pensions and bounties for services in suppressing insurrection or rebellion, shall not be questioned. But neither the United States nor any State shall assume or pay any debt or obligation incurred in aid of insurrection or rebellion against the United States, or any claim for the loss or emancipation of any slave; but all such debts, obligations and claims shall be held illegal and void.

Section 5

The Congress shall have power to enforce, by appropriate legislation, the provisions of this article.

Amendment XV

Section 1

The right of citizens of the United States to vote shall not be denied or abridged by the United States or by any State on account of race, color, or previous condition of servitude.

Section 2

The Congress shall have power to enforce this article by appropriate legislation.

Amendment XVI

The Congress shall have power to lay and collect taxes on incomes, from whatever source derived, without apportionment among the several States, and without regard to any census or enumeration.

Amendment XVII

The Senate of the United States shall be composed of two Senators from each State, elected by the people thereof, for six years; and each Senator shall have one vote. The electors in each State shall have the qualifications requisite for electors of the most numerous branch of the State legislatures.

When vacancies happen in the representation of any State in the Senate, the executive authority of such State shall issue writs of election to fill such vacancies: *Provided,* That the legislature of any State may empower the executive thereof to make temporary appointments until the people fill the vacancies by election as the legislature may direct.

This amendment shall not be so construed as to affect the election or term of any Senator chosen before it becomes valid as part of the Constitution.

Amendment XVIII

Section 1

After one year from the ratification of this article the manufacture, sale, or transportation of intoxicating liquors within, the importation thereof into, or the exportation thereof from the United States and all territory subject to the jurisdiction thereof for beverage purposes is hereby prohibited.

Section 2

The Congress and the several States shall have concurrent power to enforce this article by appropriate legislation.

Section 3

This article shall be inoperative unless it shall have been ratified as an amendment to the Constitution by the legislatures of the several

States, as provided in the Constitution, within seven years from the date of the submission hereof to the States by the Congress.] [13]

Amendment XIX

The right of citizens of the United States to vote shall not be denied or abridged by the United States or by any State on account of sex.

Congress shall have power to enforce this article by appropriate legislation.

Amendment XX

Section 1

The terms of the President and Vice President shall end at noon on the 20th day of January, and the terms of Senators and Representatives at noon on the 3d day of January, of the years in which such terms would have ended if this article had not been ratified; and the terms of their successors shall then begin.

Section 2

The Congress shall assemble at least once in every year, and such meeting shall begin at noon on the 3d day of January, unless they shall by law appoint a different day.

Section 3 [14]

If, at the time fixed for the beginning of the term of the President, the President elect shall have died, the Vice President elect shall become President. If a President shall not have been chosen before the time fixed for the beginning of his term, or if the President elect shall have failed to qualify, then the Vice President elect shall act as President until a President shall have qualified; and the Congress may by law provide for the case wherein neither a President elect nor a Vice President elect shall have qualified, declaring who shall then act as President, or the manner in which one who is to act shall be selected, and such person shall act accordingly until a President or Vice President shall have qualified.

Section 4

The Congress may by law provide for the case of the death of any of the persons from whom the House of Representatives may choose a President whenever the right of choice shall have devolved upon them, and for the case of the death of any of the persons from whom the

Senate may choose a Vice President whenever the right of choice shall have devolved upon them.

Section 5

Sections 1 and 2 shall take effect on the 15th day of October following the ratification of this article.

Section 6

This article shall be inoperative unless it shall have been ratified as an amendment to the Constitution by the legislatures of three-fourths of the several States within seven years from the date of its submission.

Amendment XXI

Section 1

The eighteenth article of amendment to the Constitution of the United States is hereby repealed.

Section 2

The transportation or importation into any State, Territory or possession of the United States for delivery or use therein of intoxicating liquors, in violation of the laws thereof, is hereby prohibited.

Section 3

This article shall be inoperative unless it shall have been ratified as an amendment to the Constitution by conventions in the several States, as provided in the Constitution, within seven years from the date of the submission hereof to the States by the Congress.

Amendment XXII

Section 1

No person shall be elected to the office of the President more than twice, and no person who has held the office of President, or acted as President, for more than two years of a term to which some other person was elected President shall be elected to the office of the President more than once. But this Article shall not apply to any person holding the office of President when this Article was proposed by the Congress, and shall not prevent any person who may be holding the office of President, or acting as President, during the term within which this Article become operative from holding the office of President or acting as President during the remainder of such term.

Section 2

This Article shall be inoperative unless it shall have been ratified as an amendment to the Constitution by the legislatures of three-fourths of the several States within seven years from the date of its submission to the States by the Congress.

Amendment XXIII

Section 1

The District constituting the seat of Government of the United States shall appoint in such manner as the Congress may direct:

A number of electors of President and Vice President equal to the whole number of Senators and Representatives in Congress to which the District would be entitled if it were a State, but in no event more than the least populous State; they shall be in addition to those appointed by the States, but they shall be considered, for the purposes of the election of President and Vice President, to be electors appointed by a State; and they shall meet in the District and perform such duties as provided by the twelfth article of amendment.

Section 2

The Congress shall have power to enforce this article by appropriate legislation.

Amendment XXIV

Section 1

The right of citizens of the United States to vote in any primary or other election for President or Vice President, for electors for President or Vice President, or for Senator or Representative in Congress, shall not be denied or abridged by the United States or any State by reason of failure to pay any poll tax or other tax.

Section 2

The Congress shall have power to enforce this article by appropriate legislation.

Amendment XXV

Section 1

In case of the removal of the President from office or of his death or resignation, the Vice President shall become President.

Section 2

Whenever there is a vacancy in the office of the Vice President, the President shall nominate a Vice President who shall take office upon confirmation by a majority vote of both Houses of Congress.

Section 3

Whenever the President transmits to the President pro tempore of the Senate and the Speaker of the House of Representatives his written declaration that he is unable to discharge the powers and duties of his office, and until he transmits to them a written declaration to the contrary, such powers and duties shall be discharged by the Vice President as Acting President.

Section 4

Whenever the Vice President and a majority of either the principal officers of the executive departments or of such other body as Congress may by law provide, transmit to the President pro tempore of the Senate and the Speaker of the House of Representatives their written declaration that the President is unable to discharge the powers and duties of his office, the Vice President shall immediately assume the powers and duties of the office as Acting President.

Thereafter, when the President transmits to the President pro tempore of the Senate and the Speaker of the House of Representatives his written declaration that no inability exists, he shall resume the powers and duties of his office unless the Vice President and a majority of either the principal officers of the executive department or of such other body as Congress may by law provide, transmit within four days to the President pro tempore of the Senate and the Speaker of the House of Representatives their written declaration that the President is unable to discharge the powers and duties of his office. Thereupon Congress shall decide the issue, assembling within forty-eight hours for that purpose if not in session. If the Congress, within twenty-one days after receipt of the latter written declaration, or, if Congress is not in session, within twenty-one days after Congress is required to assemble, determines by two-thirds vote of both houses that the President is unable to discharge the powers and duties of his office, the Vice President shall continue to discharge the same as Acting President; otherwise, the President shall resume the powers and duties of his office.

Amendment XXVI

Section 1

The right of citizens of the United States, who are eighteen years of age or older, to vote shall not be denied or abridged by the United States or by any State on account of age.

Section 2

The Congress shall have power to enforce this article by appropriate legislation.

Notes

1. The part in brackets was changed by section 2 of the Fourteenth Amendment.
2. The part in brackets was changed by section 1 of the Seventeenth Amendment.
3. The part in brackets was changed by the second paragraph of the Seventeenth Amendment.
4. The part in brackets was changed by section 2 of the Twentieth Amendment.
5. The Sixteenth Amendment gave Congress the power to tax incomes.
6. The material in brackets has been superseded by the Twelfth Amendment.
7. This provision has been affected by the Twenty-fifth Amendment.
8. These clauses were affected by the Eleventh Amendment.
9. This paragraph has been superseded by the Thirteenth Amendment.
10. Obsolete.
11. The part in brackets has been superseded by section 3 of the Twentieth Amendment.
12. See the Twenty-sixth Amendment.
13. This amendment was repealed by section 1 of the Twenty-first Amendment.
14. See the Twenty-fifth Amendment.

Source: U.S. Congress. House. Committee on the Judiciary. *The Constitution of the United States of America, As Amended Through July 1971.* H. Doc. 93-125, 93d Cong., 2d sess., 1974.

Acknowledgments

pp. 12 and 13   From "James Madison Wouldn't Approve" by Melvin Laird in the *Washington Post*, 13 February 1984. © 1984 The Washington Post.

p. 47   From "To Form a More Perfect Union" by Raymond Moley in *Newsweek*, 4 April 1955. Copyright 1955, by Newsweek, Inc. All rights reserved. Reprinted by permission.

pp. 48 and 49   From "Direct Elections: An Invitation to National Chaos" by Theodore White in *Life*, 3 January 1970. Reprinted with permission.

pp. 70-71   From "Reforming the American Presidency" by Arthur Schlesinger, Jr., in the *Wall Street Journal*, 7 April 1981. Reprinted with permission.

pp. 89 and 97   From "The Politics of Endurance" by George Will in the *Washington Post*, 30 October 1977. © 1977, Washington Post Writers Group, reprinted with permission.

p. 127   From "Budget Solution," editorial in the *Wall Street Journal*, 14 September 1983. Reprinted with permission of The Wall Street Journal © 1986 by Dow Jones & Company, Inc. All rights reserved.

p. 129   From an editorial in the *Washington Post*, 24 June 1983. © 1983 The Washington Post.

p. 152   From an editorial by George Will in the *Washington Post*, 28 July 1977. © 1977, Washington Post Writers Group, reprinted with permission; from an editorial by James Abourezk in the *Washington Post*, 10 August 1977. © 1977 The Washington Post.